The Architecture of Deconstruction

The Architecture of Deconstruction:
Derrida's Haunt

Mark Wigley

The MIT Press Cambridge, Massachusetts London, England

First MIT Press paperback edition, 1995

© 1993 MIT Press

This book was printed and bound in the United States of America.

Library of Congress Cataloging-in-Publication Data

Wigley, Mark.
  The architecture of deconstruction : Derrida's haunt / Mark Wigley.
    p. cm.
  Includes bibliographical references and index.
  ISBN 0-262-23170-0 (HB), 0-262-73114-2 (PB)
    1. Deconstruction (Architecture) 2. Derrida, Jacques—Philosophy.
I. Title.
NA682.D43W54 1993
720′.1—dc20   93-10352
                                                    CIP

For Beatriz and Andrea

Any house is a far too complicated, clumsy, fussy, mechanical counterfeit of the human body . . . The whole interior is a kind of stomach that attempts to digest objects . . . The whole life of the average house, it seems, is a sort of indigestion. A body in ill repair, suffering indisposition—constant tinkering and doctoring to keep it alive. It is a marvel, we its infesters, do not go insane in it and with it. Perhaps it is a form of insanity we have to put in it. Lucky we are able to get something else out of it, thought we do seldom get out of it alive ourselves.

—Frank Lloyd Wright
"The Cardboard House," 1931.

Contents

Preface

In 1985 the architect Bernard Tschumi called Jacques Derrida with an invitation. Architecture called on philosophy. For what? Philosophy? Not simply. The philosopher was asked if he would be interested in collaborating with an architect on the design of a section of the *Parc de la Villette* in Paris, a project that already had its own "design-philosophy" and even presented itself as being no more than this philosophy, a conceptual structure rather than a single material form. But clearly the architect thought that something was missing, that there was some kind of gap in the argument that could be filled by a philosopher, an opening that could be exploited, some kind of pocket within which another discourse could be elaborated. So Derrida was invited into the space of the project, and hence the space of architecture, which is not yet to say an architectural space.

The philosopher accepted the invitation and soon wrote an essay about the project entitled *Point de folie—maintenant l'archi-tecture* in which the architect's material is at once incorporated, rearranged, and extended, or, rather, the essay inhabits the architect's material; teasing, testing, tasting, but not judging. In no way presenting itself as criticism, the text, in a kind of strategic transference, assumes the form of what it describes. It both rehearses many of the architect's arguments and literally begins to shape itself according to the spatial logic of the architectural design in order to articulate the somewhat uneasy relationship between a certain kind of thinking and a certain kind of space.

Architecture appears to emerge for the first time as a distinct subject in Derrida's writing. After twenty years, he turns to architecture—or so it would seem.

The essay was first published in the architect's 1986 collection of drawings of the project and then in the philosopher's 1987 collection of essays, which includes other writings on architecture. By then Derrida was collaborating with the architect Peter Eisenman in the detailed design of a particular section of the La Villette project. He was occupying all the spaces of that architecture: legal, philosophical, technical, methodological, political, and interpersonal, to name but a few, in addition to what is traditionally considered to be the physical site and whatever might be projected onto it or from it.

In accepting the invitation, Derrida's work changed the architecture it occupied in a number of ways, each of which need to be carefully traced through their various complications and implications. But equally, his writing was changed by this occupation, even if it was such a brief stopover in what has become an extended itinerary through so many different discourses. The perceived limits of both architecture and philosophy were disturbed by a convoluted exchange that, like most designs, took the form of an extended negotiation. Long after the design was completed, this negotiation is still going on and is opening up on several new fronts. Some of the negotiated changes were temporary and the respective institutional spaces have already been restored and their furniture rearranged to accommodate familiar assumptions, but other spaces are, as they say, just not the same.

Spurred by this event, a vigorous discourse has developed around the question of "deconstruction and architecture" involving many names from both inside and outside the traditional institutional limits of architecture and philosophy. Just as a number of architectural theorists have turned to "deconstructive" theory, theorists of deconstruction have increasingly turned to "architecture." A multiplicity of exchanges have taken place: conferences, exhibitions, essays, special issues of journals, books, reviews, interviews, newspaper articles, editorials, debates, letters to the editor, published correspondence, dissertations, research grants, fellowships, architectural projects, architectural criticism, interdisciplinary collaborations, academic appointments and disappointments, and various forms of censorship. In these ongoing transactions, more aspects of the respective institutions have been consolidated than have been displaced, and even then some of those displacements have themselves been subsequently institutionalized according to the all too familiar economy of domestication. But still, I think a lot of important work has been done. The philosophers have had a lot to say to the architects and the architects have had a few surprises for the philosophers. Everyone has had to think again, and then again. The effects of this rethinking are considerable, if not obvious.

It is not possible to sift through all this material here, tracing the elaborate weave of heterogeneous trajectories to adequately address the question of "deconstruction and architecture." My only concern will be to trace some of the preconditions for this engagement, conditions that both made it possible and produced the sense of an event inasmuch as they are variously brought to the surface, suppressed, or displaced.

Immediately, it must be noted that this discourse, which began with the question of deconstruction and architecture and has developed in recent years into other questions in which the word "deconstruction" plays no role, did not simply emerge out of the public event of Derrida's involvement in a specific design project. On the one hand, several projects of reading Derrida's work within architectural discourse were already highly developed and would become increasingly nuanced. On the other hand, the question of architecture did not simply emerge in Derrida's work with his first essay "about" architecture. His writing already depended on a certain thinking of architecture that even surfaces in the word "deconstruction." So it is necessary to step back, to retrace some steps and identify the role of architecture in Derrida's writing before his apparent turn to it. The earlier texts need to be reread to locate the architecture that is written into them and cannot be detached, the architecture that makes those texts possible and, indeed, makes the eventual turn to architecture possible, even if that turn ignores or transforms it.

At the very least, this involves patiently tracing an intermittent subtext inscribed within Derrida's texts and following its indistinct and often circuitous trajectories. It requires a close attention to the letter of those texts, citing, reciting, repeating, and rehearsing them—not by following their more obvious lines of argument, but by locating one of the threads that passes between them and unpicking it see what it holds together, exploring the unique way in which the visible pattern and strength of Derrida's writing is maintained by this rarely visible and seemingly tenuous architectural thread.

To step back into Derrida's work to address this question will be, at the same time, to step back into the writings of Martin Heidegger, not only because Heidegger is perhaps the most rigorous thinker of the relationship between philosophy and architecture, but also because Derrida's work is itself an incessant stepping back into Heidegger, and perhaps more than anything else, it is a stepping back into Heidegger's account of the necessity of such a stepping back, an account that is itself presented in architectural terms. And this return to Heidegger needs to be made precisely when it might seem riskiest, given the current reexaminations of his association with National Socialism. But these revisions make the return even more necessary here and now because, as I have argued elsewhere, the question of architecture is implicated in them at every turn.[1]

Finally, and more personally, this book is another kind of stepping back inasmuch as it is a reworking of my doctoral thesis entitled "Jacques Derrida and Architecture: The Deconstructive Possibilities of Architectural Discourse," which is a reading of the architectural argument embedded within Derrida's work before he addressed architecture as such. When I began to write it in the splendid, if not monastic, isolation of New Zealand, architects were not yet interested in deconstruction and deconstructive writers were not yet interested in architecture, and such an interdisciplinary exchange seemed an improbable and overdetermined fantasy, which in some important sense it still is and will necessarily remain so. The thesis was finally submitted in 1986 to the University of Auckland precisely at the time that Derrida had just started to engage with architecture. I subsequently became involved in many of the different kinds of event that have constituted the lively international debate around the question of deconstruction and architecture. In returning to the thesis, I am leaving this debate behind, including Derrida's important contributions to it, in order to reconstruct my original argument, to put it on record, as it were, and to elaborate it by following its course through other texts that Derrida has subsequently published.

Despite the fact that deconstructive discourse has started to speak about architecture, I have rigidly, if not perversely, maintained my focus on the architecture embedded in that discourse before it does so. I hope this self-imposed restriction, whose brutality to the complex rhythms and nuances of the discourse cannot be overestimated, opens that discourse to some possibilities it currently resists or masks. I hope its very narrowness constitutes some kind of opening.

Earlier versions of parts of this text were originally published in the journals *Perspecta 23* and *Assemblage 8,* and the collection *Deconstruction and the Visual Arts: Art, Media, and Architecture.* My thanks to the respective editors for their criticism. I would also like to thank Melissa Vaughn for her sensitive editing; Mike Austin and Gill Mathewson, without whom I could not have finished the original thesis in New Zealand; and my colleagues and students at Princeton University, who since then have helped to construct a space for my work.

Above all, I will always be indebted to Beatriz Colomina for her intellectual and emotional support, little of which is deserved.

1

The Translation of Deconstruction

How then to translate deconstruction in architectural discourse? Perhaps it is too late to ask this preliminary question. What is left to translate? Or, more important, what is always left by translation? Not just left behind, but left specifically for architecture. What remains of deconstruction for architecture? What are the remains that can be located only in architecture, the last resting place of deconstruction? The question of translation is always, after all, a question of survival. Can deconstruction survive architecture?

It is now over twenty years since Derrida's first books were published. Suddenly his work has started to surface in architectural discourse. This appears to be the last discourse to invoke the name of Jacques Derrida. Its reading seems the most distant from the original texts, the final addition to what is by now a colossal tower of interpretations, an addition to what has become a disconcertingly stable monument to instability, an addition that marks in some way the beginning of the end of deconstruction, its limit if not its closure.

After such a long delay—a hesitation whose strategic necessity must be examined here—there is such a haste to read Derrida in architectural discourse. But it is a reading that seems at once obvious and suspect—suspect in its very obviousness. Deconstruction is understood to be unproblematically architectural. There seems to be no translation, just a metaphoric transfer, a straightforward application of theory from outside architecture to the practical domain of the architectural object. The hesitation does not seem to have been produced by some kind of internal resistance on the part of that object. On the contrary, there is no evidence of work, no task for the translator, no translation—just a literal application, a transliteration. Architecture is understood as a representation of deconstruction, the material representation of an abstract idea. The reception of Derrida's work seems to follow the classical trajectory from idea to material form, from initial theory to final practice, from the presence of a thought to its representation. Architecture, supposedly the most material of the discourses, seems the most removed from the original work, the most suspect of the applications, the last application, the representational ornament that cannot influence the substantial tradition it is added to, a veneer masking more than it reveals of the structure beneath. The last layer, just an addition, no translation. Yet.

But how to translate? Architecture can never simply be an addition inasmuch as the idea of addition is itself architectural. And deconstruction is no more than a subversion of the architectural logic of addition that sets in play a certain kind of thinking about translation. One cannot simply address translation before, outside, or above either deconstruction or architecture. The question immediately becomes complicated. There is no hygienic starting point, no superior logic to apply, no principles to be found in some domain that governs both deconstructive discourse and architectural discourse. Nevertheless, certain exchanges are already occurring between them. Architecture, translation, and deconstruction are already bound together, defining a curious economy whose pathological symptoms can be studied; it becomes a matter of identifying the logic of translation already in operation.

Because there is no safe place to begin, one can only enter this ongoing economy and begin to trace its convoluted geometry. This can be done here by locating those points in each discourse at which the others are made thematic, however fleetingly or partially—points where the other comes to the surface. The lines of argument that surface there are threads that can be forcefully pulled to see where gaps appear elsewhere in the discourse, marking covert levels of entangled relationships that bind superficially discrete areas. These hidden layers are not simply below the surface but are within the surface itself, knotted together to form its texture. To locate them involves a kind of sideways slippage along barely visible fault lines rather than the traditional scholarly labor of excavation. As there is nothing above or below the convoluted folds of the surface, it is a matter of following some circular line of inquiry, passing round and round the same small set of themes, circulating obsessively within the economy being read—within, that is, the surface itself.

Constructive Abuse

The question of translation most conspicuously surfaces in deconstructive discourse when Derrida's "Des Tours des Babel," following Walter Benjamin's 1923 essay "The Task of the Translator," argues that translation is not the transmission, reproduction, or image of an original meaning that preceded it.[1] On the contrary, the very sense of something original is but an effect of translation, the translation actually producing what it appears to simply reproduce.

A text, as Benjamin puts it, "calls for" a translation that establishes a nostalgia for the purity, plenitude, and life it never had. In answering this call, the translation necessarily abuses the text, transforming rather than transmitting it.[2] There is some kind of gap in the structure of the text that the translation is called in to cover, to cover precisely by forcing it open even further to liberate what is hidden within that structure. A text is never an organic, unified whole. It is already corrupted, already fissured, inhabited by something "alien." A translation is not simply a departure from the original that is either violent or faithful, as the original is already internally divided, exiled from itself. Not only is no text ever written in a single language, but each language is itself fractured. Languages and texts are necessarily impure. Always divided, they remain irreducibly foreign to themselves. It is the translation that produces the myth of purity and, in so doing, subordinates itself as impure. In constructing the original as original, it constructs itself as secondary, putting itself into exile from the very space that it produces. The supplementary translation that appears to be a violation of the purity of the work is actually the possibility of that very sense of purity. Its violence to the text is therefore a kind of violent fidelity, a violence called for by the text precisely to construct itself as pure. The abuse of the text is called for because of an abuse already going on within that text. The translation actually exploits this internal conflict in order to present the original as unified; the conflict becomes the basis of its own effacement.

Furthermore, as Benjamin argues, this faithfully abusive transformation also involves a certain violence to the language of the translation. Just as the translator must break open the language of the text to "liberate" what is "imprisoned" within it, the translation must equally "break through the decayed barriers" of its own language.[3] What is liberated from the text is not some fixed meaning, but a "state of flux" as "alien" to the language of the translation that releases it as to the text that concealed it. Both languages normally attempt to conceal this unstable movement. Indeed, the concealment constitutes the basic "kinship" that exists between languages that otherwise appear foreign to each other, the "central reciprocal relationship between languages" by which, in the end, they "are not strangers to one another."[4] They only appear foreign to each other inasmuch as they each repress this instability to produce the effect of languages with discrete, delimited identities. In the end, it is actually the translation itself that becomes "overpowering and alien"[5] as it releases that which is normally imprisoned and distorts the apparently secure identity of each language. Consequently, a text neither lives nor dies in translation. It does not have some original life-giving intention invested in it by an author, whose presence is either simply revived or substituted by a dead sign. Rather, it "lives on," it "survives" in a kind of spectral "afterlife" at a different level than it had before because something buried within has been released.

In elaborating Benjamin's argument about the basic kinship between languages that seem foreign to each other, Derrida argues that this "survival" [*Überleben* or *Fortleben*] of a text in its translation is organized by an unusual kind of contract that ensures that translation is never completed nor completely frus-trated.[6] The contract sustains the necessarily unfulfilled promise of translation, defining a scene of incomplete translation, an incompletion that binds the languages of the original and trans-lation in a strange knot, a double bind. Such a convoluted but constitutional bond is not like the negotiable social contracts that appear to organize each language, nor is it the fixed pre-social contract that transcends and coordinates each language dreamed of by so much of the philosophical tradition. Neither cultural nor acultural, such contracts exceed cultural transac-tions without simply being outside them. Each visible negotiable contract that organizes a particular language presupposes such a hidden contract that makes discourse possible, establishing the overt differences between languages while making certain covert exchanges between them not only possible but inevitable.

Such a translation contract is not independent of the different languages whose economy it organizes. It is always inscribed within them, albeit obliquely. The visible gap between languages actually passes through each one. And not only is each "original" already divided, but translation is occurring across those divi-sions. It is only inasmuch as each is always divided, inhabited by the other and constantly negotiating with it, that translation is possible.[7] In fact, it is the less visible translation going on within a language that makes any visible translation between it and a language outside it possible, which is to say that one language is never simply outside the other. Translation occurs across a gap folded within rather than simply between each language. The fissures that divide any text are actually folds that bind them to that which appears to be outside them, and it is precisely these folds that constitute the texts as such, producing the very sense of an inside and an outside that they subvert. In the end, the contract is no more than the strange geometry of these folds, the convoluted organization of the cracks that structure a discourse.

In these terms, any translation between deconstruction and architecture does not simply occur between the texts of philo-sophical discourse and those of architectural discourse. Rather, it occupies and organizes both discourses. Within each there is at least an ongoing architectural translation of philosophy and a philosophical translation of architecture. To translate deconstruction in architectural discourse is not, therefore, to faithfully recover some original undivided sense of deconstruction.[8] Rather, it must be one of the abuses of Derrida's texts that constitutes them as originals. To translate deconstruction in architectural discourse is to examine the gaps in deconstructive discourse that demand an architectural translation in order to constitute those texts as deconstructive in the first place. The architectural translation of deconstruction, which appears to be the last-minute, last-gasp application, turns out to be part of the very production of deconstructive discourse from the beginning, an ongoing event organized by the terms of an ancient contract between architecture and philosophy that is inscribed within the structure of both discourses. And to think of such a contract here will not only be to think of architecture as the possibility of deconstruction, but likewise to think of deconstruction as the possibility of architecture.

In the end, to translate deconstruction here will be to unearth what it is of architecture that both philosophical and architectural discourse attempt to bury and yet depend on: the irreducible strangeness of architecture that must be concealed by a range of institutional practices central to both discourses and yet also protected by them because its survival is actually their very possibility—no matter how much they disavow its existence. Indeed, it is precisely the intensity and repetition of the disavowals that marks its structural role. To exhume these repressed qualities of architecture will necessarily render the very familiarity of these discourses forever strange. This will turn out to be at once a question of the strange architecture that haunts the discourses that work so hard to entomb it and of the strange architecture of the tomb they construct for it.

The Edifice Complex Revisited

A preliminary sketch of this haunting scene of translation can be drawn here by developing Martin Heidegger's account of the idiosyncratic relationship between architecture and philosophy. A certain thinking of architecture is central to Heidegger's work.

It is not that he simply theorizes architecture as such, but that theorizing is itself understood in architectural terms. As is well known, one the most famous of his later essays, "Building, Dwelling, Thinking,"[9] literally identifies thinking with building. In fact, this identification is already written into his earliest work and, even then, he argues there that it is not so much his identification as that of the ancient and ongoing tradition of philosophy he is interrogating.

Heidegger often directly and indirectly addresses the way in which philosophy repeatedly and insistently describes itself as a kind of architecture. He points, for example, to the way Immanuel Kant's *Critique of Pure Reason* describes metaphysics as an "edifice" erected on secure "foundations" laid on the most stable "ground." Kant criticizes previous philosophers for their tendency to "complete its speculative structures as speedily as may be, and only afterwards to enquire whether these foundations are reliable."[10] The edifice of metaphysics has fallen apart and is "in ruins" because it has been erected on "groundless assertions" unquestioningly inherited from the philosophical tradition. To restore a secure foundation, the *Critique* starts the "thorough preparation of the ground"[11] with the "clearing, as it were, and levelling of what has hitherto been wasteground."[12] The edifice of metaphysics is understood as a grounded structure.

For Heidegger, the tradition of metaphysics has always understood itself as a kind of building, even before it started explicitly describing itself in these terms when René Descartes depicted philosophy as the construction of an edifice, a sound structure erected on stable, well-grounded foundations, a description that would then be institutionalized, most conspicuously by the writings of Kant. Heidegger argues that Kant's explicit attempt to lay the foundations for a building is the necessary task of all metaphysics. The question of metaphysics has always been that of the ground on which things stand, even though it has only been explicitly formulated in these terms in the modern period inaugurated by Descartes. Metaphysics is no more than the attempt to locate the ground. Its history is that of a succession of different names (*logos, ratio, arche,* and so on) for the ground.

Furthermore, Heidegger argues that philosophy's original but increasingly forgotten object, "Being" [*Sein*], is also a kind of construction, a "presencing" [*Anwesenheit*] through "standing" [*stehen*]. Each of philosophy's successive terms for "ground" [*Grund*] designates "Being," understood as "presence." Metaphysics is the identification of the ground as "supporting presence" for whatever stands like an edifice. It searches for "that upon which everything rests, what is always there for every being as its support."[13] Indeed, for Heidegger, metaphysics is no more than the definition of ground as "support."

In the terms of Heidegger's argument, it would seem that there is some kind of symptomatic transference between philosophy, as an institution that constructs arguments like a building is constructed, and the object it analyzes. At the very least, philosophy identifies with its object, seeing itself as a construction that reveals the construction of Being, not by simply representing that construction but by presenting its essential condition. The rules that organize the institutional practices of philosophy supposedly are provided by its object rather than by any sociopolitical system, which is to say that philosophy's rules are not institutional. Philosophy, in the strictest sense, does not even think of itself as an institution. The figure of architecture is therefore not simply one figure among the others that it chooses to employ. More than just philosophy's figure of itself, it is the figure by which that institution effaces its own institutional condition, an effacement that paradoxically defines philosophy's particular institutional location and sociopolitical function. It is philosophy's claim on that which precedes or exceeds the social that gives it unique social authority—the authority, precisely, to define and regulate the social. From the beginning, philosophy has represented itself as a source, storehouse, and arbitrator of order. This representation would not be possible without the architectural figure, which is to say a very particular figure of architecture, one that always has to be protected from damage even, if not especially, when it is not being explicitly invoked. Maintained in working order even when it is being held in reserve, the figure is always operative in the discourse and actually exerts the greatest force when in reserve. Philosophical discourse is more indebted to this architectural figure than it could ever say, even when it does become explicit. Indeed, the real force of the figure lies in those of its operations that philosophy cannot address.

When the figure does surface, it is that of presentation. Philosophy's structure supposedly emerges from and thereby presents the ground. The figure of the edifice, the grounded structure, is that of a standing up that presents. On the one hand, philosophy is the construction of propositions that stand up, and the ability of its constructs to stand is determined by the condition of the ground, its supporting presence. On the other hand, philosophy is the question of what the ground will withstand, of what can stand on the ground. For Heidegger, the "fundamental" question of metaphysics (why there are beings rather than nothing) asks of a being "on what does it stand?"[14] In both cases—philosophy and its object—standing up through construction makes visible the condition of the ground. An edifice is that which manifests grounding, that which exhibits the ground to an eye.

Consequently, philosophy's successive relayings of the foundations do not preserve a single, defined edifice on ever more stable footings. Rather, it is a matter of dismantling the foundations of a traditional edifice until it "begins to totter"[15] and its structure cracks open, establishing the possibility of a different building. The form of the edifice changes as the ground changes. Having cleared the ground, for example, Kant must reassess its load-bearing capacity and, as he puts it, "lay down the complete architectonic plan" of a new philosophy to "build upon this foundation."[16] The edifice must be redesigned. Re-laying the foundations establishes the possibility of a different edifice. For Heidegger, who begins his most extended reading of Kant's *Critique* by arguing that philosophy's central activity is "best illustrated if we consider the building trade," the laying of the foundation is the "architectonic circumscription and delineation of the inner possibility of metaphysics" through an interrogation of the condition of the ground. This interrogation involves the "projection" of a "building plan," the tracing of an outline, the drawing, the designing of an edifice, the drawing of the design out of the ground.[17] Interrogating the condition of the ground defines certain architectonic limits, structural constraints within which the philosopher must work as a designer. The philosopher is first and foremost an architect, endlessly attempting to produce a grounded structure.

The history of philosophy is therefore that of a series of substitutions for structure. Every reference to structure, no matter how oblique, is a reference to an edifice erected on, and marked by, the ground, an edifice from which the ground cannot be removed. As Derrida observes, when beginning a reading of Lévi-Strauss:

It would be easy enough to show that the concept of structure and even the word "structure" itself are as old as the *epistēmē*—that is to say as old as Western science and Western philosophy—and that their roots thrust deep into the soil of ordinary language, into whose deepest recesses the *epistēmē* plunges in order to gather them up and to make them part of itself in a metaphorical displacement. Nevertheless, . . . structure—or rather the structurality of structure—although it has always been at work, has always been neutralized or reduced, and this by a process giving it a center or of referring it to a point of presence, a fixed origin. The function of this center was not only to orient, balance, and organize the structure—one cannot in fact conceive of an unorganized structure—but above all to make sure that the organizing principle of the structure would limit what we might call the *play* of the structure. . . . The concept of centered structure is in fact the concept of a play based on a fundamental ground, a play constituted on the basis of a fundamental immobility and a reassuring certitude, which itself is beyond the reach of play.[18]

The figure of the edifice that philosophical discourse appears to appropriate from "ordinary" language as a metaphor of itself is that of a structure whose play is constrained by the ground, a structure with which the play of representation is constrained by presence. It is not simply a figure of the exclusion of representation in favor of presence. Rather, it represents the ongoing control of representation. The tradition of philosophy is the sustained attempt to get control by recovering something that precedes representation, restraining representation by establishing the architectonic limits provided by the ground. It searches for the most stable ground in order to exercise the greatest control.

The architectural figure is therefore never simply that of the well-constructed building. It is also the decorated building, one whose structural system controls the ornament attached to it. In the end, the edifice is as much a model of representation as of presentation. It figures a continuous hierarchy from the supposedly infinite depth, solidity, and reliability of the unmediated presence of the ground to the thin, ephemeral, dissimulating representations of ornamental layers that need to be controlled to maintain order. Order is exemplified in the control of ornament. The traditional logic of ground and structure with which philosophy organizes itself is equally the logic of structure and ornament. In the end, philosophy is no more than a theory of ornament.

In these terms, philosophy is dependent on an architectural logic of support. Architecture is the figure of the addition, the structural layer, one element supported by another. It is not just the addition of the building to the ground, but a series of assembled layers. Metaphysics' determination of the ground as support presupposes a vertical hierarchy from ground through structure to ornament. The idea of support is dependent on a particular view of architecture that defines a range of relationships from fundamental (foundational) to supplementary (ornamental). With each additional layer, the bond is weaker. The structure is supposedly bonded to the ground more securely than the ornament is bonded to the structure. But as the distance from the ground becomes greater, the threat to the overall structure diminishes. This vertical hierarchy needs to be understood as a mechanism of control that makes available the thought of the ground as support that is metaphysics.

If structure is that which makes present the ground, submitting itself to the authority of presence, ornament either represents this grounding or deviates from the line of support, detaching itself from the ground in order to represent that which is other than structural. Philosophy attempts to tame ornament in the name of the ground, to control representation in the name of presence. In the end, the philosophical economy turns on the status of ornament. In fact, it is the structure/ornament relationship that enables us to think of support, and thereby to think of the ground. The unique authority of the tradition of philosophy, its capacity to define and legitimate order, derives from its implicit theory of ornament, a theory that rarely becomes explicit.

Philosophy's traditional description of itself and its object as building invokes and sustains a particular image of architecture as a mechanism that precedes and controls the decorative images attached to it through its structural bond to the ground. This image, which itself must be controlled, is never presented in any detail, let alone subjected to any kind of philosophical analysis. It is seen as unquestionable, a truth so familiar that it is not even seen as an image—let alone an image with a particular history sustained by a complex system of institutional practices mobilized to particular sociopolitical ends. Indeed, it is not even employed as a representation of architecture as such, but as an appropriation of that dimension of architecture that supposedly precedes representation: a brute, tangible, visible, and inescapable reality of the material world that is, as a result, both immediately accessible to the reader of philosophy and unquestionable by that reader. The figure is employed to credit philosophy itself with the unmediated condition exhibited by a building, putting in place the supposed neutrality and authority of the structural and structuring gaze of philosophical argument.

The figure itself is not examined by the eye it makes possible. It is exempted from interrogation and this exemption, as it were, holds the institution of philosophy together inasmuch as it makes a whole chain of similar exemptions possible. Architecture is invoked as a kind of touchstone to legitimize certain routine practices within the discourse of philosophy, to relieve those practices from examination, to block them from view, to disavow that they are practices. The figure of architecture that supports the philosophical eye is the agent of a strategic blindness, orchestrating a system of blind spots that enable philosophy to assume and sustain a particular sociopolitical role in our culture.

Although this image of architecture is such a simplistic figure, a cartoon, it is precisely as a cartoon that it plays such an influential role in so many cultural transactions. The concern here is not to simply produce a more nuanced account of architecture. Indeed, we should not so quickly assume that this is even possible. Rather, it is a matter of trying to understand the nuances of how the implausibly simple figure operates—the complex role played by its very simplicity.

The Always Structural Ambivalence about Architecture

The strategic role of the figure can be identified more precisely by looking at the traditional site where philosophical discourse explicitly addresses the question of architecture: the philosophy of art. The already complicated relationship between philosophy's descriptions of itself and its object in architectural terms, whether explicit or implicit, is further complicated by the discourse's encounter with architecture as an art. In aesthetics, the particular image of architecture with which philosophy organizes itself interacts with an ostensibly more detailed image of architecture. These images do not necessarily, if ever, coincide. The strange relationship between them marks the particular investments that are at stake in the traditional image of architecture, an image meant to be without any investment and employed precisely to mark philosophy's absence of investment, its detached quest for the truth. The figure of architecture is used to establish the neutrality of the philosophical gaze at the world, but when philosophy is obliged to look at architecture itself through its architect's eye, the scene becomes much more complicated and is marked by certain symptomatic displacements, contradictions, evasions, and denials.

Such an overdetermination can be found in Kant's aesthetics. Although he employs architecture to describe metaphysics in the *Critique of Pure Reason*, he subordinates architecture in the *The Critique of Judgement* as an inferior art, indeed the most inferior of the arts because it is the most bound to the utilitarian realm the aesthetic supposedly transcends.[19] Architecture cannot be thought outside utility and so its beauty is merely "appendant." On the other hand, the decorations of buildings, which can be considered separately from buildings as things in themselves—

"ornamental gardens," "the decoration of rooms," "wall hangings," "wall-paper," "ornamental accessories," "beautiful furniture"—are elevated into "free" beauty, free precisely from utility. Although buildings are the lowest form of art, the decoration of buildings ("the sole function of which is *to be looked at*"[20]) is promoted into the highest form of art: painting. But much of the ornamentation of buildings is obliged to represent the function of those buildings and is therefore excluded.[21] What is promoted in metaphysics—the structural bond to the ground, which can control representation—is apparently demoted in aesthetics. The groundedness of architecture seems to get in the way of the detached aesthetic gaze.

But if we look more closely at the text, this distinction is not simply applied to architecture. Architecture organizes the very argument that subordinates it. The aesthetic eye, like the philosophical eye, is not simply directed at architecture but is framed by it. *The Critique of Judgement* begins with two architectural examples with which it defines the fundamental disposition of aesthetic taste. The first separates the aesthetic eye from the eye of reason by opposing the rational cognition of a building to taking aesthetic delight in it. The aesthetic is detached from the rational knowledge it "accompanies" and placed in a "separate faculty." The second employs the distinction between a decorated palace and functional buildings like simple huts and eating houses to establish aesthetic disinterest as a disinterest in the existence of an object, its purpose, or its utility. Before we get the concepts, we get—or are presumed to have already gotten in our everyday experience—architecture, one of the arts to which the concepts are later to be applied. And in both cases, that everyday experience of architecture is aesthetic, the very experience that the book will go on to argue is almost impossible in architecture. Architecture is used to exemplify conditions that are then excluded from it in a pathological act of disavowal.

The *Critique* attempts to subordinate architecture precisely because it is so indebted to it. Philosophical discourse is only able to preserve the image of architecture with which it organizes and describes itself by veiling its indebtedness to that image; philosophy can only preserve its self-image by domesticating architecture, confining it, taking it out of view, holding it in reserve in some secure place from which it can be used to organize the very terrain in which it is prohibited from appearing. Even the necessary appearance of architecture in the carefully delimited domain of aesthetics produces a kind of embarrassment for the discourse, which forces a series of double gestures.

It is not that architecture is simply promoted in metaphysics and demoted in aesthetics. Rather, it is stitched into the operations of philosophy in more complex ways than philosophy can describe. To understand its role, we need to know more than what philosophy can say of architecture. It is actually a question of what it will not say about architecture, the architecture that is excluded from philosophy and whose exclusion makes philosophy possible or, more precisely, the architecture that should be excluded but never can be and so must be buried by a sustained pathology of disavowal, the architecture for which even the classic image of architecture that punctuates the discourse is but a fetishistic substitute that itself must be withdrawn as much as possible. The architecture that is spoken of but always and immediately domesticated, bracketed off as a suspect figure, masks another sense of architecture, one that is unspeakable and frightening to the discourse, which nevertheless cannot avoid harboring it within its very structure, as without it there could be no sense of structure in the first place.

It is the tension between these architectures that would be at stake in any translation between deconstructive discourse like Derrida's and architectural discourse. If his work displaces the tradition of philosophy, the question here must be whether or not it displaces or reproduces the different images of architecture embedded within that tradition. These images—which are also embedded within heterogeneous cultural institutions in addition to philosophy, and even organize our sense of what an institution is—cannot be as easily detached from the discipline of architecture as it might at first appear. This seemingly all too obvious link between deconstruction and architecture, which surfaces in the very word "deconstruction," cannot simply be discarded in the interests of a more nuanced reading without effacing a critical dimension of Derrida's work. I would argue that it is precisely within this very literal association, within its very literalness, the literalness of an architectural metaphor, that Derrida's writing is mobilized. At the very least, the strategic role of what seems to be but an incidental metaphor would be one of the central issues in any engagement between architecture and deconstruction.

This is not because philosophy, when speaking of architecture, is pointing outside itself to the material condition of buildings with which the discipline of architecture is most directly concerned, offering a theory of that material practice that is necessarily transformed by Derrida's work in a way that is of interest to that discipline. Philosophy is not simply theorizing something outside itself. The apparent distance between it and a building is at once produced by and is the possibility of its own theoretical discourse. It draws an edifice rather than draws on an edifice, producing an architecture of grounded structure that it then uses for support, leaning on it, resting within it. The edifice is constructed to make theory possible, then subordinated as a metaphor to defer to some higher, nonmaterial truth. Architecture is constructed as a material reality to liberate a supposedly higher domain. As material, it is but metaphor. The most material condition is used to establish the most ideal order, which is then bound to reject the former as merely material. The status of material oscillates. The metaphor of the ground, the bedrock as the fundamental base, inverts to become base in the sense of degraded, material, less than ideal. The vertical hierarchy inverts itself, and in this inversion architecture flips from privileged origin to gratuitous supplement, foundation to ornament.

Philosophy treats its architectural motif as but a metaphor that can and should be discarded as superfluous. The figure of the grounded structure is but an illustration, a useful metaphor that illustrates the nature of metaphysics, but outlives its usefulness and must be abandoned from the final form of metaphysics, a representation to be separated from the fundamental presentation, a kind of scaffolding to be discarded when the project is complete. The scaffolding that originally supports a structure is the part of structure that becomes ornamental. The structure of structure is, in the end, ornament. When philosophy reflects on its own completion, it defines architecture as metaphorical. Metaphysics is arguably no more than the determination of architecture as metaphor. But can architecture be so simply discarded? Not if we follow Derrida's own argument about metaphor, and the architectural metaphor in particular.

Contracting Architecture

It is significant that the earliest of Derrida's lectures to be published—"'Genesis and Structure' and Phenomenology," which was originally given in 1959—is an approving reading of the particular sense of "structure" in Edmund Husserl's work, articulated in terms of the rhetoric of "grounds," "foundations," "superstructure," "excavation," and "erection" that Husserl employed, and the first essay Derrida published—"Force and Signification" of 1963—is a disapproving reading of the "privileged" role of spatial metaphors, particularly that of "structure," in a text by Jean Rousset. Husserl is supported inasmuch as he explicitly rethinks the condition of structure and the general question of spatial form, whereas Rousset is condemned for employing spatial figures uncritically. The issue is not a small one. Derrida argues that such figures are "only metaphorical, it will be said. Certainly. But metaphor is never innocent. It orients research and fixes results. When the spatial model is hit upon, when it functions, critical reflection rests within it."[22] The discourse is within the spatial metaphor rather than the metaphor is within the discourse. It is orchestrated by what it thinks it employs. For Derrida, the "aesthetic" mode in which discourse is "fascinated by the spatial image" is far from innocent; it organizes the tradition of metaphysics that can be traced back at least to Plato. To resist that tradition, he calls for a sustained suspicion of the spatial metaphor and the way its metaphoric condition is effaced:

Hence, for as long as the metaphorical sense of the notion of structure is not acknowledged *as such,* that is to say interrogated and even destroyed as concerns its figurative quality so that the nonspatiality or original spatiality designated by it may be revived, one runs the risk, through a kind of sliding as unnoticed as it is *efficacious,* of confusing meaning with its geometric, morphological, or, in the best of cases, cinematic model. One risks being interested in the figure itself to the detriment of the play going on within it metaphorically.[23]

This crucial argument does not appear to be about architecture, and yet twice Derrida clarifies the sense of the suspect metaphor in terms of architecture. At the beginning of the essay, what is figured by "structure" is said to be "somewhat like the architecture of an inhabited or deserted city"[24] and in the middle of the essay its "literal," and therefore dangerous, sense is architectural: "Now, stricto senso, the notion of structure refers only to space, geometric or morphological space, the order of forms and sites. Structure is first the structure of an organic or artificial work, the internal unity of an assemblage, a *construction;* a work is governed by a unifying principle, the *architecture* that is built and made visible in a location."[25] It is inasmuch as the spatial image is literalized as architecture that it is dangerous and its uncritical employment has to be interfered with, if not "destroyed."

Derrida's work would go on to repeatedly demonstrate that metaphysics constitutes itself with the very metaphors it claims to have abandoned as "mere" metaphors. Furthermore, at one point he argues that this very attempt to abandon metaphors in favor of something more fundamental involves the architectural metaphor itself. In his most sustained argument about metaphor, he notes that a metaphor is distinguished from the fundamental as a building is distinguished from the ground:

Thus, the criteria for a classification of philosophical metaphors are borrowed from a derivative philosophical discourse. . . . They are metaphorical, resisting every meta-metaphorics, the values of concept, foundation, and theory. . . . What is fundamental corresponds to the desire for a firm and ultimate ground, a terrain to build on, the earth as the support for an artificial structure.[26]

Philosophy can only define a part of itself as nonmetaphorical by employing the architectural metaphor. This particular metaphor organizes the general status of metaphor. In so doing, it organizes the tradition of philosophy that claims to be able to discard it. The figure of a building as a grounded structure cannot be discarded to reveal any fundamental ground, as the sense of the "fundamental" is produced by that very figure. Architectural figures cannot simply be detached from philosophical discourse. Architecture is not simply one metaphor among others. More than the metaphor of foundation, it is the foundational metaphor. It is therefore not simply a metaphor.[27]

The architectural figure is bound to philosophy, and the institutionalized discourses "responsible" for architecture and philosophy each share and maintain this bond. The bond is contractual, not in the sense of an agreement signed by two parties, but in that of a conceptual knot of which the two parties are but an effect, a translation contract in the sense of Derrida's reading of Benjamin. More than the terms of exchange and translation within and between these discourses, it produces each discourse as a discourse. The translation between architecture and philosophy works both ways. Each has a fatal attraction for the other that manifests itself in many different ways. Each depends on the other. Neither one can think of itself outside the other, and yet each can think of itself only by placing the other outside. Each constructs the other as an origin from which it is, by definition—which is to say, by self-definition—detached. Each identifies the other as other, constructing it as other by invoking it as a privileged origin, only to push it away. Philosophy appeals to architecture to constitute itself, only to immediately subordinate architecture as mere material. Likewise, architectural discourse appeals to philosophy to constitute itself, only to subordinate it as provisional and ephemeral argument that must give way to the fundamental materiality of a building. Both discourses are constantly marked by the traces of these inversions, oscillating between moments of attraction and repulsion that can never simply be separated. The translation contract, as it were, negotiates this complex and restless dynamic.

This unwritten contract, which is neither a contingent cultural artifact nor an atemporal acultural principle, establishes the possibility of the more visible social contracts that appear to organize and separate architecture and philosophy as institutional discourses. The relatively recent status of architecture as a discipline began to be negotiated by the first texts of architectural theory in the Renaissance, which drew on the canonic texts of the philosophical tradition to identify the proper concern of the newly constituted figure of the architect with drawing [*Disegno*], which mediates between the idea and the building, the formal and the material, the soul and the body, the theoretical and the practical. Architecture—architectural drawing—is neither simply a mechanical art bound to the bodily realm of utility nor a liberal art operating in the realm of ideas, but is their reconciliation, the bridge between the two. Architectural theory thus constructs architecture as a bridge between the dominant oppositions of metaphysics and constitutes itself by exploiting the contractual possibility already written into the philosophical tradition wherein it describes itself as architecture.

It is not simply that architecture has some familiar, unambiguous material reality that is drawn upon by philosophy. Rather, philosophy draws an architecture, presents a certain understanding, a theory, of architecture. The terms of the contract are the prohibition of a different description of the architectural object, or rather, the dissimulation of that object. The discipline of architecture participates in this prohibition. Even though it nominates architecture as its subject, its main concern is to maintain the assumptions about architecture that are necessary for the everyday operations of culture outside the ostensible field of architecture: assumptions about materiality, order, spacing, closure, and so on. The discipline is no more than the maintenance of the sense of a field, a defined territory ostensibly worked over by different forms of architectural practice, theory, historiographical strategies, forms of criticism, pedagogical techniques, course structures, building codes, codes of professional ethics, techniques of representation, guild mentalities, modes of publication, exhibitions, journals, galleries, museums, and so on. But this field is not so much explored by these institutional practices as defended by them. It is constituted as such by an ongoing labor of representation, which confirms that architecture has its own limits that can be demarcated and examined, but in the end does so by preventing such an examination. Even this concept of a field as a delimited space presupposes exactly those architectural assumptions that are exempted from examination by such institutionalized defenses.

It is this solid defense through a systematic blinding of discourse that defines the profoundly conservative role of architectural discourse. It is not so much that the discourse assumes a conservative position, but that it conserves certain ideas about space employed by discourses which do not appear to be concerned with space (like the ideas embedded in the very concept of "position," for example). The traditional classification of architecture as an art acts as a cover for this fundamental disciplinary work. Even, if not especially, the current discourse's endless celebration of the new and of unique architectural responses to different spatial, regional, and historical conditions, the romanticizing of creativity, the promotion of the individual architect, the production of canonic histories, the awarding of prizes and commissions, commissions as prizes, and so on, is first and foremost a labor of conservation. The solidity of architecture is in this institutional defense rather than in the structure of buildings. The resistance of architecture does not lie in its ostensible materials but in the strength of institutional resistance to their interrogation. It is not that architecture, as it were, stands up to sustained interrogation. Rather, the institution of architecture is not read as such by the many discourses it makes possible, including, but not especially, those of "architecture" and "philosophy."

The concern here must therefore be to locate certain discursive practices repressed within the pathological mechanisms of the traditional economy that bind these discourses together by tracing the impact of another account of architecture hidden within them. It must be remembered that deconstructive discourse is not outside this economy. On the contrary, it attains its force precisely by inhabiting the tradition, obeying its principles so rigorously that their internal complications and contradictions become evident. In so doing, it necessarily engages at some level with the contract between architecture and philosophy. The question is, exactly what kind of relationship does deconstructive discourse assume with the account of architecture that the traditional economy resists but cannot avoid, the always threatening architecture repressed by the tradition? Can deconstructive discourse speak about this unspeakable architecture? Or even, can a discourse be deconstructive without doing so? To what extent is deconstructive discourse no more than a certain kind of interference with the institutional mechanisms that conceal, if not incarcerate, a certain forbidden, improper, and, above all, illegitimate architecture?

Towering Ruins

It needs to be remembered here that to describe architecture's privileged role in philosophy is not to identify it as some kind of origin or pregiven reality from which philosophy derives, and which therefore must be engaged through deconstructive discourse. It is not simply that there is some fundamental material reality of architecture in the world that is being suppressed by discourse. Architecture does not precede philosophy. Space is produced as such by the particular discourse maintained by philosophy, and there is no philosophy without space. Architecture and philosophy are effects of the same transaction, effects that can never be separated. One is never simply outside the other. The sense that they are separate is actually an effect of the very contract that binds them according to complicated folds, twists, and turns that defy the institutional practices of both discourses. A deconstructive discourse would need to trace the folds of this unique topology. In so doing, it would become evident that the strange condition produced when philosophy infects itself with what appears to belong in its "outside" by drawing on architecture—but actually produces a generic image of architecture to cover over an unspeakable architecture on its "inside"—is actually internal to the architecture it represents. Architecture is cut from within. It is itself infected, and philosophy unwittingly appeals to it for precisely this internal torment, exploiting it even while officially crediting buildings with an unambiguous material and perceptual reality.

In such terms, the translation of deconstruction in architecture does not simply occur across the divide between philosophy and architecture as some kind of singular event that produces some new description of architectural objects. It is already occurring within each discourse and must already have some kind of impact on deconstructive discourse. It is not something that the discourse can choose to either address or ignore, as it is part of what constitutes that discourse as deconstructive in the first place. To make an architectural translation of deconstruction therefore involves locating the accounts of architecture already operative within deconstructive discourse rather than simply generating some new description of the architectural object for architectural discourse. The difference between these accounts and those of the tradition of philosophy marks the precise nature of deconstructive discourse's occupation and transformation of that tradition. To question the discourse's ongoing relationship to architecture is therefore to question its every gesture. Its limits are established by the account of architecture it produces and depends on, albeit unwittingly.

Such an account can even be located in Derrida's discussion of translation itself. Inasmuch as deconstruction tampers with the philosophical ideal of translation, it necessarily tampers with the philosophical ideal of architecture. And if, as Derrida argues at one point, "the question of deconstruction is also through and through *the* question of translation,"[28] its thinking about architecture is likely to surface in those texts where its thinking about translation, which is implicitly written into, if not organizing, all of the other texts, becomes explicit. In fact, Derrida's account of translation is explicitly organized around an architectural figure: the Tower of Babel. It is the failure of the tower that marks the necessity for translation, the proliferation of a multiplicity of languages, the unruly play of representation, which is to say the necessity for controlling representation. The collapse marks the necessity for a certain regulated and regulating construction. In Derrida's "Des Tours de Babel," the figure of the tower acts as the strategic intersection of translation, philosophy, architecture, and deconstruction.

The tower acts as the figure of philosophy because the dream of philosophy is that of translatability.[29] Philosophy is no more than the ideal of pure translation, the careful recovery and unmediated presentation of an original truth. But, as Derrida points out elsewhere, the univocal language of the builders of the tower is not the language of philosophy. On the contrary, it is an imposed order, a violent imposition of a single language.[30] The necessity of philosophy is actually defined in the collapse of the tower rather than in the project itself. Inasmuch as the desire for translation produced by the incompletion of the tower is, as in all translations, never completely satisfied or frustrated, the philosophical edifice is never simply finished or demolished. The building project of philosophy continues, but its completion is forever deferred. This is not to say that a single construction is slowly assembled, like the original tower, toward some unattainable goal, but that the ideal of the edifice is forever suspended in a scene of endless rebuilding, an interminable displaced discourse about building.

The tower is also the figure of deconstruction. Because deconstructive discourse inhabits the philosophical tradition, subverting it from within by exploiting its hidden resources, it necessarily inhabits the figure of the tower, lodging itself within it and transforming the representation of its construction. Inasmuch as philosophy is the ideal of translation, deconstruction is the internal subversion of that ideal, a subversion found within the very preconditions for philosophy, the incompletion of the tower: "The deconstruction of the Tower of Babel, moreover, gives a good idea of what deconstruction is: an unfinished edifice whose half-completed structures are visible, letting one guess at the scaffolding behind them."[31] Deconstructive discourse identifies the inability of philosophy to establish the stable ground—its endless deferral of the very origin it seeks, which prevents the completion of the edifice—by locating the untranslatable, unpresentable, even unrepresentable remainder, the unspeakable other that lies somewhere between the original and the translation, making translation possible yet preventing its completion, that which is located within the discourse but cannot be located by it.

Furthermore, one of the implications of Derrida's argument about translation is that the tower and its incompletion is more than simply an architectural figure for philosophy and its deconstruction. It is also a figure of architecture itself. As Derrida argues in another context, "If the tower had been completed there would be no architecture. Only the incompletion of the tower makes it possible for architecture as well as the multitude of languages to have a history."[32] The possibility of architecture is bound up with the forever incomplete project of philosophy. If the philosophical dream of pure translation is a kind of building project, the inevitable incompletion of the building marks the necessity of architecture, understood as a representation that speaks of the structural essence of building, a supplementary layer that represents the ground in its absence. If building is the presentation of the ground, architecture is the representation of that grounding. Architecture is, as it were, the translation of building that represents building to itself as complete, secure, undivided. The architectural supplement is always called for by structural failure, called in to provide a particular image of building in its absence—not just an image of a particular building but also an image of the idea of building in general, the supposedly universal sense of building as the secure grounding of material structure.

The architectural supplement (and all supplements are architectural in the end) does not simply dissimulate a structural failure that preceded it. If architecture is the translation of building, it would follow from Derrida's argument about translation that the architectural representation is not simply added as an afterthought in a moment of weakness, the weakness of the building's structure. Architecture can never be divorced from building, even though traditional discourse works hard to do so. It is not a detached, free-floating, structureless representation called in because the grounded structure of a building is incomplete, called in to cover something that is missing, a representational layer attached to the structure it covers, fastened on to the building to dissimulate its flaws. On the contrary, the original sense of building, as the paradigm of grounded material structure, is only ever produced by the representational surfaces that appear to be merely added to it or substitute for it. Building is first and foremost an architectural effect.

Such a conjunction of translation, philosophy, architecture, and deconstruction is not the result of an idiosyncratic overdetermination of the otherwise simple figure of a tower by Derrida's text or the particular reading of that text given here.

Rather, it is a question of the implicit and explicit ways in which Derrida exploits the complex economy that such architectural figures invariably put into play under the very guise of simplicity. Despite the fact that they are invoked to clarify arguments, they always mobilize a convoluted set of effects that those arguments cannot control.

In these terms, the discourses we are concerned with here turn out to be so entangled that it is necessary to trace more carefully the differences between them. Inasmuch as the figure of the tower or edifice acts as some kind of common ground shared by these apparently foreign discourses, it needs to be examined more closely in order to identify the ruses of translation marked within it that produce and maintain the sense of separate identities. The double movements of translation, which at once constitute and subvert the limits that define each discourse, are necessarily made possible by an ongoing breakdown in the sense of grounded structure that is the shared currency within them.

This breakdown is mapped by all of Derrida's texts, beginning with his first essay, which describes how Husserl rethinks philosophy by being so "respectful of that which remains open within structure" to the extent of understanding that "the opening of the structure is 'structural,' that is, essential."[33] It is precisely this enigmatic "structurality of an opening" that organizes translation. For Derrida, the incompletion of the tower is its very structure. The tower is deconstructed by establishing that "the structure of the original is marked by the requirement to be translated"[34] and that it "in no way suffers from not being satisfied, at least it does not suffer in so far as it is the very structure of the work."[35] This is to say that there is an opening in the structure, a structural opening, a gap that cannot be filled, a gap that can only be covered with some kind of supplement, an ornamental cover that cannot be removed. Inasmuch as it is a tower, the tower is always marked by a flaw—a structural flaw, a flaw that is structural, an instability concealed by the ornamental translation that produces the sense of stable structure in the first place, subordinating itself to what it produces, marking within its surfaces the line between structure and ornament. It is by patiently following the hidden twists of this seemingly clear-cut line that deconstructive discourse displaces the generic figure of architecture. This can be seen when in one of the many times that Derrida's work explicitly undermines and complicates the always political relationship between structure and ornament, it does so by thinking of it as a relationship of translation:

> I do not believe that today one can, simply, analyze anything whatever while calmly trusting the difference between an infrastructure and a superstructure. . . . at the point where a deconstructive analysis enters, this opposition cannot be considered as guaranteed, or even as a thing in which one can have confidence. . . . Conveyance is *all* there is between . . . infrastrucure and superstructure; [there is only] translation in the most open sense of the word, . . . There is no pure infrastructure. There is no pure superstructure. There is only text. . . . the economic infrastructure is text, for example.[36]

In such displacements of the traditional architectural figure, structure is no longer simply grounding through a continuous vertical hierarchy from ground to ornament, but a discontinuous and convoluted line, an enigmatic series of folds. At the very least, the building is no longer simply standing on the ground, and the whole conceptual economy it is meant to put in place is disturbed. The sense of structure is actually produced by the supplementary layers of representation that appear least structural. The sense of control sought by traditional discourse actually derives from that which the discourse identifies as being in the greatest need of that control. The fundamental sense that the building faithfully translates the ground is but an effect of the supplementary layer of architecture that is meant, in turn, to faithfully translate the building and obey its law. Architecture is made to submit to a law of its own making. This enforced submission, ritually staged in the texts of the philosophical tradition but operative throughout heterogeneous Western discourses, veils the fact that building is always only an effect of representation. The labor of construction is never more than a labor of representation. In the end, it is this fact that is the most threatening to that tradition.

The radical consequences of the thought that architecture is the possibility of building rather than a simple addition to it, that ornament is the possibility of structure, cannot be overestimated.

All of the conceptual oppositions with which the tradition organizes itself turn on this point. Its not just, or even at all, that architecture is reconfigured, that the practice of what is traditionally recognized as architecture is described in a new way. Rather, a whole conceptual economy based on a certain description of architecture is disturbed. In each site within all the discourses organized around that economy, the role of that which is tacitly understood to be like architecture is to building is disrupted. The supplementary layer is seen to orchestrate the privileged structure it is subordinated to and meant to faithfully translate. No translation is secondary. In the end, there is nothing without translation. But this of course is not the translation dreamed of by the philosophical tradition. In terms of that tradition, Derrida's tacit articulation of the structural necessity of architecture marks the structural necessity of a certain failure of translation, the structural necessity of a certain violence.

Inasmuch as translation is neither completed nor completely frustrated, the distinction between building and architecture—which is at once the contractual possibility of architectural discourse and the means by which to repress the threat posed by that discourse—is uncannily complicated. Deconstructive discourse traces architecture's subversion of building, a subversion that cannot be resisted simply because architecture is the structural possibility of building. Building always harbors the secret of its constitutional violation by architecture. Deconstructive discourse articulates the relationship between this covert violation and the overt violence with which architecture is controlled. It repeatedly locates that which is configured as ornamental within the very structure that appears to dominate and exclude it, finding the traces of the ornament's violation of structure, a violation that cannot be exorcised, a constitutional violation that can only be repressed by institutional practices that are themselves always violent.

To say this little is already to elaborate one of the implications of Derrida's discourse around deconstruction beyond the explicit focus of his writings, one of many that will have to be pursued here in more detail. But before doing so, it is necessary to go much further into his texts in order to comprehend the architectures they already produce or resist and the faint but crucial marks of a certain sustained ambivalence about architecture.

The Survival of Deconstruction

Such an in-depth reading needs to be extreme and yet cautious. A number of preliminary precautions are necessary. First, it is important to remember that deconstruction is not a method, a critique, an analysis, or a source of legitimation.[37] It is not strategic. It has no prescribed aim, which is not to say that it is aimless. It moves very precisely, but not to some defined end. It is not even an application of something or an addition to something. It is, at best, a strange structural condition, an ongoing structural event, a continuous displacement of structure that cannot be evaluated in traditional terms because it is the very frustration of those terms. Deconstruction is that which is necessary to structure but evades structural analysis (and analysis is invariably structural). It is the breakdown of structure that is the very possibility of structure, but which must be concealed to produce the effect of structure in the first place.

Rather than offering new accounts of the architectural object to replace the one that dominates the disciplines of philosophy and architecture, deconstructive discourse unearths the repressive mechanisms by which other senses are hidden within (rather than behind or underneath) that traditional figure, senses that are already threatening in their very multiplicity. It is the repression of these constitutional enigmas that is the basis of the social contract that organizes the overt discourse about architecture. The architectural figure is not simply required by philosophy because it is the paradigm of stable structure; it is also required precisely for its very instability. Just as instability must always be concealed to produce the effect of unambiguous stability, philosophical discourse, which represents itself as both the stabilizing discourse and the discourse about stability, is unable to articulate its debt to architecture. The very basis of its attraction to architecture, its most fundamental desire, is forbidden. Inasmuch as deconstructive discourse is the attempt to articulate the unspeakable, but always constitutional, desire of philosophy, it necessarily uncovers a forbidden architecture hidden within traditional discourse.

Likewise, to translate deconstruction in architecture is not to simply transform the condition of the material architectural object. It is not the source of a particular kind of architecture, but an interrogation of the ongoing discursive role of architecture. As the tradition of metaphysics is the definition of architecture as mere metaphor, any disruption of architecture's role as a figure is already a disruption of metaphysics. This is not to say that this disruption occurs outside the realm of material objects. On the contrary, it is a disruption of the line between discourse and materiality whereby the sense of a material object is understood to be a discursive effect. It is not that the traditional distinctions organized around that line that are so conspicuous in architectural discourse (theory/practice, ideal/material, project/building, and so on) disappear. Rather, they are complicated in ways that transform the status of familiar discursive operations and expose other operations that are ongoing and produce certain visible effects but cannot be recognized by the institutionalized discourses of philosophy and architecture (to name but two), covert operations that reconfigure architecture.

Such deconstructive gestures are not simply theoretical or practical. They are neither a new way of reading architecture nor the means of producing a new architecture. On the one hand, so-called material "objects" are already bisected by the institutionalized distinction between theory and practice in complex ways, according to extremely convoluted geometries. On the other, so-called theoretical discourse is itself a material site of production. To translate deconstruction in architecture does not simply lead to a formal reconfiguration of the architectural object or architectural theory. Rather, it calls into question the status of the object without simply abandoning it. If it is concerned with anything, it is concerned with theoretical objects, which is to say, objects whose theoretical status and objecthood are problematic, slippery objects that make thematic the theoretical condition of objects and the objecthood of theory. But, in the end, it does so to demonstrate that this slipperiness is not the unique property of particular discursive objects, but is the very possibility of any discourse and its objects. In the end, the solidity of an object is always a product of slippage.

These gestures cannot simply inhabit the prescribed domains of philosophy and architecture. Although philosophical discourse and architectural discourse depend on an explicit account of architecture, they have no unique claim on that account. The translation contract on which those discourses are based underpins a multiplicity of cultural economies. The concern here is with the strategic play of the architectural motif within these heterogeneous exchanges. This ongoing cultural production of architecture does not take the form specified in architectural discourse. Architecture does not occupy the domain allotted to it. Rather than the object of a specific discourse, architecture involves a number of discursive mechanisms whose operations have to be traced in ways unfamiliar to, and systematically resisted by, architectural discourse.

Consequently, the status of the translation of deconstruction in architecture needs to be rethought. A more aggressive reading is required, an architectural transformation of deconstruction that draws on the gaps in deconstruction that demand such an abuse, sites that already operate with or call for a kind of architectural violence. There is a need for a more forceful reading that locates that which deconstruction desires but cannot handle of architecture.

Certain possibilities emerge within architectural discourse that go beyond the displacement of architecture implicit in deconstructive writing. To translate deconstruction architecturally by locating these possibilities is to reproduce it by transforming it. Such a transformation would operate on the hesitation deconstructive discourse has about architecture, a hesitation that surfaces precisely within its most confident claims about architecture. At the beginning of his essay on translation, for example, Derrida writes:

The "Tower of Babel" does not merely figure the irreducible multiplicity of tongues; it exhibits an incompletion, the impossibility of finishing, of totalizing, of saturating, of completing something on the order of edification, architectural construction, system and architectonics. What the multiplicity of idioms actually limits is not only a "true" translation, a transparent and adequate interexpression, it is also a structural order, a coherence of construct. There is then (let us translate) something like an internal limit to formalization, an incompleteness of the constructure. It would be easy and up to a certain point justified to see there the translation of a system in deconstruction.[38]

This passage culminates symptomatically in a sentence that performs the classical philosophical gesture, the gesture that arguably constitutes philosophy as such. Architecture is at once given constitutive power and has that power frustrated by having its status returned to that of a "mere" metaphor that needs to be discarded. Here the tower, the figure of translation, is itself understood as a translation, the architectural translation of deconstruction, which is to say, in Derridean terms, a figure that is the possibility of deconstruction rather than simply its representation. But Derrida's texts need to be interrogated to see exactly why such an architectural reading of deconstruction is "easy" and what is the "certain point" beyond which it becomes unjustified, improper. A patient reading needs to force the already tangled surface of deconstructive writing and expose the architectural desire within it; the desire for a traditional architecture; the desire whose very properness might seem improper on the surface of this discourse that everywhere undermines propriety; the desire whose intensity is actually marked by the systematic repetition of such attempts to limit an architectural translation of deconstruction.

But perhaps even such an abusive reading of Derrida is insufficient. Inasmuch as his thinking about deconstruction is necessarily abused in architectural discourse, his account of translation—which is to say his account of the necessity of abuse—needs to be rethought. Because of architecture's unique relationship to translation, it cannot simply translate deconstruction. It is so implicated in the economy of translation that it at once preserves and threatens deconstruction. There is some kind of implicit identity between the untranslatable remainder that deconstructive discourse confidently locates and the part of architecture that causes the discourse to hesitate—the architecture it both calls for and resists. Consequently, if, as Derrida argues at one point, "everything which is living today lives through deconstruction" inasmuch as "deconstruction is survival,"[39] deconstructive discourse itself can never simply survive architecture.

2

Unbuilding Architecture

Architecture can never simply be a subject of deconstructive discourse or be ignored by it. There cannot simply be a deconstructive discourse "about" architecture inasmuch as its way of raising questions is itself architectural from the beginning. When Derrida describes "deconstruction," which he rarely does (and then only after a marked hesitation and the taking of many precautions), it is usually in architectural terms. And both the hesitation and the particular precautions taken are not unrelated to the fact that these terms are architectural.

Derrida's early work repeatedly describes deconstruction as the "soliciting" of an edifice, "in the sense that *Sollicitare*, in old Latin, means to shake as a whole, to make tremble in entirety."[1] If deconstructive discourse is anything, it is a form of interrogation that shakes structures in a way that exposes structural weaknesses. It puts structures under pressure, forcing them, taking them to the limit. Under a subtle but relentless strain their limits become evident and the structure becomes visible as such, but it becomes visible, precisely, as something unlike the culturally enfranchised image of structure. The structure does not look structural. That which is structural cannot be recognized as such by the very tradition it organizes. Derrida's texts locate the unresolvable enigmas on which the structures they interrogate depend in order to call into question the dominant tradition of thinking that is organized by a certain image of building. Each edifice is destabilized by showing that its apparent stability is but an effect of the ongoing concealment of these enigmas.

The edifice of metaphysics (and all edifices consolidate meta-physics, there being no edifice without metaphysics and no meta-physics without edifice) claims to be stable because it is founded on the solid bedrock exposed when all the insecure sedimentary layers have been removed. It is dislodged by locating the frac-tures in the bedrock that undermine its structure. The threat to the architecture that is posed by deconstruction is underground or, rather, is the underground. Subverting metaphysics always involves an underground operation. In carrying out such an operation, deconstructive discourse subverts an edifice by dem-onstrating that the ground on which it is erected is insecure, insecure precisely because it veils an underground. The suppos-edly solid base is riddled with cavities: "the terrain is slippery and shifting, mined and undermined. And this ground is, by essence, an underground."[2]

In these terms, deconstructive discourse appears to locate the fatal flaw in an edifice that causes its collapse. It appears to be a form of analysis that dismantles or demolishes structures, an undoing of construction, and it is in this sense that it is most obviously architectural. But this obvious sense misses the force of deconstruction. Deconstruction is not simply architec-tural. Rather, it is displacement of traditional thinking about architecture:

Now the concept of deconstruction itself resembles an architectural metaphor. It is often said to have a negative attitude. Something has been constructed, a philosophical system, a tradition, a culture, and along comes a de-constructor and destroys it stone by stone, analyses the structure and dissolves it. Often enough this is the case. One looks at a system—Platonic/Hegelian—and examines how it was built, which keystone, which angle of vision supports the authority of the system. It seems to me, however, that this is not the essence of deconstruction. It is not simply the technique of an architect who knows how to de-con-struct what has been constructed, but a probing which touches upon the technique itself, upon the authority of the architectural metaphor and thereby constitutes its own architectural rhetoric. Deconstruction is not simply—as its name seems to indicate—the technique of a re-versed construction when it is able to conceive for itself the idea of construction. One could say that there is nothing more architectural than deconstruction, but also nothing less architectural.[3]

To comprehend in what way deconstruction "resembles" an architectural gesture, a resemblance so emphatically opposed to what is (perhaps surprisingly) described as the "essence" of deconstruction, in order to grasp the crucial sense in which, for Derrida, nothing is more or less architectural than deconstruction, it is necessary to look at the origins of his thinking about it in Heidegger's writing.

Taking Flimsy Cover in Architecture

It is arguably Heidegger's engagement with the question of building that determines both the form and content of his writing. In *What Is a Thing?* (the text of the lectures originally entitled "Basic Questions of Metaphysics" that were given at the University of Freiburg in the winter semester of 1935–36), for example, Heidegger asks about the "inner structure" of the "building" that is metaphysics by looking at Kant's "exhibition of the inner construction of pure reason" which "draws and sketches" reason's "outline" and whose "essential moment" is the "architectonic, the blueprint projected as the essential structure of pure reason."[4] Heidegger has appropriated all of this architectural rhetoric directly from Kant as part of a general strategy of appropriation, which is itself described in architectural terms. The strategy is to occupy the philosophical structure with which Kant defines the structure of reason, identifying the limits of both these interrelated structures by inhabiting those very limits:

In our interpretation we shall not try to examine and paraphrase the structure of the work from the outside. Rather, we shall place ourselves within the structure itself in order to discover something of its framework and to gain the standpoint for viewing the whole.[5]

This strategy of occupation derives closely from the "phenomenological reduction" of Edmund Husserl. It was already formulated in Heidegger's first lectures as Husserl's assistant in 1920 and recorded in letters to his students as a matter of "destruction" (*Destruktion*) or "critical unbuilding" (*kritischer Abbau*)—the latter term being sometimes translated as "critical dismantling," or even, more recently, in a kind of reverse projection, as "deconstruction." The concept was formally introduced in the celebrated *Being and Time* of 1927, but is then more fully elaborated in the lecture course at the University of Marburg in the summer of the same year that was intended to be published as its sequel:

> All philosophical discussion, even the most radical attempt to begin all over again, is pervaded by traditional concepts and thus by traditional horizons and traditional angles of approach, which we cannot assume with unquestionable certainty to have arisen originally and genuinely from the domain of being and the constitution of being they claim to comprehend. It is for this reason that there necessarily belongs to the conceptual interpretation of being and its structures, that is, to the reductive construction of being, a *destruction*—a critical process in which the traditional concepts, which at first must necessarily be employed, are de-constructed [*kritischer Abbau*] down to the sources from which they were drawn. . . . Construction in philosophy is necessarily destruction, that is to say, a de-constructing of traditional concepts carried out in a historical recursion to the tradition. And this is not a negation of the tradition or a condemnation of it as worthless; quite the reverse, it signifies precisely a positive appropriation of tradition.[6]

Authentic construction involves taking apart unauthentic constructions from within. It is not that the "unbuilding" of the old tradition is followed by a new construction. Rather, "destruction belongs to construction."[7] The tradition contains within itself the traces of the originary construction that it has forgotten, traces that can be gradually teased out. Philosophy is therefore no more than the writing of the history of philosophy, one that must be continuously rewritten.[8] An originary construction is not something that simply lies behind the false structures of the tradition and can be revealed by demolishing them. Rather, it is built into those structures and can only be addressed by reappropriating the tradition in its own terms, taking them to their "limits."[9]

For Heidegger, the tradition of philosophy, beginning with Plato, has forgotten its original task of raising the question of Being. The institution has lost touch with the fundamental condition of beings. The identification it makes with its object, when both are understood as a kind of building that stands on a ground, is therefore more a projection of its self-image onto its object than a recovery of the essential condition of that object. Metaphysics is a particular kind of construction that actually covers the originary construction it ostensibly reveals. Inasmuch as authentic thinking is authentic building, the tradition of philosophy is at once an inadequate building and an inadequate thinking about building. Heidegger's attempt to "overcome" this tradition is necessarily a rethinking of building. This rethinking does not simply abandon the classical building of philosophy in favor of some superior construction technique, but identifies the sense of building that philosophy attempts to cover, studying the classic building for the traces of what it effaces.

Furthermore, the force of Heidegger's argument derives from its claim that the flaws in the construction of the edifice that it identifies do not simply point to another kind of building to be restored after the tradition is dismantled. Rather, they are the very structure of the building that the tradition constructs. When interrogating this edifice to reveal the condition of the ground on which it stands, Heidegger raises the possibility that the ground (*Grund*) might actually be a concealed "abyss" (*Abgrund*) and that metaphysics is constructed in ignorance of, or rather, to ignore, the instability of the terrain on which it is erected, such that "we move about over this ground as over a flimsily covered abyss."[10] Metaphysics becomes the veiling of the ground rather than its investigation, and the apparently simple sense of a building sitting on the ground, supported by it, is the very mechanism of that veiling. Architecture is a cover and philosophy takes cover in architecture.

Heidegger developed this possibility that the ground is actually an obscured abyss into a quasi-principle, or more precisely, into an argument that all principles are, in the end, unprincipled. This development is clearest in his seminars given at Freiburg in 1955–56, which studied in detail the so-called "Principle of Ground"—"nothing is without ground/reason [*Grund*]"—with which modern philosophy organizes itself. For Heidegger, this principle has been embedded in the tradition of philosophy since its origins in ancient Greece, even though it has only been formulated as such with Descartes and Leibniz.[11] The surfacing of the architectural figure in philosophy that is described in much of Heidegger's earlier writing turns out to be interdependent with the surfacing of this principle. The principle is itself architectural. Indeed, much more than this, it is the very principle of architecture. It is not just that a principled architecture is a philosophical necessity but, equally, principles are always architectural.

All principles are structural principles. They institute claims about the status of the ground that are meant to be "stabilizing for thinking."[12] The principle of ground is, as Heidegger argues "not just any principle among others"[13] as it is the principle of stability itself, the principle of principles legitimizing the concern with the "unshakable ground" that Descartes looks for in order to erect a stable construction. To philosophize about something, to rationalize it, is "to figure it as something upon which to build."[14] But this principle of secure construction is not itself examined by the tradition based around it. Rather, it is a "long-standing cognitive habit"[15] employed everywhere. The basis of thinking is itself not thought through. The principle of support is itself used for support in lieu of the thinking it ostensibly secures. In the end, it produces the very groundlessness it legislates against: "Everywhere we use the principle of reason and adhere to it as a prop for support. But it also immediately propels us into groundlessness without our hardly thinking about it in its genuine meaning."[16] Heidegger looks for the ground of this principle of grounding, examining the way the expression, and all the arguments typically invoked to explain it, are "built" on a tautological circle. In the end, the fundamental principle of ground is itself groundless. The building of philosophy is founded on an abyss. Building is always abysmal. It is founded by covering over its origin, only appearing to stand inasmuch as it conceals the absence of a ground.

Heidegger argues that philosophy has been in a state of "groundlessness" ever since the translation of the terms that organized ancient Greek thinking into the language of metaphysics, a translation that substituted the original sense of ground with that of the sense of ground as support, ground as supporting presence to which the visible world is added.[17] For Heidegger, metaphysics is groundless precisely because it determines the ground as support. It is with this image that the original sense of *logos* has been lost. Only with and through metaphysics is the origin seen as a stable ground rather than an abyss. The "modern" crisis, the "groundlessness" of the violent age of technology, is produced by philosophy's ancient determination of the ground as support for a structure to which representations may be added.[18] The crisis of representation is produced by the very attempt to remove representations in order to reveal the supporting presence of the ground. We are alienated from the ground precisely by thinking of it as secure.

Just as Heidegger displaces philosophy's sense of itself as a construction standing on a stable ground in favor of philosophy as a constructing-through-unbuilding, he also displaces the sense of the structures that philosophy describes. Although following the tradition's understanding of being as a certain kind of "standing," it is no longer a standing on a stable ground, but a standing based on a loss of ground, a construction built on an "abyss." The abyss, the rupturing of the fundamental ground of things, becomes their very condition of possibility. Heidegger argues that it is not simply that philosophy has always described its proper object as being like a founded building that stands. Rather, it is only by virtue of being readable in this way that anything is recognized as an object in the first place.[19] It is not that being is grounded but "*being in itself essentially comes to be as grounding.*"[20] Consequently, "to the extent that being as such grounds, it remains groundless."[21] In this way, both the building that is philosophy and the building that it describes are radically displaced.

The Displacement of Architecture

These closely interrelated displacements of the institutionalized, and therefore familiar, sense of construction organize Derrida's texts long before architecture becomes a discrete subject within them. Heidegger's rethinking of building is everywhere operative in Derrida's work, which significantly began with an extended reading of Husserl. The term "deconstruction" itself derives directly from Heidegger's *Destruktion* and *Abbau*. In Derrida's own words, it is literally a "translation" of those terms.[22] Furthermore, what is being translated is understood to be architectural. For

Derrida, *Destruktion* means "not a destruction but precisely a destructuring that dismantles the structural layers in the system" and *Abbau* means "to take apart an edifice in order to see how it is constituted or deconstituted."[23] Both signify "an operation bearing on the structure or traditional architecture of the fundamental concepts of ontology or of western metaphysics."[24] In remobilizing these terms, Derrida follows Heidegger's argument that this "destructuring" or "unbuilding" disturbs a tradition by inhabiting its structure in a way that exploits its metaphoric resources against itself, not to abandon the structure but to locate what it conceals.

The unbuilding that is deconstruction is not a form of demolition. It establishes the conditions of possibility of the "traditional architecture" rather than staging its fall.[25] To make a building tremble is precisely not to collapse it by subjecting it to some external force, but to explore it from within, even to consolidate the structure, imitating its every gesture, faithfully repeating its operations but in a way that exposes its limits, opening up its structure or, rather, finding the openings that are already there, the concealed points of weakness: "In the course of this repetition a barely perceptible displacement disjoints all the articulations and penetrates all the points welded together by the imitated discourse."[26] Like Heidegger's *Abbau* and *Destruktion,* this is an appropriation of structures that identifies structural flaws, cracks in the construction that have been systematically disguised, not to collapse those structures but, on the contrary, to demonstrate the extent to which the structures depend on both these flaws and the way they are disguised. That is, it identifies the structural role of what traditional philosophy would identify as structural flaws and, in so doing, displaces rather than dismantles that philosophy.

Deconstructive shaking, like the "shaking of the foundations" Heidegger describes in one of his later readings of Nietzsche,[27] produces the sense of stability as such rather than its loss. A structure does not simply collapse because it is erected on, and fractured by, an abyss. On the contrary, the fracturing of the ground is the very possibility of the edifice. The abyss, as Derrida's *Of Grammatology* argues, is a "structural necessity":

And we shall see that this abyss is not a happy or unhappy accident. An entire theory of the structural necessity of the abyss will be gradually constituted in our reading; the indefinite process of supplementarity has always already *infiltrated* presence . . . Representation *in the abyss* of presence is not an accident of presence; the desire of presence is, on the contrary, born from the abyss . . . [28]

The fissures in the ground that crack the structure are therefore not flaws that can be repaired. The subterranean cavities cannot be filled. They do not weaken a previously secure ground. On the contrary, they produce the sense of the ground in the first place. In the end, they are the ground. Buildings are erected on and by cracks. There is no more stable ground to be found, no unflawed bedrock. Consequently, the subversion of structure does not lead to a new structure. The flaws identified in the structure are the very source of its strength. When the deconstructive shaking of a building reveals structural weaknesses, they are weaknesses that are structural.

This is to say that Derrida identifies the strength of a certain weakness. Rather than abandoning a structure because its weakness has been found (which would be to remain in complicity with the traditional ideal of a grounded structure and the whole conceptual economy that follows from it), deconstructive discourse displaces the architectural figure. Structure becomes "erected by its very ruin, held up by what never stops eating away at its foundation."[29] This enigmatic sense is operative everywhere in Derrida's writing as a kind of thread stitched into each of his texts in a way that binds them together. In *Glas*, to name but one example—and within that example to point to but a few of its traces—it appears in the expression "ruin it by erecting it, perhaps"[30] which is tied in to an earlier comment that "the structure of the tower is such that its construction returns, stone by stone, to its destruction," which in turn is made in response to Genet's line, "the act of building his life minute by minute, witnessing its construction, which is also progressive destruction."[31] This sense of construction through destruction and ruin through building organizes the whole text at many different levels and binds it to Derrida's other texts.

In these terms, deconstructive discourse is a form of interrogation that shakes structure in order to identify which of its flaws are structural. Rather than demolish particular structures, it displaces the very concept of structure by locating within it that which is neither support nor collapse. As Derrida puts it in "Force and Signification," "Structure then can be *methodically* threatened in order to be comprehended more clearly and to reveal not only its supports but also that secret place in which it is neither construction nor ruin but lability."[32] The edifice is erected, that is, presents itself as a building, only by concealing this strange element that exceeds its structural logic. At the same time, that logic depends on what it conceals. Deconstruction is concerned with that which exceeds building, the confusion of structure that is hidden by it and yet makes it possible.

This anarchitectural element on which architecture depends is not simply hidden underneath the building or below the ground. It is only its repression that produces the appearance of ground in the first place. The abyss is not simply the fracturing of the ground that lies under the edifice. It is the internal fracturing of the structure, the convolution and complication of the distinction between building and architecture, structure and ornament, presentation and representation. The undermining of the security of the ground is equally the undermining of the possibility of detaching ornament from structure. If architecture always inhabits and underpins the building it is supposedly attached to, it is precisely this convolution, which philosophy will everywhere attempt to overtly deny and covertly repress, that makes possible the thought of a ground that precedes the construction of an edifice, the central thought of philosophy that will always subordinate architecture as merely a representational addition. Architecture, that is, effects its own subordination to building. There would be no building without the self-effacement of architecture. Structure is an effect of this withdrawal. Inasmuch as it is always reading this effect, deconstructive discourse is always concerned with architecture.

But to elaborate the sense in which the architectural surface is, in the end, the only building site would be to explore only one dimension of the double sense in which, as Derrida argues, nothing is more or less architectural than deconstruction. Just as deconstructive discourse offers a way of comprehending architectural discourse, it also places the very idea of architecture at risk and is only deconstructive inasmuch as it does so. This double attitude to architecture is evident in an extended passage of Derrida's *Memoires: For Paul de Man*, which responds to de Man's use of an architectural figure in speaking of allegory as the "*defective cornerstone* of Hegel's system." Derrida elaborates the figure in some detail:

We have here a figure of what some might be tempted to see as the dominant metaphorical register, indeed the allegorical bent of "deconstruction," a certain architectural rhetoric. One first locates, in an architectonics, in the art of the system, the "neglected corners" and the "*defective* cornerstone," that which, from the outset, threatens the coherence and the internal order of the construction. But it is a cornerstone! It is required by the architecture which it nevertheless, in advance, deconstructs from within. It assures its cohesion while situating in advance, in a way that is both visible and invisible (that is, corner), the site that lends itself to a deconstruction to come. The best spot for efficiently inserting the deconstructive lever is a cornerstone. There may be other analogous places but this one derives its privilege from the fact that it is indispensable to the completeness of the edifice. A condition of erection, holding up the walls of an established edifice, it also can be said to maintain it, to contain it, and to be tantamount to the *generality* of the architectonic system, "of the entire system."[33]

Having disturbed the classical architectural figure by showing how it is the very defects in certain building elements that make them central to the structure, the essay immediately distances itself from the figure, arguing that "Paul de Man's 'deconstructive' moves do not all obey this logic or this 'architectural' rhetoric,"[34] and then arguing that, rather than operating within any particular edifice, deconstruction questions the very idea of architecture, or at least the dominance of a particular account of architecture:

Nor do I think, but I will explain this elsewhere, that deconstruction—if there be such a thing and it be *one*—is bound by the link that the word suggests with the architectonic. Rather, it attacks the systemic (i.e., architectonic) constructionist account of what is brought together, of assembly.[35]

Here Derrida is again questioning "the authority of the architectural metaphor" in the same way as he does in several other texts.[36] Arguing that "one might be inclined" to reach the conclusion that deconstruction is something that is already occupying an architecture, rather than a discourse "inserting" itself into it, such that "the disruptive force of deconstruction is always already contained within the architecture of the work," he then hesitates, putting this thought on hold: "Since I want neither to accept or reject a conclusion formulated in these terms, let us leave the question hanging for a while." He nevertheless immediately returns to the original elaboration of the traditional architectural metaphor.[37] A more radical questioning of architecture is announced and immediately suspended.

This symptomatic hesitation and ambivalence around architecture punctuates much of Derrida's writing. Again, we have to ask: in what way is the architectural dimension of deconstruction only "what one might be tempted to see as" central? In what way does it, as he puts it elsewhere, merely "resemble" an architectural gesture, a gesture that is "not the essence of deconstruction."[38] What precisely is the seductive temptation of architecture that would lead us astray here? From what? What is the essential quality of deconstruction masked by architecture and where, if anywhere, might it lead us? What does it mean to be astray in deconstructive discourse anyway? In the end, what are the stakes in architecture for deconstruction?

The Elusive Politics of Architecture

Before addressing these questions in order to pursue the implications of deconstruction for the institution of architecture, it needs to be understood that deconstruction, first and foremost, bears upon the architecture of institutions. When one of Derrida's first essays describes the deconstructive solicitation of structure, it symptomatically substitutes the word "institution" for structure, even though the essay is not ostensibly about institutions:

Structure is perceived through the incidence of menace, at the moment when imminent danger concentrates our vision on the keystone of an institution, the stone which encapsulates both the possibility and the fragility of its existence.[39]

Throughout his work, when Derrida speaks of the architectural metaphor and its displacement, it is always a question of the status of the institution even if this question is raised in what appears to be, at first, an oblique way. Furthermore, it is when the question is not so oblique and he explicitly thematizes the status of institutions that the architectural metaphor is most explicit. When, for example, the interview "Ja, ou le faux-bond" rejects the impression that deconstruction is the dismantling or demolition of an architecture in favor of deconstruction as a questioning of the whole architectural rhetoric of foundation, construction, architectonics, and so on,[40] it does so in the context of discussing the politics of materialism, and beyond that, the politics of deconstruction itself: "a deconstructive practice that had no bearing on 'institutional apparatuses and historical processes'. . . which was satisfied to work on philosophemes or conceptual signifieds, discourses, etc., would not be deconstructive; no matter how original it might be, it would reproduce the auto-critical movement of philosophy in its internal tradition."[41] The questioning of the very idea of building is aligned with a questioning of institutional authority. It is the rethinking of architecture that defines the politics of deconstruction.

Whenever Derrida addresses the politics of deconstruction, he does so by identifying the centrality of its thinking about institutions; this thinking is almost invariably presented in architectural terms and is, in the end, about the status of those very terms. Institutions are understood as buildings that can be displaced only by rethinking architecture. The association between the question of materialism and architecture is not coincidental. At the beginning of "Parergon," when speaking of the political history of a particular institution—the university—institutions in general are credited with materiality by virtue of their architectural condition:

We must take account of certain specific relays, for example those of so-called philosophy teaching in France, in the institution of its programs, its forms of examinations and competitions, its scenes and its rhetoric . . . the construction of the French University and its philosophical institution—all the teaching structures that we still inhabit. Here I do no more than name, with a proper name as one of the guiding threads, the necessity of a deconstruction. Following the consistency of its logic, it attacks not only the internal edifice, both semantic and formal, of philosophemes, but also what one would be wrong to assign to it as its external housing, its extrinsic conditions of practice: the historical forms of its pedagogy, the social, economic or political structures of this pedagogical institution. It is because deconstruction interferes with solid structures, "material" institutions, and not only with discourses or signifying representations, that it is always distinct from an analysis or a "critique."[42]

This slippage between politics and architecture is repeated throughout Derrida's work but is most evident around the question of the university. In the "The Principle of Reason: The University in the Eyes of its Pupils," for example, he argues that "it is impossible, now more than ever, to disassociate the work we do . . . from a reflection on the political and institutional conditions of that work"[43] and goes on to say that this reflection must displace the traditional idea of institution: "what is meant by community and institution must be rethought."[44] This rethinking of institutional politics turns out to be architectural. The institution of the university is understood to be architectural from the beginning, a system that describes itself as a kind of building and organizes itself according to a rhetoric of ground, footing, foundation, structure, space, architectonics, and so on. In "Languages and Institutions of Philosophy," which reads "the properly architectonic or architectural figure of the institution, as a founded and structured edifice, constructed like an artifact,"[45] Derrida argues that: "One cannot think of the university institution, as an institution of reason. . . . without this role of architectonics. There is no university architecture without architectonics."[46]

In carefully reading this "institutional architecture," Derrida is following Heidegger, who at one point in his seminars on the "principle of ground" noted how the university is "built" [gebaut] on that principle.[47] Derrida's reading of those seminars focuses on the argument that inasmuch as this principle produces the institution devoted to its preservation and enforcement, it cannot itself be grounded within that institution. The "space of the university" is founded on an abyss. The structure of the building is erected on and by an instability that it cannot control even though it everywhere declares its intent to do so. This argument is continued in "Mochlos ou le conflit des facultés," a reading of Kant's architectonic description of the university, when Derrida argues that the founding, which is to say building, of a university necessarily occurs on unstable grounds inasmuch as "a founding act cannot be simply included in the logic of what it founds."[48] The edifice is built on the abyss that it is designed to conceal and that the essay is only able to identify through an extended interrogation of the ostensibly architectural concept of "foundation."

Again, this argument is explicitly concerned with politics. The essay calls for each discourse to take account of the specific politics of the institutional space that makes it possible: "I *do* say that today, for anyone who belongs to an institution of teaching and research, the minimal responsibility, and also the newest, most powerful, and most interesting, is to make as clear and thematically explicit as possible such political implications, their system, and its aporias."[49] And again, the political is understood as architectural. To think of the politics of the institution involves placing into question the traditional sense of building, not to simply dismantle any building, but rather to identify the strange ruses by which it assumes authority and to thereby disturb traditional relationships to that authority. The mechanisms of authority are not simply discredited or destroyed. On the contrary, they become more formidable. Inasmuch as a structure is founded on contradictions, it is reinforced rather than threatened by those strategies that immediately appear to be political. What is least threatening is precisely that which appears most threatening.

In this sense, the common reactions to deconstructive discourse are all too symptomatic. Clearly deeply threatened in some way by that discourse, traditionally empowered discourses (whether of the orthodox left or right) have labored very hard to construct deconstructive discourse as one of complete demolition. Ironically, to render it less threatening, they have had to construct it as totally threatening, an untenable form of nihilism that can easily be dismissed. This construction requires a sustained violence to the letter of the texts being criticized or, more typically, an almost complete ignorance of them, both of which involve the abandonment of the very academic principles supposedly being upheld. In the end, such arguments much better exemplify what they condemn than the texts they wish to dismiss. The more radical threat of deconstructive discourse lies precisely in the extent to which it does not demolish traditional structures, but identifies the contradictions on which and, more precisely, with which they are founded. In articulating the enigmas of structure, such a discourse opens up other possibilities for political action. In so doing, the status of the traditional image of building, as reproduced in Kant's text, necessarily becomes unclear:

> Reading this text today, I appreciate its assurance and sense of necessity as one might admire the rigor of a plan or structure one apprehends through the breeches of an edifice that is uninhabitable, and which leaves one unable to decide whether it is in a state of ruin or has simply never existed, never been able to do more than shelter the discourse of its own incompletion.[50]

It is precisely this suspension of the status of building, rather than any singular determination of it, that makes the reading political. The uncertainty about the edifice becomes the basis of Derrida's attempt to threaten not only "the entire architecture"[51] of Kant's text but also the entire Kantian corpus that represents itself in architectural terms and, in the end, the ancient institution of philosophy in which it is embedded.

What both institutional authority and those gestures that immediately appear to disrupt it share is a commitment to a sense of determination or decision, the sense that clear lines can and should be drawn. Derrida interferes with this sense not by, as is so often and so incorrectly asserted, promoting a generalized indeterminacy, a sense that decisions can never be made, but, on the contrary, arguing that decisions are always made, not in spite of an unavoidable indeterminacy but on the very basis of it. There is an undecidability built into every decision. And this argument is not simply applied to the idea of a building, as the sense of determination can never be separated from the sense of a building.

The specific questioning of the institutional architecture of the university and the institution of philosophy that organizes it is actually a general questioning of the institution as such. The university is not simply a specific example of the general problem of the political, one that uniquely dictates an architectural reading or rereading of architecture. Rather, the political question is first and foremost one of architecture. Derrida's essays often elaborate Heidegger's identification of architecture with institutions in general. Heidegger paid attention to the way in which the language of institution is that of building, the word *stiften* meaning both "to erect" or "to institute" and *grunden* meaning both "to ground" or "to found."[52] The traditional architectural rhetoric employed to describe the institution of the university is actually the language of institutions in general, which is to say that the idea of philosophy, which turns on a certain representation of architecture, is the idea of institution. There is no institution without that representation.

For Derrida, an institution is not simply a space within which a particular kind of discourse occurs. Institutions are built in and by discourse. Furthermore, "a concept of the institution is at work"[53] in all discourses, whether they address themselves to institutions or not. This concept involves the same principle of reason, understood as a principle of architecture, responsible for, but not specific to, university discourse. At one point, Derrida elaborates Kant's argument that "all artificial institutions . . . are grounded in reason."[54] In these terms, his reading of the university is not simply an example of his political work. It elaborates the politics of all of his work, a politics that is always architectural, even where neither architecture nor politics are made thematic, which is to say, most of the time. But it is a politics that can never simply be recognized as such even if attention is paid to Derrida's sustained argument about institutions, which is usually and symptomatically ignored by both his supporters and critics. This politics cannot be recognized as such by discourses that maintain the very sense of architecture being called into question.

The institution is not simply the walls and structures that surround, protect, guarantee, or restrict the freedom of our work. It is also and already the structure of our interpretation. Consequently, what is somewhat hastily called deconstruction is not, if it is of any consequence, a specialized set of discursive procedures, still less the rules of a new hermeneutic method, working on texts or utterances in the shelter of a given and stable institution. It is also, at the very least, a way of taking a position, in its work of analysis, concerning the political and institutional structures that make possible and govern our practice, our competencies, our performances. Precisely because it is never concerned only with signified content, deconstruction should not be separable from the politico-institutional problematic and should seek a new investigation of responsibility, an investigation which questions the codes inherited from ethics and politics. This means that, too political for some, it will seem paralyzing to those who only recognize politics by the most familiar road signs.[55]

If it is its displacement of the traditional and familiar sense of building that makes deconstructive discourse political, it is equally a displacement of the familiar sense of the political. Deconstruction cannot simply be political inasmuch as "the political" as a category is a product of the always architectural tradition of metaphysics, one of the texts that the discourse reads and overturns.[56] Hence the by now familiar scene in which the discourse is simultaneously condemned for being too political by some and for being apolitical by others. This scene has, of course, been the topic of an extended debate. All that is being added to that debate here is that deconstructive discourse is political inasmuch as it engages with architecture but precisely because that engagement takes the form of a displacement of architecture, it necessarily loses any straightforward political recognition, no matter how many times its significant interventions into traditional political sites can be pointed to.[57] In the end, it rethinks the political by rethinking architecture, and this rethinking is not simply a discursive reflection on the possibility of political action, but is itself a form of action, as the architecture that is being displaced is not detached from discourse but built into and by its every operation.

Evidence of such a tacit argument can be found within a 1985 interview with Derrida, which yet again passes from the question of the university through the issue of politics to that of architecture. In response to a question about the politics of deconstruction, Derrida describes "deconstruction as politics" by virtue of its focus on institutions and describes its effects in architectural terms, or, rather, in terms of a displacement of the traditional idea of building:

But I don't think that anything, especially an institution, could survive deconstruction in the classical form of a new wonderful building, built after the negative moment of deconstruction. If somebody thinks that—that first we have to deconstruct everything and then we'll have a new kind of society, a new kind of university . . . that would be the reproduction of the oldest schemes. What survives deconstruction should have new forms.[58]

Deconstructive discourse can never be detached from architecture. It can never be extracted from what it destabilizes. If it disturbs the architecture of institutions from within, this disturbance also occurs within itself. It is not a drifter that simply occupies and dislodges an architecture before moving on. It is never singular, never just one coherent discourse and, furthermore, each of its multiple discourses is itself divided, occupied even, by the very architecture they seem to inhabit and disturb.

The role of these internal divisions and complications can be clearly seen in Derrida's "Some Statements and Truisms," an essay that again identifies the politics of deconstruction by way of an extended tacit association between institutions and architecture, but now focuses on the architecture of deconstruction itself. The essay also removes the distinction between the content of discourse and the architecture of institutions in a way that again problematizes the traditional category of the political,[59] but it goes further by raising the question of what would be involved in institutionalizing deconstructive discourse itself, in the university, for example. Having spoken of the architecture implicit in any act of institution by describing the "hierarchizing structure of an *establishment*,"[60] it looks at the establishment of contemporary "theory" as the construction of "institutional fortifications"[61] that define a space within the university, closing it off rather than opening it up. Deconstructive discourse is seen to be divided into at least two interrelated and inevitable gestures: one that puts an architecture at risk, destabilizing an institution, and another that consolidates its own movements into some kind of stable architecture.

The destabilizing gesture with which deconstructive discourse identifies itself involves occupying the cracks in the official architecture, the hidden recesses of the institution's structure rather

than any of its officially designated spaces, forcing the cracks to
see what they hide. But the less obvious stabilizing gesture occupies the host in quite a different way. The deconstructive shaking
of structure somehow builds itself into the institution, forming
its own architecture in some kind of alignment with that of the
university, which is able to absorb its potentially disruptive movements by absorbing the shock, accommodating it through what
turns out to be a fundamentally conservative flexibility, a flexing
of its structure to house and thereby restrain the would-be rebel:
"institutional architectures are erected to respond to the seisms
or seismisms of all the new *isms* which might shake the structures."[62] The stabilizing dimension of deconstructive discourse
that can be officially accommodated, up to a point, "goes up-
wards. It stands, a station, or a stanza; it erects, institutes, and
edifies. It is edifying, essentially edifying."[63] Yet again, the bond
between this quasi-institutional architecture and that of its host
is their materiality. The stabilizing moment of the discourse, like
that of the institution it occupies, consolidates itself by way of
"the strength of materials—that which architects must carefully
calculate in order to avoid collapses."[64]

But these two gestures can never simply be separated. One is
the veiling of the other, a veiling that can never detach itself from
what it veils. The two are folded together. Deconstructive discourse is not some kind of independent argument applied to
different institutional discourses. The story it tells is also its own
story. Rather than a subversive discourse of liberation, it always
speaks of its own entrapment in the economy it describes. The
apparent stabilization of deconstructive discourse in the university is not simply a degeneration of an original, rigorous, or
authentic discourse, an unfortunate political compromise that
weakens its destabilizing movements. Rather, it is but one of the
marks of the stabilizing gestures that can be found in every one
of its texts. There can be no deconstruction without architecture.
At the same time, no deconstructive discourse is as stable as it
appears. Stability and instability cannot be separated. In the end,
what makes the institution tremble is precisely their interdependence, the sense in which the erection of a structure always conceals the violation of that structure, which is to say the sense that

architecture is always trembling, that its very stability is but an effect of the repression of the uncontrollable movements in its very foundation, the movements that found it.[65]

This sense of the trembling of architecture is invoked in the 1977 interview "Du Tout," when Derrida makes an analogy between the position he find himself in as an apparent foreigner in a meeting of a particular institution (a psychoanalytic organization) and deconstruction's position within institutions. Deconstruction is described as that which occupies the internal structure of an institution in such a way that its operations are only revealed by way of some kind of radical threat to the host architecture, a threat that is understood to be political precisely to the extent that it is a threat to that which is usually understood to be political:

[T]his evening someone from the alleged outside of your institution has been invited . . . someone who does not show himself often, a kind of beast who emerges from his hole only at the moment when he hears or feels coming toward him the vibrations of cracked walls, of collapsing partitions, of trembling supports, of threatened impermeability, etc., in a word all the signs of what I have formerly called a deconstruction; and deconstruction, as I have often had to insist, is not a discursive or theoretical affair, but a practico-political one, and it is always produced within the structures (somewhat quickly and summarily) said to be institutional.[66]

The interview goes on to describe deconstructive discourse in terms of locating that which is hidden, rather than simply enclosed, by the architecture of an institution (in this case, that of psychoanalysis), that which the architecture is designed to veil and yet is the source of its strength. Again, the basic structure of architecture, that which produces the effect of solidity and security, is understood to be its capacity to conceal. A structure is only able to stand by concealing something, something that occupies the space of the building without being visible within it, something that can only be found within the institutional discourse and yet always exceeds it, something within but inaccessible to the discourse that actually organizes its architecture.

This unanalyzed will be, will have been that upon which and around which the analytic movement will have been constructed and mobilized: everything will have been constructed and calculated so that this unanalyzed might be inherited, protected, transmitted intact, suitably bequeathed, consolidated, enkysted, encrypted. It is what gives its structure to the movement and to its architecture.[67]

The space of a building is constructed to enclose something that must never appear within it. The visible enclosure, the definition of a space with walls that makes things visible both inside it and outside it, is first and foremost a mechanism of concealment that veils another kind of space inhabited by a prohibited other, or, more precisely, veils a space that is itself the other inasmuch as it disrupts the logic of inhabitation. By shaking architecture, deconstructive discourse forces this other out into the space that is supposed to conceal it, demonstrating that its effects can actually be found throughout that space in all the routine transactions that go on within it, and even that the space itself that routinely conceals it is its first effect.

In these terms, the question being asked here about deconstruction and architecture must be: what happens when the institution whose architecture is to be shaken is that of architecture itself? What exactly is the architecture of the institution of architecture? Can there even be such a thing? And what would it conceal? What is it that is buried in and by the discourse apparently devoted to architecture?

To begin to approach these increasingly urgent questions, we need to determine more precisely what the institutionalized sense of architecture is by going further into the traditional figure of the edifice to find out what kind of interior the building has, what kind of space, if any, is constructed by the figure as it circulates through traditional discourse and what kinds of relationship Derrida's work has to that space. This necessitates a return to Heidegger, if not a succession of returns that patiently track the complicated role of architecture in his work beyond its more obvious surfacing in the concept of "destruction" or "critical unbuilding," which Derrida's work so explicitly elaborates at length.

To comprehend the prohibited sense of architecture buried within the classical figure of the edifice and whatever might be, in turn, buried within that sense, to trace their strategic role in deconstructive discourse, it is necessary to reread Heidegger more closely. Inasmuch as "deconstruction" is a translation of Heidegger, it is, as Derrida once puts it, a "deforming translation," which like all translations reconstructs, transforms, abuses, and distances itself from what it appears to translate.[68] If to translate deconstruction in architecture is to think about the senses in which deconstruction is already some kind of translation of architecture, what matters here is the precise ways in which Derrida at once reconstructs and deforms Heidegger's architecture before distancing himself from it—even, if not especially, if he never addresses Heidegger's architecture as such.

3

The Slippery Art of Space

Having identified the crucial role of a certain image of architecture in the philosophical tradition, Heidegger's sustained attempt to displace that tradition necessarily involves an ongoing displacement of that representation. At one level, this takes the form of a reconfiguration of the image but, even more important, it involves a transformation of its status, which is to say, both a repositioning of the image and a disruption of its very status as an image.

As we have seen, the figure of architecture produced and sustained by the tradition of metaphysics makes available the organizing principles of that tradition, which then appear to precede it and are actually used to subordinate it as merely a superstructural representation, a contingent figure to be discarded. But these explicit gestures of subordination only serve to cover and maintain the ongoing covert operations of that very figure within the discourse, operations that depend on it not being understood as a figure but as a special kind of touchstone, a material reality whose irreducible order can be used to stabilize and order the discourse that makes contact with it. The discourse is only able to stabilize itself with this figure of stability by effacing its figural condition and effacing the traces of that effacement. In such elaborate but routine operations, the sense of architecture becomes so familiar that it is not understood to be a representation. A sense of the irreducible solidity of construction is seen to precede representation, and this precedence is not something addressed by the discourse as such but is constantly drawn on, and only occasionally appealed to, in order to organize that discourse. Before it might choose to discuss the ground, let alone the kinds of structure it might support, the discourse has already put a building in place.

Heidegger argues that because of the very familiarity of the sense of grounded structure that organizes the current technological manifestations of metaphysics, "we most easily and for the longest time mistake the insidious nature of its violence."[1] There would be no metaphysics without this concealed violence. Both the violence and its concealment are constitutional. The tradition of metaphysics institutes itself by concealing its own violence. The architectural figure of the grounded structure sustains this violence by effecting the concealment. The vertical hierarchy it configures is a mechanism of control that dissimulates its own strategic violence. Its very familiarity marks the extent of its control.

This argument does not appear to be about architecture as such. At best it seems to call into question the architectural figure, to render it inescapably metaphysical. But Heidegger does not simply abandon architecture. The sense that architecture cannot be displaced in the way that the philosophical tradition based around it can is precisely the effect of that tradition. Heidegger's reading is made possible by another sense of architecture. The elaborate play between the traditional architecture and the often oblique effects of this other architecture in his work can be more easily followed in his reflection on the philosophy of art, or, more precisely, his use of art to displace philosophy. The complex interactions between the multiple levels of architectural argument that operate in all his texts are more conspicuous when the relationship between philosophy and art is explicitly in question.

Tasting Space

It is significant that Heidegger's well-known criticism of the traditional philosophy of art in *The Origin of the Work of Art*, like Kant's *The Critique of Judgement*, which exemplifies the tradition it is criticizing, turns on an architectural example. But unlike Kant's text, its example disturbs the familiar understanding of building, and it is arguably this disturbance that becomes the basis of his overall displacement of aesthetics, if not his entire philosophy.

Like the tradition, Heidegger appeals to architecture for its familiarity. At the beginning of the essay, he notes how "familiar" works of art are to "everyone," and architecture is his first example of this familiarity. And when architecture returns at a key point in the middle of the essay, it is again a question of familiarity. "In order to become more familiar with what the question [where does a work of art belong?] involves," Heidegger puts forward the example of "a building"—specifically, a Greek temple—which is elaborated for some pages.[2] It appears that the familiarity of architecture is going to be used to make an unfamiliar philosophical question more familiar, but in the process architecture is itself defamiliarized.

Heidegger starts with what seems to be the familiar condition of a building—"It simply stands there in the middle of the rock-cleft valley"[3]—but goes on to show how this standing is not so simple. For a start, the building is not simply seen standing in a pregiven site. Rather, the site can only be seen through the building. The edifice "makes visible" the ground on which it stands: "The temple, in its standing there, first gives to things their look and to men their outlook on themselves."[4] It is not simply looked at by an eye, aesthetic or otherwise. Rather, it constructs the eye. Furthermore, this newly constructed eye is not directed from the building toward its site. It produces what it sees. The building produces its site. It does not stand on a ground that preceded it and on which it depends for its structural integrity. Rather, it is the erection of the building that establishes the fundamental condition of the ground. The building's structure makes the ground possible.[5] The ground is constituted rather than simply revealed by that which appears to be added to it. To locate the ground is therefore necessarily to construct an edifice.

This transformation of the familiar sense of building is not limited to Heidegger's reflections on art. His texts repeatedly identify construction with the production of a view that produces the very ground it appears to be supported on, as when the third volume of *Nietzsche* argues that:

First and foremost, thinking is "constructive." Generally, that means that this thinking first *fashions* what does not yet stand and exist as something at hand, something that perhaps never was at all. It does not appeal to and depend upon something given for support; it is not an assimilation but is what announced itself to us as the poetizing nature of positing a horizon within a perspective. "Constructing" means not only producing something that is not yet at hand but also setting up and erecting, rising to the heights—more precisely, first gaining a height, securing it, and thus positing a "right direction." Thus "constructing" is a commanding that first raises the claim to command and creates a realm of command.

Insofar as construction fashions, it must at the same time and even prior to this be founded on a ground. Together with rising to the heights, it at the same time forms and opens a vista onto its surroundings. The essence of construction lies neither in piling up layers of building materials nor in ordering them according to a plan, but solely in the fact that when we set up a new space another atmosphere opens up, precisely through what is set up. Whenever that fails to happen, what has been built has to be explained afterward as a "symbol" for something else; it is established as such by the newspapers for the public. Construction in these two cases is never the same. Justice as the positing of something right, a positing that constructs—that is, founds, erects and opens a vista—is the essential origin of the poetizing and commanding nature of all knowing and forming.[6]

This displacement is also explicitly written into his general re-reading of the architecture written into the tradition of philosophy. The kind of ground clearing that Kant explicitly attempts, and that implicitly organizes the ancient philosophical tradition his texts participate in, does not precede the construction of the philosophical edifice. The ground is not independent of the edifice. The edifice is not simply added to a preexisting ground, it is simply not an addition. And, as we have seen, for Heidegger this transformation of the building of philosophy is equally a transformation of philosophy's object, which is traditionally presented in architectural terms. Being is not just a standing on a ground; it is itself grounding, a standing that grounds.[7] In the end, it is the ground and, as such, is itself not grounded. The ground is an abyss, the *Grund* is *Abgrund*.[8]

In elaborating such arguments, Heidegger is not making an analogy between architecture as a material artwork and the abstract workings of philosophy. He does not produce a new description of literal buildings in order to transform the metaphoric use of architecture by philosophy when it is not addressing architecture as such. On the contrary, he produces a different image of architecture to efface, or at least complicate, that very distinction between the literal and the metaphoric, a distinction that is an effect of the figure of architecture before it is a philosophical distinction applied to it.

The philosophy of art Heidegger opposes is produced by and for metaphysics and is therefore based on the traditional image of architecture with which that tradition constitutes itself. This image, and its symptomatic effects, can be found throughout Heidegger's essay on the artwork even though he rarely makes it thematic as such. When he does address architecture, naming it as an example, it is not one example among the other arts that could have been used to make the same point about the condition of art, all of which supposedly have the same properties inasmuch as they are arts. Architecture is operative in his argument both before and after it is named as an example. By looking more closely at the text, it becomes evident that architecture is both the agent of the subordination of art by philosophy and Heidegger's agent in overturning that subordination.

The essay begins by opposing philosophy's determination of the artwork as merely a representative "addition" to a utilitarian object, a "superstructure" added to the "substructure" which, in turn, is added to the ground. The architectural figure organizes this relationship: "It seems almost as though the thingly element in the art work is like the substructure into and upon which the other, authentic element is built."[9] The material object is the "support" to which the artwork is added; the presentation of the ground to which the artwork is added as but a representation. Which is to say that art, for metaphysics, is not structural. Art is precisely that which exceeds structure and therefore needs to be subordinated to it. What is privileged in art is necessarily subordinated in metaphysics as merely a representation of an "idea." Art is detached and subordinate to the truth it may or may not represent. In this way, one of the arts—architecture—is the mechanism of the subordination of all art.

Heidegger attempts to resist this subordination, arguing that the truth sought by the philosophical tradition is actually made possible by the very realm of art it subordinates. Art is neither a representational domain detached from the philosophical quest for the truth, nor a source of representations that can be employed strategically, but only temporarily, by philosophy to describe that quest or illustrate a point made within it. Philosophy is unthinkable outside of art. To argue this, Heidegger necessarily disturbs the image of architecture that made the subordination possible in the first place. Architecture must be his key example. Indeed, it is produced at the beginning of the central section of the essay entitled "The Work and Truth." The way the temple produces rather than represents the ground becomes his paradigm of the constitutional role of art in the very production of truth.

The revision of the relationship between philosophy and art that the example initiates is itself presented in architectural terms at the end of the essay when Heidegger argues that art is actually "foundational" to the philosophical tradition that subordinates it to the level of ornament. The whole point of the essay is to describe art as "founding truth." The reversal it seeks is itself architectural from the beginning. The essay is necessarily addressing architecture before it appears to speak about it.

In fact, the particular moment the essay speaks about architecture is in the middle of an argument framed in architectural terms not identified as such. Heidegger calls in the example of architecture to answer the question: how does a work of art "stand on its own"? The standing up of a temple is used to explain the standing up of art, the standing that he will later say, when no longer speaking of architecture, founds truth, the standing that grounds. The architectural "example" he invokes provides the key concepts with which art is now to be thought: "standing," "towering up," "erection," "arising," "placing," "founding." These terms dominate the end of the essay but they have been transformed, and it is the labor of this transformation that is the central work of the essay. The familiar sense of architecture, indeed its very familiarity, has been progressively displaced.

Its not so much that Heidegger appeals to strange elements in our familiar experience of buildings that are not acknowledged by the tradition. He does not even identify architecture as an object of "experience." Rather, experience is understood as an effect of the institutional tradition organized around a particular image of architecture, a construct that has been institutionalized to the extent that is familiar, so familiar that it can even act as a figure for the familiar. It is by defamiliarizing architecture that Heidegger disturbs the tradition. The founding of truth by art, which is exemplified by a building, becomes the establishment of the unfamiliar rather than the familiar. Indeed, the essay concludes by defining founding as the unfamiliar "overflowing" the familiar. This founding is itself understood as the possibility of the institution of philosophy, even if that institution seeks to efface the unfamiliar, which is to say that philosophy effaces its own conditions of possibility. The enigmatic and self-effacing question of architecture is, as it were, built into the institution.

When architecture comes up in the essay, it is in response to a question that is at once architectural and institutional. To ask how the work of art stands on its own is explicitly, for Heidegger, to ask how it stands unimpeded by the institutions of the "art-industry" that frame it: the spaces of "collections and exhibitions," "connoisseurs," "critics," "art dealers," and "art-historical study." He argues that the "setting-up" of the art-work by these institutions, including that of philosophy, which ostensibly put them in place, is somehow produced by the art-work itself, its fundamental condition as a setting-up, the condition exemplified by a building. The art-work produces its institutional sites just as the temple produces its site, even if those institutions fail to recognize the essence of the art-work. Although the structure of such institutions is different from, and insensitive to, that of a building, it is called for and made possible by such building.

In these terms, Heidegger's displacement of architecture is first and foremost a rethinking of institutional authority. The philosopher-architect who attempts to produce a grounded structure is not simply adding a building to the ground. Philosophy does not emerge from and present the ground; it produces the effect of ground, an effect of stability that veils a fundamental instability. The figure of architecture acts as a veil, enabling philosophy to disguise its active ordering of the world as the neutral discovery of the world's preexisting order. In this way, Heidegger's rethinking of architecture appears to provide the terms for a radical dismantling of the tradition.

But in the end Heidegger's account reproduces much of what it critiques. His untraditional thinking of architecture is eventually detached from architecture. Architecture is once again subordinated to and by the very arguments it has made available. Heidegger's account of architecture remains one of presentation. Indeed, when the essay speaks of architecture, it does so precisely to bracket off representation: "For this attempt let us deliberately select a work that cannot be ranked as representational art. A building, a Greek temple, portrays nothing. It simply stands there in the middle of the rock-cleft valley."[10] Heidegger's progressive displacement of this "simply," his complication of what it is to stand, continues to draw a clear distinction between standing and representation. It redraws rather than abandons the line that the institutions of philosophy have always been concerned to maintain, and have done so by appealing to architecture.

Inasmuch as that distinction is redrawn, architecture is inevitably maintained in its traditional place. This can be seen at the end of the essay, where the concepts that were earlier put in place with the example of architecture are appropriated by the art of poetry, the highest art that then "governs" the lower arts like architecture. Architecture is subordinated to the immediacy of poetic speech in the very terms that it has provided (a gesture that he elaborates in more detail in his lectures of 1942–43 on Parmenides[11]). If, as Heidegger argues, philosophy routinely subordinates the arts that are its possibility, Heidegger's own argument ends up subordinating the art of architecture on which it is based, reconstituting the tradition he critiques, and opening up his text to its own criticism.

Spaced Out

Derrida's work is shaped by a reading of this systemic duplicity in Heidegger's texts. In "Restitutions of the Truth of Pointing," his extended reading of Heidegger's essay on the artwork, he notes, "I have always been convinced of the strong necessity of Heidegger's questioning, even if it *repeats* here, in the worst as well as the best sense of the word, the traditional philosophy of art. And convinced of its necessity, perhaps, to the very extent that it does this."[12] This comment marks his consistently complicated and ambiguous relationship to Heidegger, and must in some way mark his relationship to Heidegger's thinking of architecture. Yet while Derrida's essay goes on to address the question of ground, foundation, and support that is always at stake in the figure of architecture, it does not explicitly identify architecture's role in either Heidegger's displacement or repetition of metaphysics.

Nevertheless, at the beginning of "Parergon," his reading of Kant's *The Critique of Judgement*, Derrida tacitly identifies the way in which Heidegger's account of the philosophy of art is, in the end, defined by its treatment of the question of space. Pointing to the ultimate subordination of the plastic arts to speech by Heidegger's essay, Derrida argues that the way it "subjected the whole of *space* to the discursive arts, to voice and the *logos*"[13] repeated the traditional philosophy of art it was attempting to resist. This point had been made much earlier in the 1967 interview "Implications," in which he singles out the way Heidegger's essay privileges speech as the best evidence of his general complicity with the tradition of metaphysics. And again, the privileging is understood as the demotion of space. Derrida points to the essay's subordination of architecture and sculpture to poetry, the spatial arts to the "space of the poem," material spatiality to abstract space:

But doubtless there is a certain Heideggerian phonologism, a noncritical privilege accorded in his works, as in the West in general, to the voice, to a determined "expressive substance." This privilege, whose consequences are considerable and systematic, can be recognized, for example, in the significant prevalence of so many "phonic" metaphors in a meditation on art which always returns, by means of examples chosen in a very marked way, to art as the "appearance of truth". . . . Thus is explained that according to Heidegger all the arts unfold in the space of the poem which is "the essence of art," in the space of "language," and of the "word." "Architecture and sculpture," he says, "occur only in the opening of saying and naming. They are governed and guided by them."[14]

To understand the importance of this apparently incidental point about space, and why Heidegger's essay on the artwork is singled out to exemplify it, it is necessary to pay closer attention to the argument about space embedded within Derrida's early work. Such an argument can be found, for example, in *Of Grammatology* of 1967, perhaps the most read of Derrida's books. A concern with space punctuates the text without ever appearing to be the central issue. It is a fragmentary subtext whose significance can only be established here by piecing together what seem like isolated fragments to see the coherent argument they assemble that runs through the book, stitched into it like a fragile thread that holds together the more visible arguments.

As is well known, the text calls into question the way the tradition of metaphysics organizes itself around a privileging of the immediacy of speech over the mediations of writing, but little attention has been paid to the way in which Derrida explicitly presents this privileging as a subordination of space. He repeatedly shows how writing is traditionally identified with space by tracing its role in a number of canonic thinkers including Plato, Hegel, Saussure, Husserl, Rousseau, and Lévi-Strauss. Each in turn is seen to locate writing "in space,"[15] the "space of inscription . . . the spatial *distribution* of signs,"[16] and to subordinate space, using a concept of the unmediated presence of speech to effect this subordination. In each writer, speech "sublimates space."[17] The tradition of metaphysics they participate in rejects writing understood as "the invoking of an 'exterior,' 'sensible,' 'spatial' signifier interrupting self-presence."[18] Metaphysics is that which subordinates space, associating it with "death," "decay," "degeneration," "representation," "dissimulation," "interruption," "seduction," "materiality," "sensuality," "monstrosity," and so on. In Rousseau, for example, space is opposed to speech as death is opposed to life: "voice. . . . transgressing space, mastering the outside, . . . That is to say a certain death signified by space. The arts of space convey death within themselves."[19] Metaphysics is no more than the mastery of space, and space is mastered by being kept outside. Speech supposedly precedes space and is therefore able to control it. Writing, with all its dangerous spatiality, is cast out to the subordinate exterior.

But although speech "does not fall into the exteriority of space,"[20] this does not mean that it simply "occupies" an interior. The privileged interior from which writing is excluded is not a space. On the contrary, it is the absence of space. Speech is precisely that which is without space, and space is always that which is outside.[21] And just as speech does not simply occupy the interior, writing does not simply occupy the exterior. When Derrida speaks of the "spatial exteriority of the signifier,"[22] the exterior is space itself. It is the very gesture of exclusion that produces space in the first place. Writing is not simply located "in" space. Rather, it is the production of space. There is no space before the writing that appears to go on within it. Consequently, Derrida refers to writing as "the possibility of inscriptions in general, not befalling an already constituted space as a contingent accident but producing the spatiality of space."[23] Furthermore, he not only speaks of writing as spatial but also of space as writing. Space is inscription rather than its site. Writing does not have a site. Sites are an effect of writing. This sense of space can be found in all of Derrida's work, as when "Plato's Pharmacy" speaks of "the space of writing, space *as* writing,"[24] which is taken further when *Speech and Phenomena* speaks of "the externality of space, externality as space."[25] If space is writing, it is not simply placed in the exterior. The exterior is always, and only, space.

Inasmuch as space is not a static receptacle of inscriptions but an effect of ongoing inscription, what the tradition attempts to subordinate is not so much space as the gesture of inscription that produces space. For this, Derrida deploys the term "spacing" [*espacement*], describing writing as spacing and "spacing as writing."[26] Speech is only able to subordinate space inasmuch as it is "unconnected to *spacing*." It is in this sense that the supposed immediacy of speech is by definition opposed to the mediations of space. Spacing is that which produces both the sense that things are exterior to each other, that they are spaced out in some kind of space, and the sense that space is itself exterior to some other domain, that the spatial world is detached from one that is without space. Spacing is the "distance" of representation: both the spatial intervals between signifiers and the effect of substitution, the production of the sense that the material signifier "stands in for" something detached from it, the sense that space is an exterior domain of representation detached from that of presence, which is to say, the sense of an exterior divided from an interior. In such terms, theories of representation are necessarily theories of space. Inasmuch as Derrida complicates the classic account of representation, which his work is everywhere doing, he necessarily reconfigures the thinking of space and the role of space in thinking.

Derrida attempts to resist the tradition of metaphysics by showing that space is never a contingent element that can be simply bracketed out in favor of some higher immutable and immaterial constant. As *Of Grammatology* puts it, "that language must traverse space, be obliged to be spaced, is not an accidental trait but the mark of its origin."[27] Space does not befall the pure voice sought by philosophy but is its very possibility. There can be no voice, let alone the philosophical desire for such a voice, without the spatiality that appears to contaminate it: "For the voice is always already invested, undone [*sollicitée*], required, and marked in its essence by a certain spatiality."[28] The contamination of the dream of philosophy by space turns out to be the very possibility of that dream.

Speech, that which is supposedly without space, is "fissured" by a demand for space and this fissure is itself a "spacing" that cannot be removed.[29] The supposedly stable prespatial interior so revered by the tradition of philosophy is already fractured, opened up, contaminated from the beginning, by the very movements of space it supposedly precedes, subordinates, and excludes. Inasmuch as Derrida shows that "spacing insinuates into presence an interval"[30] such that "spacing is not the accident"[31] but the possibility of the rule, the simple opposition between space and presence upon which the tradition of philosophy

depends is confused.[32] Space cannot simply be subordinated
inasmuch as it harbors the possibility of that which attempts to
subordinate it. Equally, space is no longer what the tradition
constructs it as in order to subordinate it. Derrida's reading does
not simply reverse the tradition by inverting the classic opposition and making space dominant. The traditional sense of space
is only produced in the very gesture of its subordination. To
interfere with that gesture is to produce a very different sense of
space, a sense that at once disturbs and produces the tradition.
It is to mark this sense that Derrida uses the word "spacing," a
word that carries some of the connotations that the tradition
attaches to space in its attempt to dismiss it but also carries senses
that cannot be recognized by the tradition.

To disturb the tradition involves subverting its attempt to detach itself from space by identifying that attempt as a form of
institutional resistance that attempts to conceal the convoluted
structure of the tradition that makes it. The exclusion and subordination of space produces an orderly facade, or, rather, the
facade of order, to mask an internal disorder. The traditional
anxiety about space marks a forbidden desire that threatens to
collapse the edifice of philosophy from within.

This internal conflict can be seen when *Of Grammatology* shows
how the simultaneous need for space and the desire to subordinate space, by configuring it as merely a degenerate and regret-
table event, sustains a strangely contradictory but normative
economy: "even while saying that spacing assures the possibility
of speech and song, Rousseau *wishes* to think of space as a simple
outside by way of which disease and death . . . make their entry."[33] The texts of the tradition are marked by an ongoing debt
to space that is only partially veiled by their repeated subordina-
tions of space, insistent declarations of the integrity of the interior that take the form of a denial, if not a disavowal. The overt
desire to expel space marks a subterranean and structural desire
for space, a desire that can itself only be understood in spatial
terms. Derrida's essays relentlessly track the strategic effects of
this desire. Inasmuch as the subordination of space is tied to a
certain image of architecture, the question of deconstruction
and architecture must be, from the beginning, a question of

repressed desire or, more precisely, of the repression of what *Of Grammatology* calls the "spacing between desire and pleasure."[34]

While Derrida goes out of his way to disassociate his general reading of Rousseau's texts from a literal psychoanalysis, (arguing that the texts of psychoanalysis need to be subjected to the same type of reading[35]) the specific question of space invites such an analysis. In "Desistance," his more recent text on Philippe Lacoue-Labarthe's work, for example, the strange role of space in the tradition is described as a "haunting," and its concealment as a symptomatic gesture of repression. The particular spatiality of "rhythm" (which often acts as Derrida's figure for spacing) is said to have "such effective deconstructive power" because it destabilizes the metaphysics of speech it "insensibly" "structures." This insensibility to spacing is itself an institutional effect produced to mask the threat posed by spacing to the system it at once organizes and disorganizes. Through its ongoing "repression" by institutions, "the inscriptive force of a spacing . . . has always *haunted* our tradition, without ever reaching the center of its concerns."[36]

Derrida's work involves a recovery of this repressed sense of space that haunts the tradition, the spatiality disavowed in and by the space of philosophy, the sense of spacing hidden by the tradition's attempt to control space, but whose presence is at the same time revealed by the very intensity of that attempt. If, as he puts it in another interview, the "distance" of writing from philosophy "provides the necessary free space from which to interrogate philosophy anew,"[37] this "space" is, in the end, spatiality itself. Derrida's work is everywhere concerned with that which is subversive insofar as it spaces.

A concern with space can easily be found throughout Derrida's work, from the earliest texts to the latest. On the one hand, they raise the general philosophical question of space in the writings of Husserl, Plato, Bergson, Leibniz, Hegel, Heidegger, and so on. On the other hand, they are concerned with general spatial conditions, like line, border, interior, exterior, threshold, closure, frame, margin, invagination, and so on, and with particular spatial figures: the labyrinth, ear, pyramid, hymen, circle, column, and so on. The general theories of space and their strategic roles in the tradition are analyzed and rethought, while the spatial

terms are reread in a multiplicity of registers and each of the
spatial figures is examined in detail and their specific incongrui-
ties are mobilized to become the basis of a general shaking of
the tradition, by showing how each is invested with the very
authority the tradition attempts to deny them. All of these interrelated interrogations of space are of interest to architectural
discourse, but the first concern here must be with something
between them: the question of spacing. In the end, it is spacing
that the tradition represses, not space in general or spatial properties or the particular spaces that are overtly addressed and
subordinated.

Spacing is precisely not space but what Derrida describes as
the "becoming space"[38] of that which is meant to be without
space (presence, speech, spirit, ideas, and so on). It is that which
opens up a space, both in the sense of fissuring an established
structure, dividing it or complicating its limits, but also in the
sense of producing space itself as an opening in the tradition.
Spacing is at once splintering and productive. As Derrida puts it,
"spacing is a concept which also, but not exclusively, carries the
meaning of a productive, positive, generative force . . . it carries
along with it a *genetic* motif: it is not only the interval, the space
constituted between two things (which is the usual sense of
spacing), but also spac*ing*, the operation, or in any event, the
movement of setting aside."[39] Spacing, as distinct from space, is
first and foremost not a thing but a movement. If it is anything,
it is no-thing: "*Spacing* designates *nothing*, nothing that is, no
presence at a distance; it is the index of an irreducible exterior,
and at the same time of a *movement*, a displacement that indicates
an irreducible alterity. I do not see how one could dissociate the
two concepts of spacing and alterity."[40] This argument renders
alterity internal or, rather, problematizes the very sense of interior and thereby the whole economy of identity, propriety, immediacy, presence, and so on, which is based on it: "spacing is the
impossibility for an identity to be closed on itself, on the inside
of its proper interiority, or on its coincidence with itself. The
irreducibility of spacing is the irreducibility of the other."[41]

This sense of "spacing" can be found throughout Derrida's
texts. Symptomatically, he employs Mallarmé's use of the word as
the epigraph for the collection of his earliest essays.[42] It is a key

term in his work, and he usually includes it in his occasional lists of the chain of strategic terms successively deployed in his work, most of which have received more attention. But he resists any treatment of it as some kind of master term in the same way that he resists such a privileging of any of the other terms. Nevertheless, its role is unique inasmuch as he singles out the term as marking precisely this impossibility of privileging any one member of the chain in which it participates.[43] Its trajectory needs to be followed here in more detail than it is usually accorded, but without monumentalizing it and thereby freezing its at once constructive and disruptive movements.

The Space of Inscription

The sense of the term "spacing" is not fixed or singular, by definition. Its trajectories in Derrida's writing are necessarily multiple, and it is this very multiplicity that becomes the issue here. While *Of Grammatology*, for example, attempts to bring the sense of spacing to the surface by paying attention to the moments in which it already marks the surface of a number of the canonic texts despite their sustained attempt to efface it, this does not involve tracing the role of a singular element that can be monumentalized as some master term. The quasi-concept is deployed in the text in many different ways. In addition to marking the "becoming space" of space, the opening up of spatial distances, the opening of another kind of distance between the world of those distances and that of prespatial presence, and the internal division of that world, its primordial opening to its other, it also marks the literal spatiality of writing, the materiality of each inscription and the "architectonics" of each text, which is not simply its visible and static formal structure, but the complicated and less obvious movements that produce and maintain it as such.

Having begun his reading of Rousseau by speaking of the hidden "spacing" that produces a text and contrasting it with what a text may say about its own production,[44] Derrida later becomes concerned with the literal spacing of Rousseau's *Essay on the Origin of Languages,* addressing "the space of its structure," and the tension between this "architecture" and the text's declared intention, including its avowed intention to subordinate space.[45] While closely reading the text, Derrida notes that the structure of "its space" reflects the very structure of language it attempts to describe. Like the text, language is understood as a spatial structure, a "system of oppositions of places and values" with a particular "orientation."[46] There is a complex interaction between the spatial structure of the text, what it says about that space, and the role it ascribes to space in general. Derrida looks into this interaction for the structural inconsistencies, the variations in the structural and conceptual orders, whether visible or concealed, acknowledged or not. It is these variations that not only mark the forces at work in the text but give the text its force in the first place.

This concern with the spacing of the text, the strategic role of its "architectonics," is evident throughout Derrida's work, not only in his close readings of the spatial organization of so many texts but also in the organization of his own. His essays often focus on the traditional spatial logic of the text (title, footnotes, preface, divisions, order, columns, and so on[47]), but also on the less obvious spacing that organizes the main body of a text, the gaps in its fabric and argument.[48] This is particularly evident in his essay "Mallarmé," which looks at the tension between the idea of blank space that "permeates" Mallarmé's writing and the actual blank spaces in that writing, the "rhythm" of white spaces whose meaning is undecidable and yet establishes the basic structure of the texts. These spaces are seen to at once define the space of the text and yet prevent it from being closed, installing its structure yet leaving it "as if without support."[49] In not signifying anything, while setting the system of signification in motion, they can only mark "the spacing of reading," which is to say, "the space of writing itself."[50] This sense of spacing as that which at once institutes an architecture and undermines it becomes the basis of Derrida's own writing, which he elsewhere symptomatically describes as the production of "blank spaces" in the institutions of philosophical discourse.[51] Most of his texts engage with their own spatiality, spacing themselves out in polemical ways and interrogating their own spatial structure. This interrogation is carried out as much by the spatial structure as it is by the words it appears to structure. Indeed, Derrida's texts only attain their force inasmuch as they undermine the traditional distinction between space and discourse.

This is most graphic in *Glas* with its multiple and parallel fragments of text whose quasiargument is both structured by the white spaces that fragment it and is left unresolved by them. This double sense is itself registered within one of the fragments when it moves from addressing "writing's spacing"[52] to declaring, in a quasi-religious tone, "Let us space."[53] Again, this call is understood in architectural terms. It is primarily a question of columns, both in the literal organization of the text as two apparently heterogeneous columns that are fractured and entangled and in its central theme which, from the very first page, turns on the question of the column in Hegel and Genet, or more precisely, the inevitable doubling of the column that at once reasserts and undermines the traditional psycho-architectonic logic of erection.[54] To name but one other of so many examples, the multiplication of similar strategies is evident in *The Truth in Painting*. The central theme of the collection of essays is the structure of a frame. Its four essays are presented as the four sides of a frame; the preface, itself understood as a frame, is divided into four parts; the "Parergon" essay that opens the collection is itself continuously structured by the disjointed corners of frames inserted into its interior; and so on. In each case, the argument engages with its own space, subjecting itself to what it describes, making itself an example of what it addresses, disrupting the traditional sense that a text is simply "about" something completely outside it, embedding the text in the very spaces it appears to read.

But it must immediately be noted that such overt plays are no more spatial, let alone architectural, than any of Derrida's other texts, no matter how indirect their concern with space or conventional their spatial strategy may seem. In the end, Derrida is precisely attempting to demonstrate that the same kind of play organizes the structure of all texts. He merely exaggerates certain spatial slippages, which is to say certain internal slippages of the architecture, to identify their ongoing structural role in all texts.

The importance of this concern with the architecture of the material space of the text can be seen in "Implications" where, having identified Heidegger's subordination of space to speech—a gesture understood as not just a particular example of a complicity with the tradition of metaphysics, but as the central gesture of that tradition—Derrida goes on to identify his own work as a concern for the materiality of writing, the "textual spacing of differences"[55] that are effaced by the metaphysical tradition they make possible. Without naming architecture, his work is a theorizing of space—and perhaps it is no more than that. And inasmuch as it draws on, follows, and yet critiques Heidegger, it is necessarily a rereading of Heidegger's architecture even though it does not present itself as such.

In following this rereading further in terms of architectural discourse, it must be remembered that Derrida has radically displaced the traditional sense of writing and, even then, this displaced sense does not fully register the sense of spacing in his texts. There is a need to hesitate here, as can be seen by looking more closely at his early essay, "The Pit and the Pyramid: Introduction to Hegel's Semiology," which, in the way that has been described here, pays attention to the "space" of Hegel's argument (seen as "the ultimate reassembling of metaphysics"), its "architectonics" or "topography," the "topical scheme" that assigns a "place" for each philosophical question. This "architectonic reading" locates Hegel's theory of the sign within a supplement to a certain section of the *Encyclopedia of Philosophical Sciences*. In that designated and carefully circumscribed space, the sign is understood as a certain kind of negation of "spatiality." It is necessarily spatial, but it supposedly effaces its spatiality in favor of what it signifies. Hegel's figure for this transcendence of "cold space" is architectural. The sign is like a monument that preserves the soul in the face of death, a tomb, specifically, a pyramid. As Derrida argues, the "construction" of a sign is a kind of "shelter" or "dwelling" for that which exceeds it and remains "foreign" to it, foreign not just to that particular space but to space itself. He compares this use of the architecture of the pyramid as a sign of the sign to the way in which architecture is "studied for itself" as a kind of sign in Hegel's *Aesthetics*. Even though the figure is employed as the paradigm of the sign in one part of Hegel's system, all such "plastic works of art" are subordinated in his aesthetics inasmuch as they are irreducibly spatial, like writing. The purest sign is that which "erases its own spacing." The one least contaminated by the mediations of space in this sense is speech. Although there is no sign without space, that spatiality must be effaced. Space is understood as a contingent prop that must never be mistaken for the truth it makes available: "If the passage through . . . spacing, externality and death . . . is a necessary passage . . . this necessity becomes perversion and regression as soon as it is taken as a *philosophical model*."[56]

Implicit in Derrida's essay is the strategic role of architecture we have been following here. If the spatial sign always gives way to what it signifies, the figure of the building, as the sign of the sign, must give way to the conceptual system it makes available. There would be no philosophical model without architecture, but the generic image of architecture cannot be mistaken for it and indeed is subordinated by it. Derrida appears to understand architecture as a kind of writing, the pyramid being, as he puts it, a "hard text of stones covered with inscription," the literal "inscription" of the "facade of a monument." Even though the essay does not move beyond reading the writing on the surface of the stone toward thinking of the stone itself and the space it defines as an effect of writing, his general account of writing as spacing would seem to open up a persuasive account of architecture, an account he occasionally touches on but does not elaborate.

But it is precisely at this promising point that we must hesitate. When Derrida's essay argues that the immediacy of the "phonic makes every spatial language—and in general all spacing—remain *inferior* and *exterior*," he immediately notes that "writing, according to an extension that transforms our notion of it, may be considered as an example or as the concept of this spacing."[57] Even if the sense of writing is transformed from an example of spacing to its very concept, it should not itself be monumentalized as spacing or vice versa. Just as writing is necessarily exceeded by the sense of spatiality it might exemplify, the subversive quality of that spatiality is frozen whenever it is treated as a "concept." Spacing, by definition, can never be a concept. It is, in the end, precisely that which exceeds the conceptual. Derrida everywhere tries to think beyond the regime of concepts, the philosophical regime that is always that of a fixed space.[58] Spacing is of interest only inasmuch as it exceeds the conceptual order it makes possible. In fact, it is spacing only in this very excess. Writing is only the concept of spacing for the tradition of philosophy, a concept that cannot fully comprehend the threat that spacing poses to that conceptual tradition, let alone the spacing involved in the very construction of that specific concept. The traditional concept of writing (as being like the inscriptions on a pyramid) is an important part of the resistance to spacing.

What is provocative in Derrida's work for architectural discourse is therefore more than just his writing "about" space, the role of spatial figures in writing and the spatiality of writing. Rather, it is the spacing between the architecture implied in the traditional sense of writing and the architecture implied in the sense of writing it attempts to conceal, what Derrida at one point calls "the immense problem of figurative spatialization (both *in* speech or writing in the current sense and in the space *between* the current sense and the other, of which the current sense is only a figure)."[59]

In these terms, what marks writing is its spatiality and what marks space is writing but, in the end, it would be more valuable for architectural discourse to think of Derrida's work as being committed to the question of spacing rather than to that of writing, especially since most of his readers have simply associated writing with written words, if not the institution of literature, even though his texts explicitly warn against this limitation. At the same time, it has to be said that his texts equally repeatedly invite this very association through a sustained privileging of the literary as a strategic response to the traditional subordination of writing. This strategy leaves open the possibility that the texts sustain the equally traditional displacement of thinking away from material space and therefore away from architecture. Even if writing is being subversively privileged for its materiality and spatiality, this would reproduce the tradition being subverted if these were seen to be fundamentally different from the materiality and spatiality of buildings.

Such a conservation of the tradition has been sustained by over twenty-five years of conferences in which the readers of Derrida's work have employed an architectural rhetoric to enthusiastically embrace the loss of foundations, the subversion of structure, and so on, while actively resisting the possibility that such arguments could be deployed to analyze the architecture of the very rooms within which these claims were being made (unlike Heidegger, who repeatedly elaborated his arguments by analyzing the room in which he was lecturing[60]). It is not that the extensive use of this rhetoric requires that it be employed in the architectural domain from which it appears to have been appropriated. Indeed, one of the consequences of paying attention to the specificity of that domain may be, ironically, to conclude that an entirely different rhetoric would be involved in the deconstruction of architecture. Rather, the issue is simply (although its consequences are far from simple) the sustained absence of such attention and, furthermore, a tacit prohibition against it. Many different kinds of gestures made within the evolving discourse around deconstruction can be understood as forms of resistance to such an interrogation of architecture, a resistance that faithfully maintains the very logic ostensibly being threatened and renders much of that threat illusory.

Consequently, it is necessary to carefully study each of Derrida's gestures to see if it disturbs or reproduces the traditional economy within which architecture has a unique role, only to be subordinated to some conceptual order. If Heidegger explicitly addresses architecture only to detach his thinking from it in a way that reproduces metaphysics, Derrida's work is of interest to architectural discourse only inasmuch as it rethinks space in a way that radically transforms architectural thinking and cannot be detached from architecture, even if architecture is never discussed as such. Rather than applying Derrida's discussion of space to architecture, its architectural condition needs to be more precisely identified. Instead of thinking of architecture as a kind of writing (as so many readings of deconstructive theory in architectural discourse have attempted to do), it is at the very least a matter of thinking of writing as a kind of architecture and tracing the architecture already embedded within Derrida's discourse.

In these terms, the question here becomes whether or not Derrida distances himself from Heidegger in a way that rethinks the subordination of space in general and architecture in particular. And, given that the traditional scene of architecture in philosophical discourse is one of identification sustained by repression, this raises the additional question of whether there is a relationship between the way Derrida draws so extensively on Heidegger's work, only to detach himself from it, and the way Heidegger draws so extensively on architecture, only to detach himself from it. Does Derrida detach himself from Heidegger at precisely the point at which Heidegger detaches himself from architecture? Could Derrida's work be understood as continuing the rethinking of architecture that Heidegger prematurely abandoned?

To approach these questions, which can so easily, and necessarily, be multiplied here, involves carefully tracing the role of space in Derrida's thinking as distinct from his thinking about space. It is a matter of identifying the relationship between spacing and the traditional architectural figure, which is to say, between spacing and the space of the edifice. This must be a uniquely complicated relationship inasmuch as the figure of the edifice is already that of the ongoing control of writing by speech. Architecture already appears to stand for the repression of spacing. Indeed, it seems to appear only inasmuch as it represses. It is, as it were, the very appearance of repression.

The figure of the grounded structure designates the fundamental project of metaphysics, the identification of a universal language that controls representation in the name of presence: the *logos*. As we have seen, Derrida traces the way in which the tradition of metaphysics maintains this logocentric protocol, which privileges presence over representation, with an account of language that privileges speech over writing. While speech is promoted as presentation of pure thought, writing is subordinated as the representation of speech. The role of architecture in establishing this hierarchy can be seen in Heidegger's identification of the original sense of the word *logos* as a "gathering" in a way that lets things "stand," the standing of "construction." A link between structure and presence organizes traditional accounts of language. The means by which language is grounded is identified with structure. Speech is identified with the way the structure of a building makes visible the condition of the ground it is bonded to. Phonetic writing, as the representation of speech, is identified with the ornamentation of a building that represents the structure to which it is added. And writing that ceases to be phonetic, losing its bond to speech, representation detached from presence, is seen as ornamentation that refers away from the structure to which it is attached, dissimulating the building. The hierarchical protocol of metaphysics (presence-presentation-representation) is sustained by the architectural figure (ground-structure-ornament).

In these terms, the figure of the edifice is employed to subordinate spacing, where spacing is understood as the detachment of writing. The structure's attempt to control the ornament that exceeds it is the attempt to control spacing, an attempt that turns on the division of ornament. The line between space and spacing cuts through ornament. But the architectural figure is not just the figure of the control of spacing, a metaphor for the ongoing work of the tradition, it is the figure itself that controls, the metaphor itself that does the work. Architecture, the "art" of space, is called in to subordinate spacing, and, in the end, to subordinate space. If space is configured as the control of spacing, it is then itself subordinated. Architecture ends up subordinating itself. And this complication is, as it were, structural. To trace the role of space and spacing in Derrida's work, it is therefore necessary to follow the role in it of the architectural figure that is traditionally employed to subordinate them, a figure whose widespread strategic operations can never be pinned down and that remains elusive even in those moments in which it seems to be clearly articulated, an enigmatic figure that is always, at the very least, double.

The Structure of Ornament

It is significant that Derrida's reading of Kant's philosophy of art distances itself from Heidegger's by focusing on the question of ornament. He argues that Kant's text turns on the possibility of making a clear distinction between the inside and the outside of the artwork, between its internal meaning and its external circumstances. All philosophical discourse on art from Plato on (including Heidegger) is seen to attempt to draw this line, but it is always disturbed by ornamentation (*Parergon*), which is neither simply inside nor simply outside the work (*Ergon*). For Kant, ornament is "only an adjunct, and not an intrinsic constituent."[61] It is supposedly that which can be detached from the work, that which has been added to it, an external addition, a supplement subservient to the work, in the service of the work.

The Critique of Judgement handles the question of ornament by splitting it in two. The work of philosophy is not to separate structure and ornament but to separate good ornament from bad. The *Critique* explicitly authorizes ornament to enter the work it is attached to inasmuch as it is "form" or "design," but inasmuch as the ornament is material, bodily, sensual, it is excluded from the interior as seductive, a dangerous object of desire, dangerous because desirable. In the fine arts "the *design* is what is essential. Here it is not what gratifies in sensation but merely what pleases by its form, that is the fundamental prerequisite for taste."[62] In this way, the critique employs the distinction between form and matter with which the tradition of metaphysics has always organized itself. Aesthetics is subservient to metaphysics. It is the application of metaphysics to art—or so it would seem.

This attempt to control ornament does not only come up when philosophy comes across art. It is written into every operation of metaphysics. Metaphysics is a certain thinking of ornament that only manifests itself within aesthetics where the philosophical tradition is bound to address ornament as a subject, but this thinking is operative throughout the tradition, actually constituting it as such.

Derrida disturbs this tradition by questioning its ability to control ornament. He notes that what Kant's three examples of ornament (the frame on a painting, drapery on a statue, and the colonnade on a palace) share is that they cannot be detached without destroying the work. There is a gap, a lack, a crack in the structure of the work that must be filled by the ornament. The work not only admits the external ornament, in all its sensuality, into its interior but is constituted by that entry, made possible by that which appears to be excluded from it, that which serves it, that which it supposedly masters. The ornament is an outsider that always already inhabits the inside, an intrinsic constituent of the interior from which it is meant to be banished. There could be no work without the play of that which appears to be merely its supplement.

This argument might not seem architectural, architecture being but one of Kant's three examples, but in each case the rhetoric employed is architectural. The issue is invariably that of structure. In each ornament, Derrida identifies the "internal structural link which rivets them to the lack in the interior of the *ergon*."[63] And this argument, in turn, is not limited to the question of art. On the contrary, it is raised throughout Derrida's writing, which is always concerned with the status of such supplements, that which appears to be added, whether it be the title, preface, metaphor, signature, and so on. And in each case, it is a question of its "structural" role. Indeed, at one point, *Of Grammatology* identifies its concern with what it elsewhere calls the "structure of supplementarity"[64] as a concern with "supplementary as *structure*."[65] Ornament is therefore not just an example of the operations of the supplement, one of a long chain of equivalent terms in Derrida's writing. Each of these terms is understood as an ornament, and the issue is always that of the "structural link" that binds it to what it appears to be detached from. Most of Derrida's work is work on ornament. Inasmuch as it always involves identifying the structural role of a supplement, ornament is not just an example of the work of deconstructive discourse but its ongoing theme. And this thematic question of ornament, which is not simply, if ever, a question of or for art, is always architectural.[66] It involves a thinking about space that cannot be as easily separated from the question of a building as might at first appear. What is at stake in ornament is the distinction between inside and outside. It is ornament that defines space. There may be no space without ornament, and no thought about ornament that is not a thought about space.

Derrida's thinking of ornament has many implications for architecture, not because it can be simply applied to architecture, but because it is from the beginning a rethinking, a repositioning, of architecture. Indeed, such a thinking might not, in the end, be very different from certain subtexts of traditional theories of ornament in architectural discourse. Much of what Derrida argues is already explicitly written into canonic architectural theory. It is relatively easy to point to similar theories of the enigmatic centrality and structural role of ornament, like Gottfried Semper's in the nineteenth century, for example, whose traces are everywhere manifest in the very canonic tradition of architectural discourse that suppresses it.[67] At the very least, deconstructive discourse redirects attention to the traditional resources of architectural discourse. It may be that deconstruction is not so much a transformation of architectural discourse as an appropriation of certain architectural enigmas already built into that discourse. Derrida's work may appropriate more from architecture than it offers in return. Indeed, that appropriation of certain architectural qualities may, ironically, be precisely what it offers inasmuch as it initiates a sustained self-reflection in architectural discourse. What is at issue then in reading Derrida's work in architectural discourse is not a new architecture, or even a new theory of architecture, but a repositioning of architecture, a different space for architecture rather than a different architectural space.

Clearly, Derrida is not writing "about" architecture as such. Indeed, on those few occasions when his earlier work addresses architecture as an art, he seems to rehearse some of the most routine assumptions about architecture and resist their complication, accepting and reinforcing the familiar image even in the middle of pointing to the ways in which that image could be opened up but symptomatically not doing so in the end. This ambivalence about architecture is not so much an isolated event in Derrida's discourse, but a structural condition that pervades the discourse and surfaces most clearly in those isolated moments when architecture is addressed.

This structural ambivalence can be seen in the two moments of his essay on Kant's *The Critique of Judgement* that explicitly address architecture as such by discussing the properties of buildings. The first elaborates the architectural "analogy" in Kant's text by distinguishing between the material structure of a building and the view at it:

A spatial, so-called plastic, art object does not necessarily prescribe an order of reading. I can move around in front of it, start from the top or the bottom, sometimes walk round it. No doubt this possibility has an ideal limit. . . . In terms of the analogy (but how to measure its terms) one ought to be able to begin anywhere and follow any order, although the quantity and the quality, the force of the reading may depend, as with a piece of architecture, on the point of view and on a certain relation to the ideal limit—which acts as a frame. There are only ever points of view: but the solidity, the existence, the structure of the edifice do not depend on them. Can one say the same, by analogy, of a book. One does not necessarily gain access to a piece of architecture by following the order of its production, starting at the foundations and arriving at the roof-ridge. And we must distinguish here between perception, analysis, penetration, utilization, even destruction. But does one read a book of pure philosophy if one does not begin with the foundations and follow the juridical order of its writing. What then is it to read philosophy and must one only read it.[68]

While Derrida appeals to the ability to engage with architecture relatively independently of the ground-foundation-structure-ornament logic that it represents to reconfigure the reading of philosophy that preserves the same logic, the passage preserves a clear separation between the angle of view and the material building it is directed at—a separation, that is, between subject and object. This is significant inasmuch as it can be argued that architecture is not merely an example of this split but is its very possibility, as can be seen in the way Heidegger explicitly understands his attempt to identify the building as the construction of a view, rather than something that is viewed, as the disruption of that split. When speaking of architecture, Derrida hesitates to track the complications he everywhere else relentlessly pursues.

Likewise, in the second moment in which Derrida addresses the material building, he takes apart Kant's architectural example of the detachability of ornament (the colonnade on a building) but, in so doing, echoes the claim that a building "does not represent anything" that Heidegger's essay originally asserted precisely in order to be progressively displaced:

> Why would the column be external to the building? Where does the criterion, the critical organ, the organum of discernment come from here? . . . the *parergon* is added this time to a work which *does not represent anything* and which is itself already *added to* nature. We think we know what properly belongs or does not belong to the human body, what is detached or not detached from it even though the parergon is precisely an ill-detachable detachment. But in a work of architecture, the *Vorstellung*, the representation is not structurally representational or else is so only through detours complicated enough, no doubt, to disconcert anyone who tried to discern, in a critical manner, the inside from the outside, the integral part and the detachable part. So as not to add to these complications, I shall leave to one side, provisionally, the case of columns in the form of the building, those that support or represent the support of a window (and does a window form part of the inside of a building or not? And what about the window of a building in a painting?), and which can be naked or clothed, . . . [69]

Again, the complications of architecture are successively invoked rather than pursued, left "to one side." Furthermore, it can be argued that just as their invocation has a decisive affect on the course of the argument, which then appears to proceed without them (enabling Derrida to immediately identify "the internal structural link" that binds the ornament to a gap in the structure), so too does the reluctance to follow them further. Again, this is significant because architecture is not simply an example of the relationship being explored. It is precisely the relationship between structure and representation that is always at stake in the architectural figure and, indeed, that relationship can only be thought in terms of that figure. The figure is routinely invoked by the tradition for its capacity to articulate the distinction between presentation and representation. By invoking but ultimately bracketing out the complication of this distinction in architecture itself, Derrida short-circuits the question even while elaborating an argument that necessarily bears on the figure of architecture and would transform it precisely through those very "detours" that confuse inside and outside.

In the end, Derrida doesn't hesitate and follow this interruption of the trajectory of his argument as it passes through architecture, which raises the possibility that his thinking might already be coming to a stop with architecture in a way that calls into question its ostensible force everywhere else, that architecture—which is to say, a certain image of architecture—is itself acting as some kind of stable ground on which the rest of his work plays, without putting it into question. We must remain constantly alert to this possibility here. But it is equally possible that the force of Derrida's work derives from a particular rethinking of architecture that might not be identified as such, or cannot be identified inasmuch as it is a rethinking of that which is supposedly the focus of the discipline of architecture but actually constitutes its central blind spot, that which might not be recognized as architecture precisely because it is so central, that which is hidden in and by the center of the discourse, making the very institutional mechanisms that veil it possible.

Again, it has to be said that this is not a question of what Derrida says about architecture, but of the role a certain image of architecture plays in his thinking. It does not involve reading his texts from some external position—that of the institution of architectural discourse—and adjudicating their thinking of architecture to be sophisticated or naive, radical or reactionary, and so on. The very idea that architecture is "external" to philosophical discourse and the role of that idea in the organization of both institutions is precisely what is at stake here. Rather, it is a matter of following the texts, tracing their contours in detail to see how they construct themselves, following the way they themselves follow other texts. Such a parasitic reading, endlessly indebted to its host texts, is not so much concerned with locating the architecture hidden in, if not by, Derrida's work, but of seeing what it might say about such a hiding, seeing what it reveals about concealment, what it opens about closure, and so on. In the end, these are the architectural questions.

The Threat of Architecture

It is in these terms that it is necessary to return to Derrida's reading of Kant's aesthetics and look at the other level at which architecture comes up in the essay. Its rethinking of ornament has been set up by a certain thinking about architecture, or, rather, a thinking about Kant's thinking of architecture. If Heidegger identifies and undermines the way in which aesthetics defines art as a superstructural addition to an object, Derrida identifies and undermines the way that aesthetics is itself treated as a superstructure added to the substructure of philosophy. Philosophy understands itself as a grounded structure to which is attached the ornament of art. It subordinates the arts, including architecture, by employing the vertical hierarchy dependent on a certain understanding of the art of architecture. Art is subordinated by being located furthest from the ground. The subordination is made possible by the traditional image of architecture, the image that will itself be subordinated within the arts and detached from philosophy as merely a contingent metaphor superfluous to the fixed structure of philosophy. Everywhere, architecture is involved in its own subordination.

Derrida's essay points to this strange economy by paying attention to the way *The Critique of Judgement* introduces itself in terms of the design project for an edifice sketched out in the *Critique of Pure Reason:*

For if such a system is some day worked out under the general name of Metaphysic . . . the critical examination of the ground for this edifice must have been previously carried down to the very depths of the foundations of the faculty of principles independent of experience, lest in some quarter it might give way, and, sinking, inevitably bring with it the ruin of all.[70]

Aesthetic judgment depends on rules but, unlike metaphysics, it cannot give them. It is only the presumed universality of the immaterial voice listened to when faced with the material art object that establishes the rationality of aesthetic judgments—a presumption that cannot be confirmed without contaminating taste with reason. Aesthetic judgment is recognized "*a priori* as a law for everyone without being able to ground it upon proofs," without, that is, being able to identify its "determining ground."[71] Consequently, aesthetics cannot be constructed on the ground like metaphysics. *The Critique of Judgement* constructs itself as a "bridge" over the "abyss" between Kant's first two critiques and their respective theoretical and practical realms. From this bridge, the ground at the very bottom of the abyss, on which the projected metaphysics will eventually stand, can be surveyed. *The Critique of Judgement* is constructed to produce a groundplan, a plan for the foundations of metaphysics. It is only a temporary structure which, like scaffolding, precedes the building but becomes an ornament to it which must be detached. But the convoluted logic of ornament ensures a certain difficulty in detaching art from the interior of philosophy, a difficulty that binds architectural discourse to philosophy. In describing metaphysics as an edifice, Kant organizes philosophy in terms of a certain account of the art of architecture before the architectural object, or any of the other arts, has been examined in aesthetics. As Derrida puts it:

Kant proposes another metaphor. He borrows it, already, from art, which has not yet been discussed, from the technique of architecture, architectonics: the pure philosopher, the metaphysician, will have to operate *like* a good architect, like a good *technitēs* of edification. He will be a sort of artist. Now what does a good architect do, according to Kant? He must first of all secure the ground, the foundation, the fundament . . . the architect of reason excavates, sounds, prepares the terrain, in search of a solid foundation, the ultimate *Grund* on which all metaphysics may be erected . . . Here philosophy, which in this book [*The Critique of Judgement*] has to think art through—art in general and fine art—as a part of its field or of its edifice, is here *representing itself* as part of its part, philosophy as an art of architecture. It represents itself, it *detaches itself*, dispatches from itself a proxy, a part of itself outside itself to bind the whole, to fill up or heal over the whole that suffers from detachment. The philosophy of art presupposes an art of philosophizing, a major art, but also a miner's art in its critical preliminaries, an architect's art in its edifying erection. . . . if this pure philosophy or fundamental metaphysics here proposes to account for, among other things, desire, pleasure and unpleasure, it exposes itself and represents itself first of all in its own desire. The desire of reason would be a fundamental desire, a desire for the fundamental . . . a metaphor of reason to account for all other metaphors. It would figure the being-desire of desire, the desire of/for reason as desire for a grounded structure. Edifying desire would be produced as an art of philosophizing, commanding all the others and accounting for [*rendant raison de*] all rhetoric.[72]

By representing itself as a work of art, metaphysics is subject to its own analysis of art. Just as it admits ornament into the artwork only inasmuch as it is "design," it admits its own ornament—aesthetics—into its own interior only inasmuch as it is architecture. Architecture must be admitted to cover some kind of gap within metaphysics.

Derrida's argument can be developed further by suggesting that architecture enters by virtue of its claim on "design." The "trace" that is the signature of the divine artist is design and, for Kant, fine art is only able to give life to the dead body of an object because it is authorized by that signature: "no one would ascribe design, in the proper sense of the term, to a lifeless material."[73] Fine art imitates the original productivity of the divine artist, the capacity to produce originals, to be original, by presenting design rather than imitating his products by representing specific designs. It must have the appearance of design and yet "must have the appearance of being undesigned and a spontaneous occurrence."[74] In this way, the *Critique* produces its famous formulation of the beautiful as the presentation of purposiveness without the representation of a specific purpose, like "nature which in her beautiful products displays herself as art, not merely by chance, but, as it were, designedly, in accordance with a regular agreement as purposiveness without purpose."[75] The *Critique* depends on the traditional argument that the appearance of design in the world presupposes the presence of a designer, an architect, a "supreme Architect."[76] It is only by employing such an argument from design that the philosophical tradition can describe itself as architecture and the philosopher as an architect.

Architecture, then, plays a curious strategic role. It is able to pass between philosophy and art in a unique way. It is involved in a kind of translation. The metaphor circulates between and within the two systems, complicating them as it folds back on itself. A convoluted economy is sustained by the description of architecture as ornamented structure that enables art to be subordinated to philosophy even while philosophy describes itself as architecture. Philosophy describes itself in terms of the very thing it subordinates.

In organizing itself around an account of objects as grounded structures, philosophy projects an account of architecture outside itself, which it then appeals to as an outside authority. In so doing, it literally produces that architecture. The divisions between inside and outside, structure and ornament, philosophy and architecture, and so on, do not precede the exclusion of architecture—they are produced by it. The production of architecture is at the same time the production of the space of philosophy. Architecture, which appears to be the good tame ornament of philosophy, is actually the possibility of philosophy. But it is so only inasmuch as it secretly wild, exceeding philosophy's attempts to describe it, let alone define and thereby position it, which is to say that architecture is the possibility of philosophy only inasmuch as it is not strictly architectural.

Architecture can only be subordinated as such inasmuch as it can be rendered metaphoric, that is, only inasmuch as a clear distinction can be maintained between material space and immaterial space. The maintenance of this line takes the form of a denial, a fetishistic disavowal that becomes the very basis of both philosophy as a cultural institution and each the arguments it sanctions. If, as Derrida suggests, philosophy, in appealing to architecture, "represents itself, it *detaches itself,* detaches from itself a proxy, a part of itself outside itself to bind the whole, to fill up or heal over the whole that suffers from detachment,"[77] it does so to cover some kind of gap, some internal fracture of its structure. Metaphysics produces the architectural object as the paradigm of ground as support in order to veil its own lack of support, its ungrounded condition. Philosophy represents itself as architecture, it translates itself as architecture, producing itself in this translation. The limits of philosophy are established by the metaphorical status of architecture.

Derrida closely follows the part of Heidegger's work that interferes with that status before his texts restore it and return architecture to its "proper place." One implication of Derrida's reading of ornament is that it is the way in which the thought of architecture as a simple addition to building covers the structural role of architecture that actually makes possible the thought of the naked ground as support. This possibility could be developed by looking again at Heidegger's later essays, which explicitly address architecture and seem to undermine the division between building and architecture in order to displace the traditional sense of the ground. For example, "Building, Dwelling, Thinking" asserts: "But the nature of the erecting of buildings cannot be understood adequately in terms either of architecture or of engineering construction, nor in terms of a mere combination of the two."[78] This description of actual building is sustained when he employs architecture as a figure for philosophy, as, for example, when his *Schelling's Treatise on the Essence of Human Freedom* locates philosophy in the "uneasy" place "between" structure and ornament, between the closure of a foundation and the openness of that which needs no ground.[79] In these terms, the thought of that which is neither building nor architecture that is elided by traditional discourse is the thought of the original ground that precedes the ground-as-support—the sense of support being no more than an effect of that elision. The linear logic of addition that architecture is invariably called in to reinforce is confused. The building is not simply added to the ground, the ornament is not simply added to the structure, art is not simply added to philosophy. The vertical hierarchy of ground/structure/ornament put in place by the architectural figure is radically convoluted. The architectural figure undermines itself and, ironically, in so doing, it undermines its own subordination. Inasmuch as the figure subverts what it supposedly stands for, it can no longer be dismissed as a mere ornament. On the contrary, it derives its force precisely from its ornamental role.

But while certain Heideggerian moves subvert the logic of addition by displacing the traditional account of architecture, Heidegger ultimately contradicts that possibility, confirming the traditional logic by looking for a stable structure while bracketing off architecture, or, more precisely, he establishes a stable structure by bracketing architecture. In his reading of "The Origin of the Work of Art," Derrida argues that Heidegger is in the end unable to abandon the tradition of ground as support, ground as that which is "underneath," even while "discovering a few cave-ins of the terrain, some abysses too in the field where we advance so tranquilly."[80] Indeed, Heidegger retains it in the very account of translation he uses to identify the way its emergence conceals the abyss:

> At the very moment when Heidegger is denouncing translation into Latin Words, at the moment when, at any rate, he declares Greek speech to be lost, he also makes use of a "metaphor." Of at least one metaphor, that of the foundation and the ground. The ground of the Greek experience is, he says, lacking in this "translation."[81]

The thought of ground as support is not just produced by a mistranslation. It is itself no more than a certain account of translation. Translation is traditionally understood as presentation of the ground, and mistranslation is understood as detachment from ground, loss of support. It must be recalled that it is the collapse of the Tower of Babel that establishes the necessity of translation as one of reconstruction, edification.[82] Heidegger's account of translation undermines itself when dealing with the translation of the original ground into the idea of the edifice with which philosophy organizes itself. He appears to employ an account of translation similar to Derrida's inasmuch as he argues that the violation of the original ground is already there in the Greek original. But then he attempts to go "underneath" this sense to erase the violation, and, in so doing, restores a traditional account of translation.[83] He rebuilds the very edifice he appears to have undermined, putting the subversive qualities he drew from architecture into play but only after he detaches them from buildings, rendering architecture metaphoric, putting architecture back in its place and, in so doing, putting philosophy back in its place.

Derrida's work disturbs this metaphoric status. Having pointed to the figure in Heidegger's account of translation, he immediately calls it into question: "What I have just too hastily called 'metaphor' concentrates all the difficulties to come: does one speak 'metaphorically' of the ground for just anything?"[84] The relevance of Derrida's work for architecture and vice versa hangs on this question. His work attains its greatest force when it interferes with the traditional categorization of architecture as either a literal, irreducible, and inescapable material reality—the almost hyperreal status credited to buildings in our culture—or a contingent and immaterial metaphor. The two categories are actually interdependent. The more fundamental buildings are seen to be, the more metaphoric their role in discourse seems. Architecture, as it were, clarifies the opposition between material object and immaterial discourse, acting as philosophy's paradigm. Derrida can only disrupt this opposition by disrupting the image of architecture that constitutes it, rather than being its product.

If Heidegger ends up reconstituting the tradition of metaphysics sustained by subordinating architecture and prohibiting other accounts of it, this prohibition marks a repression. Something about architecture cannot be said without calling into question the whole system. Deconstructive discourse is of interest to architectural discourse inasmuch as it can be used to identify the threat that architecture poses to the tradition of metaphysics to which it is contracted, the threat that causes that tradition to subordinate architecture. Such an appropriation of deconstructive discourse makes available accounts of architecture prohibited by the terms of the ancient contract that binds architecture into discourse, and continues to orchestrate "theoretical" discourse, including those discourses that identify themselves, however cautiously, as "deconstructive."

4

The Domestication of
the House

Heidegger's "late" work develops his early motif of the edifice—
the grounded structure—into that of the house. As his writing
becomes increasingly committed to the question of language, the
traditional architectonic structure of language discussed in the
early work becomes a "house." Language as grounding becomes
language as "dwelling" [*Wohnen*]. The figure of "standing" becomes that of "enclosing." The structural system binding signifiers to the ground becomes an enclosure. In the famous
formulation of the 1947 "Letter on Humanism": "Language is
the house of Being. In its home man dwells."[1] This focus on the
house is often identified with Heidegger's so-called turn. In turning, he turns to the house. This is not so much a turn from the
edifice of the early work toward the house. Rather, the edifice is
turned into a house, building is now understood as housing.

In this way, Heidegger develops a whole architectural rhetoric
out of the traditional architectural metaphor with which philosophy institutes itself. Philosophy becomes no more than thinking
about housing or, more precisely, the institutions of philosophy
are to be displaced by a thinking that houses. This displacement
is first and foremost a rejection of philosophy's construction of
space. Beginning with the central argument of *Being and Time*,
Heidegger's texts present an extended critique of the conception
of space that has been progressively institutionalized since ancient Greece, a conception that is, for him, the institution of
space itself. The moment that philosophy's central architectural

metaphor becomes explicit as such—with Descartes—is also the moment its ancient basis in a certain account of space becomes explicit. To deconstruct this tradition, Heidegger employs a spatial rhetoric—"house," "enclosure," "shelter," "abode," "lodging," "inner," "proximity," "neighborhood"—but asks us not to hear it spatially. The familiar sense of architecture as the definition of space is invoked and then displaced, highlighted then withdrawn. What we unproblematically take to be the space of the house (as the paradigm of space itself) is seen to both emerge from and veil a prior and more fundamental condition from which we have become alienated. But what distinguishes Heidegger's arguments from so many other similar-sounding critiques of modern life is that the process of alienation is understood to be an ancient one that is only becoming manifest with modernity and, furthermore, that the basic condition it alienates us from is itself one of profound alienation. The alienating space of the home veils a more fundamental and primordial homelessness. To be at home in such a space is precisely to be homeless.

To dismantle the tradition of metaphysics, Heidegger has to dismantle our most familiar experiences of architecture, which are but the product of the tradition of metaphysics and are therefore complicitous with the necessarily violent regime of technology that is its contemporary manifestation. He employs an architectural rhetoric in a way that dispels, among other things, the apparent innocence of architectural space. But this gesture, which has so much to say about architecture—and a certain dimension of it has been influential in architectural discourse—is susceptible to its own criticism in a way that opens further possibilities for that discourse. Indeed, it is precisely the dimension that has already been so eagerly appropriated by the discourse that is the focus of this criticism. In the end, Heidegger's architectural rhetoric sustains the very tradition it is deployed to displace.

Disfiguring the House

Heidegger's work is almost always double sided. It repeatedly performs a rigorous dismantling of some aspect of the tradition of philosophy, only to later revive that very aspect in a displaced form that consolidates whatever had been destabilized. The risk built into Heidegger's original argument that construction depends upon, and is no more than, an ongoing destruction from within ultimately, and perhaps necessarily, turns on his own writing, his critical unbuilding becoming constructive of the very system it places in question. As Derrida argues, when reading *Being and Time,* "At a certain point, then, the destruction of metaphysics remains within metaphysics, only making explicit its principles."[2] All of his many readings of Heidegger's texts locate this point by applying those texts' own strategies to themselves. Consequently, his relationship to Heidegger is, at the very least, "enigmatic" as he once put it.[3] He thinks through Heidegger in detail in order to depart from him, taking each text to the limit, elaborating each of its arguments further, but not simply as "an extension or a *continuous* radicalization," as he points out elsewhere.[4] He departs from Heidegger by following him in a maneuvre that is far from straightforward. Heidegger's writing is seen to both exemplify the often subtle and elusive operations of the hegemonic tradition that need to be unbuilt and to provide the strategies for doing just that.

I do maintain . . . that Heidegger's text is extremely important to me . . . That being said . . . I have marked quite explicitly, in *all* the essays I have published, as can be verified, a *departure* from the Heideggerian problematic . . . I sometimes have the feeling that the Heideggerian problematic is the most "profound" and "powerful" defence of what I attempt to put into question under the rubric of the *thought of presence.*[5]

Derrida is at once closer to and further away from Heidegger than is usually acknowledged. The "departure" is never simple or complete. His writing never simply moves beyond or outside Heidegger's discourse. Rather, it interrogates that discourse from within, locating and exploiting certain openings in it.

Architecture plays an important role in this interrogation. One of the key symptoms of Heidegger's allegiance to the very tradition he appears to displace—which Derrida identifies and which is equally, and necessarily, a point of departure for Derrida's own work, an opening for a radical displacement of that tradition—is the figure of the house. When reading the "Letter on Humanism," Derrida argues that it is by employing the chain of metaphors that surround the house that Heidegger "remains within" metaphysics:

Whence, in Heidegger's discourse, the dominance of an entire metaphorics of proximity, of simple and immediate presence, a metaphorics associating the proximity of Being with the values of neighboring, shelter, house, service, guard, voice, and listening. As goes without saying, this is not an insignificant rhetoric; . . . the choice of one or another group of metaphors is necessarily significant. It is within a metaphorical insistence, then, that the interpretation of the meaning of Being is produced.[6]

By making the house thematic, Heidegger identifies the figure that organizes the tradition he attempts to dismantle, but in the end he fails to dismantle the house. On the contrary, he repeatedly advocates a return to it, a withdrawal to the primal shelter, the site of unmediated presence, in order to take refuge from the modern—which is to say technological—age of representation that is condemned inasmuch as it produces a generalized "homelessness." He inhabits metaphysics in a way that does not threaten the authority of the house, succumbing to the risk implicit in his strategy of destruction, the same risk that faces the contemporary appropriations of that strategy by deconstructive discourse that Derrida pointedly describes in terms of the house:

To attempt an exit and a deconstruction without changing terrain, by repeating what is implicit in the founding concepts and the original problematic, by using against the edifice the instruments or stones available in the house, that is, equally, in language. Here, one risks ceaselessly confirming, consolidating, *relifting* (*relever*), at an always more certain depth, that which one allegedly deconstructs. The continuous process of making explicit, moving toward an opening, risks sinking into the autism of the closure.[7]

Secure housing is the greatest risk of deconstructive discourse. It is always possible to rearrange the stones of the house without, in the end, disturbing its capacity to house. Derrida's prolonged elaboration of Heidegger's displacement of the architecture of the edifice, problematizing the cumulative logic of building (ground-foundation-structure-ornament), which plays such a decisive role in organizing discourse in our culture, must therefore also be, in some way, a displacement of the architecture of the house.

But deconstructive discourse cannot simply reject Heidegger's use of the traditional figure of the house, or even its "dominance" in his work, since Heidegger's first argument, picked up so insistently by Derrida, is that it is necessary to inhabit metaphysics in precisely this way, exploiting all its resources, especially its central metaphorical figures, in order to overcome it. Such metaphors cannot simply be abandoned. Rather, they have to be affirmed, elaborated, and redeployed to identify exactly what their use both constructs and covers over. Heidegger's writing never simply upholds the tradition it occupies. Rather, it is "at once contained within it and transgresses it"[8] through an ever shifting double movement. By occupying metaphysics, it establishes the strategic roles of the metaphors that organize it. Heidegger's appropriation of the house from the tradition is a key example of this. But in occupying that house, he has to transgress it to disrupt the tradition, appropriating it in a way that recovers that which even this forgotten image forgets, identifying the image's own transgressive potential. Heidegger does not, at first reading, appear to do this despite his explicit rejection of the modern sense of the house as a spatial interior, a space that is itself understood as an alienating technology of control that operates as an agent of metaphysics. The house appears to be simply consolidated rather than deconstructed.

Such a deconstruction would be uniquely complicated because the motif of the house, like that of the edifice, is not simply another metaphor (if metaphors are ever simple), but is that which determines the condition of metaphor in the first place. Metaphor is supposedly defined by its detachment from a "proper" meaning. In "The *Retrait* of Metaphor," one of Derrida's most extended readings of the question of metaphor that is always at stake in his work, this sense of the proper is seen to be bound to that of the house. The essay points to "the economic value of the domicile and of the proper both of which often (or always) intervene in the definition of the metaphoric."[9] Throughout his writing, Derrida draws on the Greek association between the household (*oikos*) and the proper (*oikeios*). When speaking of Freud, for example, the house is described as the "familiar dwelling, the proper place."[10] And elsewhere Derrida notes that in Hegel "the general form of philosophy, is properly familial and produces itself as *oikos:* home, habitation, . . . the guarding of the proper, of property, propriety, of one's own."[11] All of these readings follow a consistent trajectory from his point in "The Ends of Man" that it is precisely in Heidegger's writing that "the themes of the *house* and the *proper* are regularly brought together."[12] This point can be elaborated by looking at the way Heidegger binds the metaphor of the house to language by linking it to his concept of "appropriation" (*Ereignis*). Building, understood as housing, is repeatedly described as appropriation.[13] Language is a house because it is a mode of appropriation whereby thought recovers presence in the face of alienating representations rather than a form of representation. It is a house because it appropriates, making proper by excluding representation and establishing a "proximity" to presence.[14]

In these terms, the house is the metaphor of that which precedes metaphor. It determines the condition of the proper, from which the metaphorical is then said to be detached and inferior. As the traditional figure of an interior divided from an exterior, it is used to establish a general opposition between an inner world of presence and an outer world of representation that is then used to exclude that very figure as a "mere" metaphor, a representation to be discarded to the outside of philosophy. But the figure always resists such an exclusion. Inasmuch as the condition of metaphor is established by the metaphor of the house, the house is not simply another metaphor that can be discarded. And, more than this, although metaphor is understood as a departure from the house, it is still not a departure from housing. Rather, it is the temporary occupation of another house, a borrowed house. Metaphor is an improper occupation, a being at a home without being at home. Consequently, the figure of the house is neither metaphorical nor proper. It is, as Derrida argues in "The *Retrait* of Metaphor," "not only metaphoric to say that we inhabit metaphor . . . it is not simply metaphoric. Nor anymore proper, literal or usual."[15] As the figure of the house is what makes the distinction between metaphor and proper possible, it is not, according to "White Mythology":

one metaphor among others; it is there in order to signify metaphor *itself;* it is a metaphor of metaphor; an expropriation, a being-outside-one's-own-residence, but still in a dwelling, outside its own residence but still in a residence in which one comes back to oneself, recognizes oneself, reassembles oneself or resembles oneself, outside oneself in oneself. This is the philosophical metaphor as a detour within (or in sight of) appropriation, parousia, the self-presence of the idea in its own light. The metaphorical trajectory from the Platonic *eidos* to the Hegelian Idea.[16]

What Derrida, echoing Heidegger, refers to so often as "the metaphysics of presence" is sustained by the figure of the house in the same way as it is sustained by the figure of the edifice. Since Plato, the house has always been that tradition's exemplar of presentation. The governing concept of "Idea" as presence, and of the visible world as informed matter, the material presentation of immaterial ideas, is traditionally established with the metaphor of the house produced by an architect, the house as the presentation of an "idea," as can be seen in Marsilio Ficino's commentary on Plato:

If someone asks in what way the form of the body may be similar to the form and reason of the spirit and the Angel, I ask this person to consider the edifice of the Architect. From the beginning the Architect conceives in his spirit and approximately the Idea of the edifice; he then makes the house (according to his ability) in the way in which he has decided in his mind. Who will deny that the house is a body, and that it is very similar to the incorporeal Idea of the artisan, in whose image it has been made? It must certainly be judged for a certain incorporeal order rather than for its matter.[17]

It is only possible to abruptly point to this canonic form of the metaphor here in lieu of tracing its long history in detail by following the curious trajectories and slippages between terms like "maker," "builder," "architect," "demiurge," "*techne,*" and so on. Such a detailed reading would show the way in which architecture, and, in particular, the house, is not simply the paradigm of the operations of the idea. Rather, the idea is itself understood as a paradigm—literally, for Plato, a *paradeigma*—or architectural model. This particular image plays an important role in the traditional analogy between the philosopher and the architect that has been exploited by both discourses.

Philosophy does not depart from itself to illustrate its concepts with the figure of the house. On the contrary, it forever circulates around the house, departing from it only to stage a return to it. This can be seen when, in defining the essence of technology, Heidegger notes that the original sense of *techne,* from which philosophy has departed, is "to be entirely at home [*zu Hause*] in something."[18] But to define essence, he uses the example of the "essence of a house [*Haus*]" and then draws on Plato's theory of "Ideas" to describe the house's condition. To determine the essence of *techne* as housing, he determines the sense of essence by reference to the house. The house is not simply an example of essence. It does not simply illustrate presence or essence. Rather, it is used to define them. Neither can be thought outside the house.

In such involuted circulations between concepts and the image of a house, which regularly punctuate the tradition of philosophy, the sense of the house as an interior never goes away, even in Heidegger's texts, despite their insistent attempt to discard it. The house is always first understood as the most primitive drawing of a line that produces an inside opposed to an outside, a line that acts as a mechanism of domestication. It is as the paradigm of interiority that the house is indispensable to philosophy, establishing the distinction between the interiority of presence and the exteriority of representation on which the discourse depends.

In all the binary pairs of terms with which metaphysics organizes itself, as Derrida argues when reading Plato, "each of the terms must be simply *external* to the other, which means that one of these oppositions (the opposition between inside and outside) must already be accredited as the matrix of all possible opposition."[19] Consequently, the philosophical system is organized by spatial metaphors it cannot abandon. It is itself necessarily spatial. When noting the way in which Freud's theoretical system both invokes and discredits spatial metaphors, Derrida claims "a certain spatiality, inseparable from the very idea of system, is irreducible."[20] This argument is even more explicit in his early reading of the way Emmanuel Levinas identifies being as an "exteriority" only to argue that it is not spatial. Insisting on "the necessity of lodging oneself within traditional conceptuality in order to destroy it," Derrida argues that "one would attempt in vain, in order to wean language from exteriority and interiority . . . for one would never come across a language without the rupture of space."[21] Space is the very possibility of language and the tradition of thinking that believes it can transcend space and employ language as merely a temporary and necessarily inadequate vehicle for its pure (which is to say, aspatial) thought. Consequently, one must "inhabit" the spatial metaphor that is "congenital" to philosophy in order to question it:

[I]t is necessary still to inhabit the [spatial] metaphor in ruins, to dress oneself in tradition's shreds and the devil's patches—all this means, perhaps, that there is no philosophical logos which must not *first* let itself be expatriated into the structure Inside-Outside. This deportation from its own site toward the Site, toward spatial locality is the *metaphor* congenital to the philosophical logos. Before being a rhetorical procedure within language, metaphor would be the emergence of language itself. And philosophy is only this language . . . one must not expect, henceforth, to separate language and space, to empty language of space.[22]

Here Derrida is clearly following Heidegger's claim in *Being and Time* that spatial significations (*Raumbedeutungen*) are irreducible in language: "Is it an accident that proximally and for the most part significations are 'worldly,' sketched out beforehand by the significance of the world, that they are indeed often predominantly 'spatial'?"[23] In a later reading of Heidegger Derrida draws on this argument, briefly elaborating it by simply restating it, but in a way that identifies a spatiality within the philosophical tradition in its very attempt to exclude spatiality: "The phenomenon of so-called spatializing metaphors is not at all accidental, nor within the reach of the rhetorical concept of 'metaphor.' It is not some exterior fatality."[24] The concept of metaphor cannot be thought outside that of exterior. Space cannot simply be excluded, as any act of exclusion constructs a space by dividing an inside from an outside.

To this we can add that this irreducible spatiality turns around the figure of the house. The spatial metaphor that must be "inhabited" is actually the metaphor of inhabitation itself. The house is constitutionally bound into the metaphysical tradition and cannot simply be subordinated as a metaphor. It can never be exterior to philosophy, as it produces the very sense of interior on which that tradition is based. The edifice of metaphysics is necessarily a house. Within every explicit appeal to the necessity of stable construction is an implicit appeal to the necessity of a secure house. The philosophical economy is always a domestic economy, the economy of the domestic, the family house, the familiar enclosure. Deconstructive discourse must therefore be first and foremost an occupation of the idea of the house that displaces it from within.

Taking Shelter in the Uncanny

A rhetoric of the house can be found throughout Derrida's texts without it ever being their ostensible subject. It is a kind of subtext that surfaces in radically different contexts and usually in small and scattered fragments. A sense of this house and its strategic role can be built by assembling some of these fragments here.

In Derrida's work all of the associations with the traditional figure of an edifice on secure foundations slide into that of the secure domestic enclosure. If to ground a structure is to build a house, to constrain the unruly play of representations is to house them, to domesticate them. Just as Derrida's sporadic but multiple references to the edifice identify speech as structural and writing as superstructural, his references to the house identify speech as inside the house, whereas writing is outside. In his account of Plato, for example, the *logos* "does not wander, stays at home," whereas writing is "unattached to any house,"[25] such that "in nothing does writing reside."[26] To sustain the tradition that privileges presence by rejecting the "other" is therefore, as he puts it in another essay, "to take shelter in the most familial of dwellings."[27] And in another context, the "*law of the house,* the initial organization of a dwelling space" represses play when difference is "enclosed."[28] Elsewhere, the economy of metaphysics literally attempts to "arrest, domesticate, tame"[29] the other. In these terms, all his work "'analyzes' philosophical power in its domestic regime,"[30] as he once describes his earliest readings of Husserl. This domestic regime is both the space that philosophy claims for itself and the arguments made within that space. In appropriating the space as its own and delimiting its territory, it is defining its law, defining it precisely as a law of domesticity, philosophical law as the law of enforced domesticity. The space of philosophy is not just a domestic space, it is a space in which a certain idea about the domestic is sustained and protected.

The house's ability to domesticate is its capacity to define inside and outside, but not simply because that which is located inside is domesticated. For Derrida, the "outside" of a house continues to be organized by the logic of the house and so actually remains inside it. By being placed outside, the other is placed, domesticated, kept inside. To be excluded is to be subjected to a certain domestic violence that is both organized and veiled by metaphysics.[31] Metaphysics is no more than a determination of place, the production of the sense of a pure interior divided from an improper exterior, a privileged realm of presence uncorrupted by representation. Whatever disrupts metaphysics disrupts this sense of interior. Derrida's work is concerned with that which "threatens the paternal *logos*. And which by the same token threatens the domestic, hierarchical interior."[32] His texts everywhere, albeit obliquely, question the sense of the house ultimately reinforced by Heidegger.

But, significantly, Derrida's "departure" from Heidegger is not a departure from the house. The interior space of presence is not simply abandoned for that of representation, nor is the realm of representation simply seen to occupy the interior. Rather, the economy of representation is seen to structure the interior as such. The sense of interior is actually an effect of representation. It is produced by what it supposedly excludes. Derrida departs from Heidegger by tacitly locating a violation within the structure of the house that is repressed by a systematic domestic violence that is itself in turn concealed by the apparent structure of the house. The constitutional violation of the edifice by the abyss that Heidegger demonstrated to be necessary for that structure to stand is equally the constitutional violation of the house that makes its capacity to house possible. The fracturing of the ground is equally, in Derrida's hands, a fracturing of the walls. The house of metaphysics is deconstructed by locating the "traces of an alterity which refuses to be totally domesticated"[33] and yet cannot be excluded, that which resists metaphysics because it cannot be placed either inside or outside, and is therefore "undecidable," and yet is indispensable to the operations of metaphysics.

In a footnote in "The Double Session," Derrida identifies its account of undecidability as a "rereading" of Freud's essay "The Uncanny" (*Das Unheimliche*) which, as is well known, describes the uneasy sense of the unfamiliar within the familiar, the unhomely within the home. Freud pays attention to the way the term for homely (*heimliche*) is defined both as "belonging to the house, not strange, familiar, tame, intimate, friendly, etc." and as what seems at first to be its opposite: "concealed, kept from sight, so that others do not get to know of or about it, withheld from others."[34] In this structural slippage from *heimliche* to *unheimliche* that which supposedly lies outside the familiar comfort of the home turns out to be inhabiting it all along, surfacing only in a return of the repressed as a foreign element that strangely seems to belong in the very domain that renders it foreign. Derrida's footnote goes on to say that "we find ourselves constantly being brought back to that text."[35] But despite, or perhaps because of, the unique attraction of this text or, more likely, its subject, it is never explicitly analyzed in the essay other than as a brief point in another footnote. Nor is it read in depth anywhere else in Derrida's writings. Like the figure of the house to which it is bound, it is a theme that can be traced throughout Derrida's work without it ever becoming a discrete subject, as if it is itself repressed, returning only occasionally to surface in very isolated and what seem, at first, to be minor points. But precisely for this reason it can be argued that its effects actually pervade all the texts that are unable or unwilling to speak about it.[36]

Derrida repeatedly, one might almost say compulsively, identifies the undecidables that uncannily intimate the violence within the familiar domain, which is to say, the domain of the family, the homestead, the house. Being, as he puts it, "domestic but utterly foreign,"[37] the uncanny exposes the covert operations of the house. For this reason its constitutional violation of the ostensible order of the house is itself repressed, domesticated by the very domestic violence it makes possible. Metaphysics is no more than the disguising of this domestic violence that in turn represses the fundamental strangeness of the house. The house of metaphysics represses the violation that made it possible. More than a domestic violence, this is the violence of the domestic itself. Derrida locates within the house that which is actually, as *Of Grammatology* puts it, "the sickness of the outside (which comes from the outside but also draws outside, thus equally, or inversely, the sickness of the homeland, a homesickness, so to speak)."[38] Heidegger's sickness for the home is displaced by Derrida's sickness of the home.

As their shared insistence on the necessity of a strategic inhabitation of the tradition would lead us to expect, this revision of the status of the house still closely follows Heidegger—indeed, goes even further into his work. Long before Heidegger explicitly raised the question of the house, his *Being and Time* had argued that the familiar everyday world is precisely a "fleeing in the face of uncanniness" that "suppresses everything unfamiliar."[39] The concept had already been introduced in his 1925 lectures at Marburg in terms of the feeling of dread when "one no longer feels at home in his most familiar environment."[40] Through the systematic concealment of the uncanny in everyday life, the familiar is actually a mode of uncanniness.[41] Just as the alienation of modern life is not simply produced by the abyss underlying all structures but by the covering over of that abyss, it is equally produced by covering over the uncanniness behind and of the familiar.[42] The apparent innocence of the familiar is but a mask that alienates by masking a more fundamental alienation: "the obviousness and self-assurance of the average ways in which things have been interpreted are such that while the particular *Dasein* drifts along towards an ever-increasing groundlessness as it floats, the uncanniness of this floating remains hidden from it under their protecting shelter."[43] The mask of the familiar is a primitive shelter, a house, or rather a pseudohouse, which veils a fundamental unfamiliarity. The uncanny is literally a "not-being-at-home," an alienation from the house experienced within it. With its discovery, "everyday familiarity collapses," and the "*not-at-home*" concealed by this familiarity "*must be conceived as the more primordial phenomenon.*"[44] Heidegger attempts to interrogate the familiar to discover what he later describes as the "danger" concealed within it: "Such questions bring us into the realm of what is familiar, even most familiar. For thinking, this always remains the real danger zone, because the familiar carries an air of harmlessness and ease, which causes us to pass lightly over what really deserves to be questioned."[45] From the beginning, his work attempts to displace the familiar, or at least place it at risk, in a way that raises the question of the danger in and of the familiar house. This question would be tacitly raised but symptomatically never answered by his later work.

To comprehend Derrida's thinking of the house, we need to go even further into Heidegger's thinking about it. Instead of simply rejecting Heidegger's ultimately reactionary use of the figure,[46] we have to locate the circuitous openings within his argument that can be used to displace it.

The Violence of the House

The symptomatic way in which Heidegger's questioning of the familiar through a questioning of home begins to slide into a questioning of the house can be seen when the 1935 essay "The Origin of the Work of Art" locates the uncanny danger within the very comfort of home:

We believe we are at home in the immediate circle of beings. That which is familiar, reliable, ordinary. Nevertheless, the clearing is pervaded by a constant concealment in the double form of refusal and dissembling. At bottom the ordinary is not ordinary; it is extraordinary, uncanny.[47]

This sense was developed in the same year by *An Introduction to Metaphysics,* which again argues at length that metaphysics is the mechanism of the concealment of the uncanny by the familiar, but does so in a way that redefines inhabitation. A reading of Sophocles' *Antigone* (itself described as a "poetic edifice") is used to affirm that "man"[48] is the "uncanniest of all beings"[49] and to identify two sides of this uncanniness, each of which involve a certain violence. On the one hand, man is violent, violating both enclosure and structure ("he who breaks out and breaks up"[50]) and violently domesticating things with technology ("he who captures and subjugates"[51]) in defining a home. On the other hand, there is the "overpowering" violence of Being, which the familiar space of the home attempts to cover over but which compels a certain panic and fear within it, and inevitably forces man out of it. The endless conflict between these two forms of violence is constitutional rather than simply a historical event. And it is not that one is an act of violence by a subject while the other is an act of violence against that subject. Rather, the conflict between them is the very possibility of the subject's existence, indeed, the existence of any thing as such. "Man" does not build a home in the same way that man does not build a language. Rather, "man" is built by the home. But, equally, it must be emphasized here, "man" is built by its destruction.

Heidegger is not speaking about literal houses, that is, spatial enclosures erected on particular sites. Significantly, he always describes the home as a kind of interior, but it is the very sense of spatial interior that masks the interiority he is describing. From his earliest texts, Heidegger always insists that the fundamental sense of the word "in" is not spatial in the sense of the occupation of a "spatial container (room, building)" but is the sense of the familiar.[52] Through the endless double movement of the "fundamental violence"(*Gewalt-tätigkeit*), man "cultivates and guards the familiar, only in order to break *out* of it and to let what overpowers it break *in*"[53] [my emphasis]. Man both occupies the enclosing structure and "tears it open," but cannot master the overpowering and so is "tossed back and forth between structure and the structureless,"[54] between using the structure to violently master and violating it—both of which "fling him *out* of the home"[55] [my emphasis], the "homeland," the "place," the "solid ground," and into the "placeless confusion" of the "groundless" "abyss" as a "homeless" "alien":

We are taking the strange, the uncanny [*das Unheimliche*], as that which casts us out of the "homely," i.e. the customary, familiar, secure. The unhomely [*Unheimische*] prevents us from making ourselves at home and therein it is overpowering. But man is the strangest of all, not only because he passes his life amid the strange understood in this sense but because he departs from his customary, familiar limits, because he is the violent one, who, tending toward the strange in the sense of the overpowering, surpasses the limit of the familiar [*das Heimische*]. . . . not only that in so doing he *is* a violent one striving beyond his familiar sphere. No, beyond all this he becomes the strangest of all beings because, without issue on all paths, he is cast out of every relation to the familiar. . . . without city and place, lonely, strange, and alien . . . Man embarks on the groundless deep, forsaking the solid land. . . . he abandons the place, he starts out and ventures into the preponderant power of the placeless waves.[56]

This is not just an argument using spatial metaphors to make a point that is not itself spatial. The text is organized around an explicit argument about space. Its rejection of the sense that material building is an act of man, rather than its possibility, is developed into a rejection of the familiar sense that a building is produced in space, as distinct from producing space (*Raum*), or, more precisely, place (*Ort*). For Heidegger, this sense is seen to be sustained by the basic claim of metaphysics inaugurated by Plato that material objects stand in a preexisting space, offering surfaces to the eye of a subject who also occupies that space, an "outward appearance" that presents an immaterial idea. The degeneration of philosophy is seen to begin with its ancient account of space. Heidegger argues that the Greeks had no word for "space" and refers to Plato's *Timaeus* to demonstrate that the theory of ideas as models (*paradeigma*) is actually the original theory of space.[57] In speaking of ideas, Plato is seen to have invented space and thereby initiated the degeneration that is only reaching its most extreme and explicit form with modernity.

This argument was picked up in Heidegger's lectures on Nietzsche of the following year. At one point, they closely follow a section of Plato's *Republic* that explains the doctrine of the ideas with examples of objects produced by a craftsman (*demiourgos*). Plato's tripartite distinction between the idea, the way the craftsman's object presents the idea, and its representation in a painting is exemplified for Heidegger in the way that "the amassed stone of the house" is a "presencing" that acts to "bring the *idea* into appearance" differently than its representation in a painting.[58] Against Nietzsche, Heidegger attempts to argue that for Plato this difference is, in the end, but one of degree. The house itself becomes an image, albeit a superior one as it is closer to truth. But Plato's text does not actually talk about the house. It refers to objects that, as Heidegger notes, "we find commonly in use in many homes,"[59] namely, tables and bedframes, but not the home itself. And Heidegger does not just add this example. He begins and ends his reading with it, reframing and refocusing the original argument. Clearly, he cannot separate the question of metaphysics from the question of the house. His argument about the violence of home inevitably heads toward the house.

The violent construction of a home and exile from it that he describes are not simply historical events. They are built into the home as its very structure in the same way that the abyss is the possibility of any edifice erected upon it. Like the loss of ground, this violence is "fundamental" but is covered over by the interdependent senses of secure structure and secure enclosure. The house is made possible by the very violence it conceals. Heidegger's revision of the condition of building—such that structure rises rather than falls with the loss of ground—is also a revision of the condition of enclosure, as can be seen when he addresses the question of the house more directly in a later essay: "Language speaks. If we let ourselves fall into the abyss denoted by this sentence, we do not go tumbling into emptiness. We fall upward, to a height. Its loftiness opens up a depth. The two span a realm in which we would like to become at home, so as to find a residence, a dwelling place for the life of man."[60] It is the absence of the ground that makes a residence. Housing, like building, is abysmal.

Just as the edifice conceals itself in concealing the abyss, the house conceals itself in concealing the uncanny (the theme of the abyss being entangled with that of the uncanny throughout Heidegger's work). It is because the house conceals the unhomeliness that constitutes it that the "mere" occupation of a house, which is to say the acceptance of its representation of interior, can never be authentic dwelling. Those "residing" *in* the home—

"the merely casual possession of domestic things and the inner life"[61]—are not *at* home. Home is precisely the place where the essence of home is most concealed.

Homecoming is therefore not simply the return to the space of the home, because it is within that space that the home most "withdraws" itself, "shuts away" its own essence. Within the spatial interior there is another kind of interior, within which the essence of the home resides. The home is therefore "mysterious" to those who occupy it: "proximity to the source is a mystery."[62] To be at home is precisely to be at home with this irreducible mystery. Heidegger plays on the way the word for mystery—*Geheimnisvoll*—has the home's capacity to conceal, to make secret (*Geheim*), built into it. It is therefore the homeless that come nearest to the essence of home that can never simply be occupied. Just as it is only by falling into the abyss that a poet can determine the condition of the structure,[63] it is only the poet's exile from the home that can establish its strange condition, the unfamiliarity of its apparently familiar enclosure: "In his exile from home, the home is first disclosed as such. But in one with it and only thus, the alien, the overpowering, is disclosed as such. Through the event of homelessness the whole of the essent is disclosed. In this disclosure unconcealment takes place. But this is nothing other than the happening of the unfamiliar."[64] In the end, it is only the alien that dwells.

In this way, the origin around which the tradition of philosophy organizes itself is not a "primitive" innocence: "A beginning, on the contrary, always contains the undisclosed abundance of the unfamiliar and extraordinary, which means that it also contains strife within the familiar and ordinary,"[65] which is to say that the origin itself becomes uncanny. It is already defined by an exchange between internal violation and external violence. The original sense of *logos* on which metaphysics is based necessarily participates in this violence. It is itself, for Heidegger, an "act of violence."[66]

This fundamental sense, however, has been lost. Metaphysics is institutionalized by repressing the originary violence, making familiar that which is actually a departure from the familiar, a departure from the original sense of the house. Metaphysics produces homelessness by repressing the originary homelessness "insofar as the home is dominated by the appearance of the ordinary, customary, and commonplace."[67] "Man" is detached from the house and the ground precisely by following philosophy in thinking of them as secure. The radical insecurity of the uncanny is concealed by the familiar sense that "man" speaks language, rather than language speaking "man," that "man" builds, rather than building constructing man as such.[68] "Man" occupies the familiar, which is "out of" its essence rather than being "at home in" it, which is not to say that its essence lies elsewhere, in some other interior. On the contrary, it is the uncanniness that "resides" in the familiar that is his essence.

Heidegger's argument convolutes traditional thinking about space. Spaces are not simply built and occupied. It is only with metaphysics that a stable ground is seen rather than an abyss, a secure house rather than an exile from it. Because of the very familiarity of these images, their violence is concealed. And more than this, they become generic figures of the exclusion of violence. For Heidegger, the "supreme" act of violence is to conceal the originary violence behind the mask of the familiar.

It is this constitutional violence of the house that is the opening within Heidegger's discourse that could be exploited to displace the philosophical tradition from within. But whereas Heidegger explicitly identifies the violence of the figure of the edifice, associating violence with the uncanny,[69] and arguing that it is precisely because violence is built into the apparent innocence of building that violence is itself uncanny,[70] he never directly identifies the violence of the house itself. He identifies the uncanniness of "housing" but not the uncanniness of the house. Like Freud, he seems to preserve the familiar status of the house while defining an unfamiliar scene within it. The house becomes the site of a violence of which it is innocent.

Interior Violence

It is in these terms that we must reread Derrida's work before it explicitly addressed architecture as a subject, let alone engaged with specific architectural projects. The question to be asked of that writing becomes something like: If Derrida locates the uncanny within the house by following Heidegger who, in the end, restores the very space of the house he repeatedly undermines, what about the house itself in Derrida's work? But, of course, the question is still too quick. Can we even speak of such a thing as "the house itself"? To expose houses to deconstruction, which is actually to expose ourselves to the deconstructive movements that are the very possibility of the house, would surely be to problematize the distinction between the literal and the metaphorical house. To raise the question of the material house, and therefore, of architectural spaces and practices in general, in Derrida's writing would not be to look for "houses" as such but to look for the problematization of such an idea.

Yet again, such a gesture can first be found in Derrida's reading of Heidegger. He appropriates that dimension of Heidegger that neither consolidates the traditional space of the house nor dismantles it, but is the side-effect of an oscillation between these gestures. Heidegger's repeated attempts to detach the literal sense of the house from his argument have already radically transformed the house in a way that is covered over when he equally repeatedly slips and restores the literal figure. The literal sense is never simply abandoned in favor of the metaphorical. In "The Ends of Man," Derrida argues that the "Letter on Humanism" makes the house uncanny by locating it beyond or before that opposition. The house is no longer simply the site of the uncanny, the familiar space within which the unfamiliar resides. It is itself already uncanny.

Just as Heidegger had argued in 1935 that Kant's architectural rhetoric is no "mere 'ornament'"[71] of his philosophy, he argues in the "Letter on Humanism" that his own thinking about the house is not an independent ornament added to an otherwise self-sufficient philosophy in order to reveal its inner structure; the house is no "mere" image for philosophy. The relationship between the figure and the philosophy that appears to employ it is subtle and convoluted: "[it] is no adornment of a thinking . . . The talk about the house of Being is no transfer of the image 'house' to Being. But one day we will, by thinking the essence of Being in a way appropriate to its matter, more readily be able to think what 'house' and 'to dwell' are."[72] This displaces the traditional status of architecture, radically subverting the tradition of philosophy that is defined by its determination that the architectural images it employs are "merely" metaphorical, temporary supplements to the main body of the argument that will eventually, and necessarily, be abandoned. Philosophy's familiar image of presence—the house—becomes doubly unfamiliar when it is no longer seen as an innocent image of innocence, separable from the arguments it is attached to, but is a construction of those very arguments whose dependence on them is veiled in order that it can act as their guarantee, an independent witness to their truth, a testament to their very innocence.

In this way, that which is most familiar becomes unfamiliar. The house is no longer the paradigm of presence. It is first and foremost a representation (albeit of the absence of representation). It is not just that the house's status as an institutionally produced and sustained image is simply exposed, but that the familiar itself becomes an image. The ostensible realm of proximity, immediacy, nearness, and so on becomes a realm of extreme detachment. To remove the metaphorical status of the house fundamentally displaces the tradition of metaphysics that maintains it as such. The whole economy turning around the house is disrupted. "Being," that which is, by definition, nearest, is no longer simply explained by the image of that which is nearest, the house. But, as Derrida points out, nor is the house to be simply explained by the study of Being. Both are made strange. The opposition between that which is known and that which is unknown, that which is near and thát which is far, is radically disturbed. And the loss of the innocence of the house is somehow written into the structure of the philosophical tradition that constitutes itself by endlessly denying that loss.

"House of Being" would not operate, in this context, in the manner of a metaphor in the current, usual, that is to say, literal meaning (*sens*) of metaphor, if there is one. This current and cursive meaning . . . would transport a familiar predicate (and here nothing is more familiar, familial, known, domestic and economic, one would think, than the house) toward a less familiar, and more remote, *unheimlich* (uncanny) subject, which it would be a question of better appropriating for oneself, becoming familiar with, understanding, and which one would thus designate by the indirect detour of what is nearest—the house. Now what happens here *with* the quasi-metaphor of the house of Being, and what does *without* metaphor in its cursive direction, is that it is Being, which, from the very moment of its withdrawal, would let or promise to let the house or the habitat be thought. . . . One could be tempted to formalize this rhetorical inversion where, in the trope "house of Being," Being says more to us, or promises more about the house than the house about Being. But this would be to miss what is most strictly proper in what the Heideggerian text would say in this place. In the inversion considered, Being has not become the proper of this supposedly known, familiar, nearby being, which one believed the house to be in the common metaphor. And if the house has become a bit *unheimlich*, this is not for having been replaced, in the role of "what is nearest," by "Being." We are therefore no longer dealing with a simple inversion permutating the places in a usual tropical structure.[73]

It is this double displacement that organizes the figure of the house in Derrida's writing. The link between the house, law, economy, and family is an important theme throughout his work. The house is always invoked as the familiar abode, the abode of the family but equally the abode of the familiar. But although he repeatedly identifies the chain of house-economy-law-family with metaphysics, the family scene he reconstructs is not simply a metaphor of metaphysics, a familiar image that offers access to an unfamiliar conceptual structure. On the contrary, metaphysics is, if anything, a kind of metaphor of the family, the familiar means of access to the endlessly strange structure of the family.[74] In this Heideggerian gesture, the very familiarity of the family is the product of metaphysics, which is no more than the institution of domestication itself. It is the violence of the "household" of metaphysics that produces the family in producing the image of individual subjects independent from the house whose interior they occupy. That is, of subjects as that which can be housed, violently domesticated by a structure that can dissimulate that violence. Derrida's displacement of metaphysics' capacity to domesticate must also be a displacement of the figure of the house, which is its paradigmatic mechanism of domestication. To displace metaphysics is already to displace domesticity. The house no longer simply houses. The paradigm of security becomes the site of the most radical insecurity—indeed, the very source of

insecurity. Security becomes but the uncanny effect of the repression of insecurity.

Yet again it is important to note that this displacement of
architecture in Derrida's work does not occur in explicitly architectural terms. To raise the question of the unfamiliarity of architecture, the strangeness of even its most routine definitions
of space, the terms of the discourse must shift. It is not a question
of simply applying the discourse to something seemingly outside
it, like "material space," but of rethinking the space of discourse
itself. That which seems most proper to material architectural
practices, the articulation of space, is actually the product of
multiple systems of representation that construct the very sense
of a material world that can be shaped or read by discourses
detached from it. Architecture is first and foremost the product
of mechanisms of representation that seem to be independent
of it and whose disguise produces this sense of independence on
which its unique cultural role is based. These mechanisms are
exemplified by the institution of philosophy, but are also embedded within the multiple cultural practices of so-called everyday
life.

The deconstruction of this institution therefore does not simply have architectural consequences. It must be architectural
from the beginning, which is to say that as long as architecture
is seen to remain outside, or even after, the "unbuilding" of
philosophy, then that philosophy is actually being consolidated
by what appears to deconstruct it. It is precisely when deconstructive discourse "turns to" architecture—by describing particular
buildings or even by simply raising the question of buildings—
that it runs the greatest risk of reestablishing the tradition of
metaphysics, which defines itself by keeping architecture in a
certain place. The tradition's capacity to domesticate literally
depends on the domestication of architecture. In the end, the
philosophical economy turns on the domestication of the idea
of house. But, equally, deconstructive discourse is bound to run
the risk of domesticating architecture, as any refusal, or even
delay, to engage with buildings also reinforces their traditional
status. Buildings can no more be isolated from deconstruction
than particular houses can be isolated from Heidegger's writing

and its politics. It is in terms of the risk of architecture, which is necessarily a political risk, that Derrida's engagement with architecture must be read.

It is important to note here that before it begins to speak of architecture, all of Derrida's writing is a rethinking of interiority. This rethinking had already begun with his original appropriation of Heidegger when "deconstruction" is itself understood as a certain way of inhabiting the tradition. When Heidegger says "we shall place ourselves within the structure itself,"[75] "keeping it [destruction] within its [the tradition's] limits,"[76] he has already given the edifice of philosophy an interior. In fact, it is already a house. In rethinking that space, both Heidegger and Derrida address the question of housing long before either uses the word "house." They already participate in the tradition organized around a certain image of housing inasmuch as they describe that tradition as something that can be occupied, something that has an interior and can be inhabited:

The movements of deconstruction do not destroy structures from the outside. They are not possible and effective, nor can they take accurate aim, except by inhabiting those structures. Inhabiting them in a certain way, because one always inhabits, and all the more when one does not suspect it. Operating necessarily from the inside, borrowing all the strategic and economic resources of subversion from the old structure, borrowing them structurally.[77]

Deconstructive discourse, if it is anything, is no more than a rethinking of inhabitation. It never involves a simple departure from an enclosure. On the contrary, it goes further into the structure, running the risk of consolidating it in order to locate the cracks that both hold it up and produce the sense of interior in the first place. In so doing, it locates the subtle mechanisms of institutional violence, which is to say the violence that makes institutions possible but is concealed by them in a way that produces the effect of a space. There is no violence without institution, no institution without space, no space without violence. And more than this, violence is always domestic, but not because it goes on within an interior. Rather, it is the violence of the interior as such, a violence that is at once enacted and dissimulated by familiar representations of space, representations that are so familiar that they are not even understood to be representations. The question of deconstruction is therefore first and foremost a question of the uncanniness of violence. To speak here of "deconstruction and architecture" is not to simply speak of an uncanny or violated architecture but the uncanniness of architecture as such, the violence of even, if not especially, the most banal of spaces, spaces that are violent in their very banality.

5

Throwing Up Architecture

To disrupt the house by identifying its constitutional uncanniness is at the same time to disrupt the place of architecture, as there is a structural relationship between the house's ability to position things and the tradition's ability to position the house. To understand exactly how deconstructive discourse displaces architecture, it is necessary to return again to the institutional contract that positions architecture and elaborate some of its terms in more detail, paying attention to the fine print and looking for the loopholes, openings in the structure that are constantly being exploited in unrecognized, and often unrecognizable, ways. This can be done here by returning to the positioning of architecture by Kant's texts.

If, as we have seen, architecture, understood as an edifice (an ornamented structure in which the ornament is meant to be subordinate to the structure it articulates) is doubly subordinated by philosophy (located within the inferior aesthetic domain and then subordinated within that domain) yet plays a central role in establishing the very mechanism of that subordination, the question becomes: what is the strategic role of architecture when it is understood as housing? What role does the image of the house play in the positioning of architecture? And, more precisely, what role do the hidden complications of the house play in that positioning?

To ask these questions does not involve looking for "houses" in the discourse, but for the discursive effects of particular ideas about housing; ideas that often do not manifest themselves as such but are embedded within the discourse and surface only by way of various forms of displacement. These displacements even operate within those moments where the discourse is explicitly addressing or deploying the figure of the house. Talk of houses usually acts as a cover for that which is threatening about houses. Furthermore, there can be no talk about anything without this cover. The idea of a discourse can never be separated from a certain talk about houses, that is really to say a certain silence, not the absence of talk but a certain fold within the fabric of the discourse which hides something unspeakable. To locate these folds in order to comprehend the strategic role of the house cannot involve simply listening to the overt discourse. It requires a different kind of reading, one that actively employs gestures that are at once more oblique and more brutal. And, in the end, the question of the house turns out to be precisely one of obliqueness and brutality.

The Taste of Derrida

Within *The Critique of Judgement* we can easily find the subordination of space to speech that Heidegger reproduces and Derrida undermines, a subordination made possible by the architectural figure of the edifice. Kant describes fine art as a form of expression in which the dead body of an object is given life by an artist, animated in a way that presents the artist's soul: "through these figures the soul of the artist furnishes a bodily expression for the substance and character of his thought, and makes the thing itself speak, as it were, in mimic language . . . attributes to lifeless things a soul suitable to their form, and . . . uses them as its mouthpiece."[1] Fine art speaks. It is listened to rather than read. Aesthetic judgment depends on the belief that the internal "voice" attended to when confronted by a beautiful object is common to all mankind and is, therefore, the voice of nature rather than culture. Whereas cultural conventions organize signs that remain in the bodily realm detached from and subordinate to what they represent, aesthetic taste requires a complete disinterest in the bodily existence of the object: its utility, function, or purpose. Taste is that encounter with an object in which the object is not consumed, not mastered through appropriation, not made servile, not used as a means to some independent end. Aesthetic pleasure is attained through the suspension of all bodily desire and its "gratification" in the "mere enjoyments of sense found in eating and drinking."[2] To taste is to spit the object out before it is consumed, to detach oneself from the object.

Aesthetic detachment is explicitly opposed to the consumption (use) of an object in an economy. For Kant, fine art transcends the economic realm in which the exchange of objects is organized by contracts, by being "free" precisely "in a sense opposed to contract work, as not being a work the magnitude of which may be estimated, exacted, or paid for according to a definite standard."[3] This exclusion of the economic from the aesthetic is also the exclusion of representation (the contractually organized exchange of signs for things). *The Critique of Judgement* is organized by the need to privilege expression over representation by preventing the contamination of fine art by the bodily economy from which it detaches itself, but on which it nevertheless depends. It establishes a hierarchy of the arts in which poetry is the most privileged because it most resembles the immateriality of speech, and architecture is the least privileged because it remains in the contractual economy of consumption—representing bodily function rather than presenting the soul:

The determining ground of whose [architecture's] form is not nature but an arbitrary end . . . In architecture the chief point is a certain *use* of the artistic object to which, as the condition, the aesthetic ideas are limited. . . . adaption of the product to a particular use is the essential element in a *work of architecture*.[4]

Buildings are subordinated to speech because they are bound to consumption. For philosophy, there is a structural affinity between architecture, physical desire, eating and drinking. The art of space is degenerate. But if the figure of the house, like that of the edifice, is employed by philosophy to effect this very subordination by being aligned with speech, the house must be seen as detached from digestion, not to mention indigestion. Indeed, it must act as the very figure of this detachment. If the figure of the house is that of the privileged interior, the space of unmediated presence, or, more precisely, the site of the exclusion of space by presence, it must be unlike a stomach. There should be no consumption in the ideal house, no exchange within or across its borders. The architectural figure is again double, sometimes acting as the model of philosophy's desire and sometimes the model of what that desire attempts to transcend. When architecture is explicitly addressed, it is excluded as the paradigm of consumption. But when it is understood as a figure, it is the paradigm of that very exclusion. For philosophy, there is a world of difference between architecture and its figure. But what is it about architecture that allows this reversal to take place? How can the figure of architecture "stand" against architecture? This cannot simply involve a reversal. The figure must be tied in some way to what it appears to detach itself from. Philosophy's opposing constructions of architecture cannot be separated. Its fundamental ambivalence about architecture, an ambivalence without which it couldn't function, actually occurs within both its ideal construction of architecture as some kind of abstract spatiality and its construction of architecture as a material spatiality.

The digestive system that the house both exemplifies and opposes is the site of the internalization of the outside. The figure of the house is that of exclusion that maintains a line between inside and outside, while the digestive system is that which confuses inside and outside, endlessly folding the limit, transforming one into the other. At the same time, digestion's messy realm of confusion is also the space of separation, that which makes possible the sense that the body has an interior in the first place. The digestive system, which is neither inside or outside the body, maintains the limits of the body. Likewise, the sense of the house depends on that which subverts it. The two senses of architecture are interdependent. It is the labor of philosophy to preserve the sense that they can be separated.

It is significant that Derrida's work, which is everywhere concerned with such confusions of limits that actually makes them possible and always understands the house as a mechanism of consumption whose "domestic law" is economic, an "assmilatory power"[5] that works to preserve what he once calls its "intestine"[6] condition, does not simply abandon the aesthetic but exploits a subversive possibility within it. His reading of *The Critique of Judgement* in "Economimesis" argues that fine art only detaches itself from the representational economy of material objects in order to participate in a "divine economy" in which the artist imitates God by transcending the world of products for that of pure productivity. The human artist's non-exchangeable productivity becomes exchangeable with that of God. This exchange takes place on the basis of what Kant describes as a "regular agreement," an "accordance," a "compact," sealed by the "trace" inscribed in nature that authorizes nature as a work of art. In the moment of transcending the realm of contracts, a divine economy constitutes itself on the basis of a contract sealed by the signature of the divine artist. This hidden contract provides the rules for fine art by organizing an expressive language: "the cipher in which nature speaks to us figuratively in its beautiful forms."[7] The human artist is able to imitate the divine artist by speaking this natural language.

Derrida examines the conditions of this contract to see if it does sustain an economy of expression rather than representation, taste rather than consumption. He notes that as fine art is a form of speech, the aesthetic turn away from bodily consumption toward taste does not leave the mouth. The mouth is the site of both bodily consumption and ideal detachment. The privileging of expression, of speech over writing, of production over consumption, by the tradition of metaphysics disguises an economy of secret consumption, covert representation governed by repressed desire.

Throughout his work, Derrida argues that to exclude something by placing it "outside" is actually to control it, to put it in its place, to enclose it. To exclude is to include. The very gesture of expelling representation appropriates it. Metaphysics appropriates whatever it places in "its" outside, such that "*its* outside is never its *outside*."[8] To expel representation to the "outside," for example, is to place it in "the exteriority, that it represses: that is expels and, which amounts to the same, internalizes as one of *its* moments."[9] Expulsion is consumption. To lock something up doesn't involve simply imprisoning it within four walls. It is imprisoned simply by being banned. In fact, it is enclosed even before it is officially excluded inasmuch as it can be defined, portrayed as some kind of object that can be placed, whether inside or outside. It is not so much a question of placing it within visible limits as declaring that it has limits: "expulsed, excluded, objectified or (curiously amounting to the same thing) assimilated and mastered as one of its moments . . . *constituting* its contrary as an object in order to be protected from it and to be rid of it. In order to lock it up."[10] Each official prohibition marks the presence of a forbidden desire, the covert assimilation of that which should not be eaten: "to renounce the other (not by being weaned from it, but by detaching oneself from it, which is actually to be in relation to it, to respect it while nevertheless overlooking it, that is, while knowing it, identifying it, assimilating it)."[11] The metaphysics of production is always a secret economy of consumption. Everywhere, the tradition carries out its work of consumption behind the disguise of detachment, consuming what it claims to detach itself from.

In these terms, aesthetic detachment only excludes bodily consumption in order to master the object by consuming it ideally: "it also passes through a certain mouth . . . assimilates everything to itself by idealizing it within interiority . . . refusing to touch it, to digest it naturally, but digests it ideally, consumes what it does not consume and vice versa."[12] The divine economy is an economy of consumption like the material economy it seeks to transcend. *The Critique of Judgement* attempts to exclude the sensual as "positively subversive of the judgement of taste . . . it is only where taste is still weak and untrained that, like aliens, they are admitted as a favor, and only on terms that they do not violate that beautiful form."[13] Derrida exploits the subversive possibility of aesthetics by demonstrating that the constitutional possibility of pure form is precisely its violation by a subversive alien; a foreign body that already inhabits the interior and cannot be expelled without destroying its host; an alien that can only be repressed. This constitutional violation of ideal form by the body in aesthetics is the constitutional violation of presence by representation, speech by spacing.

Derrida's work is full of such gestures, which locate the aliens within that have been consumed to produce the effect of presence, arguing that, as he states when reading Hegel, "the act of consumption . . . is not the *negative* of presence."[14] What makes his reading of aesthetics so pivotal in this extended series of readings is that in the case of aesthetics, the alien that is secretly consumed is itself a certain kind of consumption. What is being ostensibly excluded by Kant's text, and therefore covertly consumed by it, is consumption itself. In aesthetics, the already convoluted economy of metaphysics is doubled again, and this doubling involves the architecture of the house. When Derrida's "Ja, ou le faux-bond" refers to "exclusion enclosing what it wants to neutralize or cast out,"[15] he is speaking of the production of an enclosure, the sense of an interior, a space. But what is unique about this space, and crucial to the question of deconstruction and architecture being raised here, is that it is a domestic space that attempts to domesticate space.

On the one hand, the space is domestic inasmuch as the very form of domestication is that of an exclusion that covertly includes. When another of his essays refers to that which is "excluded or mastered—that is to say domesticated—by philosophy,"[16] Derrida is tacitly describing the production of a particular domestic space, the house of the philosophical tradition. On the other hand, what philosophy excludes from that house, the designated "outside" that is actually repressed on the inside of the domestic space, is space itself, and philosophy's paradigm of space is the house, that which divides an inside from an outside. What is excluded is the material building that supposedly produces an unquestionable sense of interior and, as such, is repeatedly pointed to in order to legitimize philosophical practice. What is excluded from the inside of philosophy is the material production of an inside that it employs to guarantee the very idea of interior, including its own. Philosophy is only able to organize itself around the idea of interior by excluding its paradigm of that idea in order to repress certain effects of that paradigm, effects that are threatening inasmuch as they are structural, which is to say, internal. The house of philosophy is produced as such by repressing something about houses.

What is repressed is not simply something about the material reality of houses that must be hidden to cleanse the immaterial discourse, but something in the representational system of that discourse that makes the idea of house possible in the first place, something that must be hidden precisely because, among other things, it calls into question the opposition between immaterial and material. To identify this repression does not involve looking for some architectural reality the traditional discourse overlooks, but looking more closely at the architecture built into that discourse, the architecture that allows the discourse to look in the first place. Indeed, what is at stake here is the tradition's representation, which is to say construction, of the house as something that precedes representation, first in the sense of being some kind of object standing in the world that can be represented and is independent of its representations, and second and more crucially, in the sense that this object is not in itself a mechanism of representation, that it is so detached from representation that it can act as the very figure of presence.

The question here becomes: what disruptions of the house are ostensibly excluded, while being systematically repressed within the discourse, in order to sustain this generic image of the house as that which simply and unproblematically excludes through the institution of a spatial division like a wall?

This is an even more complicated question than it might at first appear, because the house can never simply be repressed inasmuch as it is repression that makes possible the image of the house and, equally, the idea of repression is unthinkable "outside" that of the house. It has to be recalled that Freud often employs the figure of the house, its rooms, and the doorways between them to describe the mechanism of repression. Likewise, he employs the figure of digestion. For the tradition to constitute itself as a house by repressing a certain part of the house must involve secretly digesting that disturbing part, secreting it inside, secreting it to produce the very sense of inside. The tradition consumes the threatening aspect of the house and conceals that consumption, or, rather, conceals the indigestion that it produces. What the tradition represses, in order to at once represent itself as a house and represent the house as unmediated presence, is its own indigestion. In the end, metaphysics is the suppression of the indigestion of the house, the indigestion that must be repressed in order that any house can appear as such; the indigestion that makes the house possible; literally, the internal structure of the house, its always veiled constitution.

A house, then, is no more than the repression of a constitutional indigestion. There is no house without either indigestion or its concealment. The line drawn by a house is not that between what appears as an inside and what appears as an outside, but the less clearly defined and much more convoluted one between the visible and the invisible. The security of a house is not its capacity to enclose or exclude, but its capacity to conceal.

The Indigestion of the House

To understand how indigestion and the house are bound together, it is necessary to see how architecture, and the house in particular, are written into aesthetics and its argument about consumption rather than simply being subjected to it. The argument is put in place by architecture before it is used to put architecture in its place. In fact, as we have already seen, the very first example in *The Critique of Judgement*, the one that establishes the sense of aesthetic disinterest, is architectural. The book begins by distinguishing a rustic hut from a palace, building from architecture. The disinterested eye is opposed to the hungry stomach by splitting building and architecture:

> If any one asks me whether I consider that the palace I see before me is beautiful, I may, perhaps, reply that I do not care for things of that sort that are merely made to be gaped at. Or I may reply in the same strain as that Iroquois *sachem* who said that nothing in Paris pleased him better than the eating-houses. I may even go a step further and inveigh with the vigor of a *Rousseau* against the vanity of the great who spend the sweat of the people on such superfluous things. Or, in time, I may quite easily persuade myself that if I found myself on an uninhabited island, without hope of ever again coming among men, and could conjure such a palace into existence by a mere wish, I should still not trouble to do so, as long as I had a hut there that was comfortable for me. All this may be admitted and approved; only it is not the point now at issue.[17]

The degeneration of taste into consumption is the degeneration from the house detached from consumption (the palace) to the house of consumption (the eating-house). Kant contrasts the utilitarian concern with bodily consumption of the primitive with the aesthetic disinterest of the cultivated: "taste that requires an added element of *charm* and *emotion* for its delight . . . has not yet emerged out from barbarism."[18] To become cultivated is to "raise ourselves above the level of the senses,"[19] to move from the bodily to the ideal, from gratification to pleasure, from the unadorned utilitarian rustic hut to the ornamented house that is superfluous to utility, the house of the aristocracy: the palace. The desire to transcend the body by adorning it begins with the social acquisition of language: "with no one to take into account but himself a man abandoned on a desert island would not adorn either himself or his hut."[20] *The Critique of Judgement* privileges the very thing that Rousseau condemns: fine art based on the transcendence of bodily function that is only available to the aristocracy.

For Rousseau, architecture is a corruption of the purity, the innocence of building. The primitive hut, the basic house that does no more than define an interior space, occupies the privileged place between nature and its substitution with language, a substitution first required with the weaning of the child. Language originates as a substitute for mother's milk, the voice of mother nature, and so is itself a form of speech, a form of expression organized by a "social contract" still tied in to the order of nature. But with the rise of luxury came what *A Discourse on the Origin of Inequality* describes as "the easiness of exciting and gratifying our sensual appetites, the too exquisite foods of the wealthy which overheat and fill them with indigestion," upsetting "the good constitution of the savages."[21] The unnatural excesses that produced this indigestion also produced art through the adornment of the naked body of the primitive and "his" hut with representations detached from the purity of nature and, therefore, in the words of *A Discourse on the Moral Effects of the Arts and Sciences,* a form of perversion, a "vice":

It is beneath the rustic clothes of a farmer and not beneath the gilt of a courtier that strength and vigor of the body will be found. Ornamentation is no less foreign to virtue, which is the strength and vigor of the soul. The good man is the athlete who likes to compete in the nude.

He disdains all those vile ornaments which would hamper the use of his strength, most of which were invented only to hide some deformity.[22]

This degeneration from expression to representation, from the living voice of nature to the dead body of a sign, is also for Rousseau a degeneration from building to architecture, from the unadorned rustic hut to the ornamented temple that conceals some structural deformity: "Then came the height of degeneracy, and vice has never been carried so far as it was seen, to speak figuratively, supported by marble columns and engraved on Corinthian capitals."[23] For Rousseau, the undecorated house precedes indigestion. But again we are bound to ask, what exactly is it "to speak figuratively" here?

The Social Contract attempts to remove the excesses of fine art by restoring a contract, a restoration that itself turns out to be a building project: "Before putting up a large building, the architect surveys and sounds the site to see if it will bear the weight."[24] Rousseau appeals to this architectural image again in *A Discourse on the Origin of Inequality* in order to argue that the institution of the social contract turns out to be grounded in nature: "all human institutions seem at first glance to be founded merely on banks of shifting sand. It is only by taking a closer look, and removing the dust and sand that surround the edifice, that we perceive the immovable basis on which it is raised, and learn to respect its foundations."[25] Kantian aesthetics, on the other hand, is governed by the same architectonic figure but attempts to restore a divine contract by cultivating fine art based on excess. Whereas Rousseau attempts to reject ornament, Kant attempts to tame it.

Nevertheless, Kant's privileging of fine art and Rousseau's condemnation of it veils a fundamental complicity between them. Kant's *Anthropology from a Pragmatic Point of View* significantly explains the standard use of the "organic" word "taste" (which usually refers to the sensuous surface of "the inside of the mouth") for the "ideal" power of aesthetic judgment by arguing that the host's selection of a variety of food at a dinner party is the model.[26] His early lecture "On Philosopher's Medicine of the Body" not only addresses the dinner party when discussing the relationship between thinking and eating, but raises the question of what it is for a cerebral philosopher like him to address such a bodily scene.[27] In his *Metaphysics of Morals*,[28] Kant shares Rousseau's condemnation of overeating as an immoral "vice." In these terms, his *The Critique of Judgement* remains bound to Rousseau's account of the primitive. It employs the metaphor of taste precisely for its links with the mother's breast—such that it is the mother's voice that is listened to when appreciating fine art. Equally, Rousseau's account maintains the same aesthetic as Kant, in which color is subordinated to design as "purely a pleasure of the sense."[29] Both argue that expression has been, as the *Critique* puts it, "violated and rendered impure"[30] by the sensuality of representation, and both attempt to restore its purity, its innocence and primacy. In so doing, they sustain the tradition of metaphysics that attempts to domesticate representation. Both are committed to a regime of domestication—committed, that is, to maintain the house.

The strategic operation of this domestication in the maintenance of metaphysics is very literal in Rousseau. His explicit rejection of slavery, for example, is based on a horror of the domestication of "man," which implicitly establishes the necessity of the domestication of man's other as slave. The house is the mechanism of this mastery. In the *Discourse on the Origin of Inequality*, men and women ceased to be equal with the origin of the house: "The sexes, whose manner of life had been hitherto the same, began now to adopt different ways of living. The women became more sedentary, and accustomed themselves to mind the hut and their children, while the men went abroad in search of their common subsistence."[31] Language is acquired by the men outside the hut rather than within it, as can be seen in *Essay on the Origin of Languages:* "genuine languages are not at all of domestic origin. They can be established only under a more general, more durable agreement. The American savages hardly speak at all except outside their homes. Each keeps silent in his hut."[32] The expressions sustained by this fraternal contract are violated by representations when the woman assumes the man's authority by leaving the house.

The same oppressive sense can be found throughout Kant's writing, but is most explicit in his "political" texts, as can be seen when *The Philosophy of Law* speaks of the "equality" of the partners in a marriage contract only to immediately argue that the husband's "supremacy" over the wife does not violate this equality because of the "natural superiority of the husband compared with the wife."[33] The same duplicity is evident in his insistence on the political equality of all subjects in the essay "On the Common Saying: 'This May be True in Theory, But it Does Not Apply in Practice,'" which immediately goes on to conclude that the only thing that disqualifies any person from citizenship is being a woman, a person who has no property precisely because she is property.[34] This exclusion from the public domain presupposes both physical and legal confinement to the domestic as well as the confinement of authority to the domestic, as can be seen when *Anthropology from a Pragmatic Point of View* argues that the wife's "legal voicelessnes with regard to public transactions makes her all the more powerful in domestic matters."[35] Kant repeatedly associates the figure of the woman with the superficiality of material ornament, the seductions of representation that distract reason, while the man is associated with the supposed penetration of reason to the infinite depth of immaterial ideas.

For both Kant and Rousseau, woman is the figure of the dispossession of the authority of immediate expression by the mediations of representation. She is a double figure: the paradigm of nature when domesticated in the house and the paradigm of the alienation from nature when outside the house, untamed. In *Of Grammatology*, Derrida looks at the way in which, for Rousseau, women's power is the "paradigm of violence and political anomaly" hence the necessity of "containing them within domestic government" such that "woman takes her place, remains in her place."[36] This domestic order is understood as the basis of all political order. The threat the woman poses to that order is, for Derrida, "directly linked" to the subversive spacings of writing. Its not that writing is like a woman who must be domesticated. Rather, the woman has to be domesticated inasmuch as she is like writing. In the face of this threat, which is that of a supplement, an ornament that is somehow necessary to the system and yet violates it, Rousseau attempts to "*arrest it, domesticate it, tame it.*"[37] The logic of ornament installed by the architectural figure of the edifice is inseparable from that of the house.

Femininity is not simply one example of the supplements that must be placed under house arrest. All supplements are constructed as feminine. The feminine being that which is domesticated, produced as such in the moment of domestication, or, rather, produced in the ongoing but always frustrated attempt to domesticate. Metaphysics is a determination of place that attempts to domesticate the other, as it domesticates woman, rendering whatever it domesticates "feminine" by placing it. The feminine is that which is placed. The mastery of philosophy is that of the master of the house, the patriarchal authority that makes the other a slave within the house, a domestic servant or servant of domesticity. Whatever threatens the authority of the "man of the house" threatens metaphysics. Again, this is not so much a matter of placing the other in a particular space as it is of placing it in the subordinate realm of material space. The institution of space that Derrida obliquely interrogates is, from the beginning, organized around a certain thinking about—which is to say, construction of—the space of the house.

And if the question of architecture is most explicit in deconstructive discourse when it is addressing politics, the politics of architecture become more explicit when the edifice is figured as a house. Not because of the literal politics of the house—the oppression of women, for example, as a political reality (something both more "political" and more "real" than other subjects of deconstructive discourse)—but because the very sense of the political, the classical definition of politics, (not to mention the sense of reality) comes from a certain representation of the house. The law is always, in the end, the law of the house. The question of politics is always one of domestic economy. As Derrida argues in "Interpretations at War": "*oikonomia* here names the law of the family *oikos* as the *law,* period."[38] Whether it addresses politics or not, philosophy can never be apolitical. It can never be detached from the violent law of the domestic. On the contrary, it is at once its manifestation and its defense, as alluded to in a passage from *Glas* that identifies the domestic regime in and of Hegel's philosophy:

Economy: the law of the family, of the family home, of possession. The economic act makes familiar, proper, one's own, intimate, private. The sense of property, of propriety, in general is collected in the *oikeios.* . . . And so political. The political opposes itself to the familial while accomplishing it . . . The *eidos,* the general form of philosophy, is properly familial and produces itself as *oikos:* home, habitation, apartment, room, residence, temple, tomb [*tombeau*], hive, assets [*avoir*], family, race, and so on. If a common sense is given therein, it is the guarding of the proper, of property, propriety, of one's own . . .[39]

This identity between the law of the house and the tradition of metaphysics is one of the most insistent themes throughout Derrida's work. But the sense that philosophy is the defense of the politics of the house is not, as it were, forced onto the tradition. It is already written into it, often explicitly, as when Rousseau's *A Discourse on Political Economy* identifies the domesticity of politics: "The word Economy, or Oeconomy, is derived from *oikos,* house, and *nomos,* law, and meant originally only the wise and legitimate government of the house for the common good of the whole family."[40] Furthermore, the privilege of the house is not written into the texts of the tradition as one theme among others. Whether explicit or not, it operates as their organizational principle.

The sense of security associated with the material space of the house that philosophy draws on can never be detached from the violent subordination of the feminine, where the feminine is understood as spacing. To subordinate is to suppress spacing in favor of space, or, more precisely, to produce the effect of space by suppressing spacing. The house is not simply the site of a particular subordination, a particular kind of violence. It is the very principle of violence. To dominate is always to house, to place in the *domus.* Domination is domestication.

Yet the house does not simply precede what it domesticates. The house is itself an effect of suppression. The classical figure of the feminine is that which lacks its own secure boundaries,

producing insecurity by disrupting boundaries, and which therefore must be housed by masculine force that is no more than the
ability to maintain rigid limits or, more precisely, the effect of
such limits, the representation of a space, a representation that
is not only violently enforced by a range of disciplinary structures
(legal, philosophical, economic, aesthetic, technical, social, and
so on), but is itself already a form of violence. Masculinity is not
only erection but also enclosure, the logic of the house is as
phallocentric as that of the tower. The tower, in the end, is a
house. Kant discloses this implicit agenda that organizes the
architectural figure in philosophy at the very end of the *Critique
of Pure Reason* when he redesigns the edifice it attempts to construct as a house: "although we had contemplated building a
tower which should reach the heavens, the supply of materials
suffices only for a dwelling house . . . building a secure home for
ourselves."[41] This house is not simply a substitute that will be
abandoned when the tower of metaphysics is finally completed.
Rather, the house is what is always installed behind the more
visible dream of philosophy.

Architecture is bound to metaphysics because it represents the
capacity to domesticate. It is not simply a question of the solidity
of its foundations. Rather, it is the apparent solidity of its walls,
the security of its enclosure, its definition of space, its production
of place. Deconstructive discourse threatens the tradition of
metaphysics by disturbing the ability of its constructions to put
things in their place. It produces this displacement by identifying
the series of undecidable figures that resist domestication inasmuch as they can be neither housed nor evicted. In so doing, it
necessarily disturbs architecture.

The Disgusting Truth

As the house is the privileged site of the ideal speech of *logos*
dreamed of by philosophy, to locate that which resists domestication is to locate that which resists the mastery of the mouth,
eluding the relentless economy of consumption. Derrida's
"Economimesis" interrogates the limits of both the overt bodily
economy and the covert ideal economy of metaphysics by look-

ing closely into the mouth they share for that which resists consumption because it is neither bodily nor ideal and therefore cannot be digested, assimilated, appropriated, or mastered, that which "cannot be eaten either sensibly or ideally and which . . . by never letting itself be swallowed must therefore *cause itself to be vomited.*"[42] He notes that *The Critique of Judgement* explicitly identifies this inconsumable other that removes the distinction between representation and presentation and resists the aesthetic eye as the "disgusting":

One kind of ugliness alone is incapable of being represented conformably to nature without destroying all aesthetic delight, and consequently artistic beauty, namely, that which excites *disgust.* For, as in this strange sensation, which depends purely on the imagination, the object is represented as insisting, as it were, upon our enjoying it, while we still set our face against it, the artificial representation of the object is no longer distinguishable from the nature of the object itself in our sensation, and so it cannot possibly be regarded as beautiful.[43]

Aesthetics is defined by its exclusion of the disgusting. It is a disgust for that sensuality which imposes enjoyment, enslaving the observer by seducing it and thereby reversing the mastery of the ideal over the bodily dictated by metaphysics, a mastery that can never be separated from the mastery of the house. What is truely disgusting is not simply what is seen but the disruption of vision it produces. At one point in his *Anthropology from a Pragmatic Point of View,* Kant symptomatically associates vomit with the extent to which certain visual perceptions can remove the distinction between mental and physical:

The illusion caused by the *strength* of our imagination often goes so far that we think we see and feel outside us what is only in our mind . . . The sight of others eating loathsome things (as when the Tunguse rhythmically suck out and swallow the mucus from their children's noses) moves the spectator to vomit, just as if he himself were forced to eat it.[44]

Vomit marks the limit of vision, its inability to be aesthetically detached. As Kant argues in his *Observations on the Feeling of the Beautiful and the Sublime:* "Nothing is so much set against the beautiful as disgust."[45] Symptomatically, he says so in defining the difference between the sexes. Inasmuch as the "beauty" of the domesticated woman is the very figure of the aesthetic, the disgusting is that which threatens her domestication. Women are meant to be "cleanly and very delicate in respect to all that provokes disgust,"[46] such that their most "painful" insult is "being called *disgusting*," as distinct from the man who, as the "natural" agent of reason which is the force of domestication, is most offended by being called a "*fool*."[47] Kant's whole system turns on a phallocentric resistance to the contaminations of the disgusting.

In naming the disgusting as that which cannot be consumed, that which belongs "outside" aesthetics at the greatest distance from reason, the philosophical economy attempts to appropriate it, consume it as its "other." But as the real other of this economy that consumes whatever it represents (consuming it in representing it) is that which cannot be represented, words like "disgusting" still do not name it. As Derrida argues: "the word *vomit* . . . is then for philosophy still, an elixir, even in the very quintessence of its bad taste."[48] The expulsion of any threat to the "outside" represses the horror of that which violates the philosophical economy but cannot be detached from it, the subversive alien that inhabits the very mouth that represses it, the "inassimilable, obscene other which forces enjoyment and whose irrepressible violence would undo the hierarchizing authority"[49] of metaphysics. In the end, the distastefully enslaving violence of the visceral is not outside the tradition that condemns it. On the contrary, it is the very possibility of both taste and the reason that cultivates it.

This argument draws on Nietzsche's identification of the strategic role of disgust in the constitution of institutions, which Derrida briefly discusses in a footnote to "Otobiographies":

Nietzsche constantly draws our attention to the value of learning to vomit, forming in this way one's taste, distaste and disgust, knowing how to use one's mouth and palate, moving one's tongue and lips, having good teeth or being hard-toothed, understanding how to speak and to eat (but not just anything!). All this we know, as well as the fact that the word *"Ekel"* (disgust, nausea, wanting to vomit) comes back again and again to set the stage for evaluation . . . it is disgust that controls everything.[50]

In such terms, Derrida does not identify the distasteful alien in order to simply escape the regime of metaphysics. The disgusting is not outside the institution, as the outside is as much a mechanism of consumption as the inside. To simply go "outside" metaphysics is not to escape its mouth but to remain inside it, even to be "swallowed" by it as "Structure, Sign and Play" reminds us: "The step 'outside philosophy' is much more difficult to conceive than is generally imagined by those who think they made it long ago with cavalier ease, and who in general are swallowed up in metaphysics in the entire body of discourse which they claim to have disengaged from it."[51]

Derrida locates the gastric disorder within the institution of metaphysics itself, within the line it constantly draws between inside and outside. In maintaining the traditional economy of consumption, the texts of Rousseau and Kant, for example, privilege the scene in which, as Rousseau puts it in *Emile*, "indigestion is unknown,"[52] the scene set, as Kant argues in *Education*, by regulating the woman's behavior such that the child does not "throw up" its mother's milk.[53] Rather than abandoning this tradition, deconstructive discourse disturbs its authority by tracing the effects of an indigestible other within it, philosophy's indigestion, the irreducible and irresistible foreignness within philosophy that disseminates itself cryptically throughout philosophic practice. It begins to do so by demonstrating that each of the binary oppositions of concepts that organize the tradition of metaphysics is made possible by a double figure that radically convolutes the opposition, that the tradition is made possible by that which violates it by resisting consumption and giving it permanent indigestion. These "undecidables" uncannily occupy the house but cannot be domesticated by it. Neither inside nor outside the house, unable to be swallowed or spat out, they are the very possibility of the house. The uncanniness of the house itself is produced by its constitutive indigestion.

Violating the Crypt

Freud's essay on the uncanny with which Derrida identifies his thinking about undecidability tracks the "double" gesture by which the familiar becomes frightening, the *heimliche* resonating with what it supposedly excludes, such that what doesn't "belong in the house" somehow belongs and the unfamiliar remains all too familiar. Within the security of the homely is an impropriety that is horrifying if exposed, precisely because it does not befall an innocent subject. Indeed, it constitutes the subject as such, being "in reality nothing new or alien, but something which is familiar and old-established in the mind and which has become alienated from it only through the process of repression."[54] It is not simply that the subject is frightened. Rather it is the constitution of the subject that is frightening. The secret of this constitutional violation haunts the house in the same way as the "residues" and "traces" of primitive people haunt the supposedly civilized person and those of the child haunt the adult. For Freud, the passage from child to adult is that from primitive to civilized. Rather than a passage from innocence to violation (as in Rousseau's account), it is a passage from (what will be seen in adulthood as) violation to its repression. The uncanny horrifies because it exposes an originary violation that has been repressed.

Freud argues that the gesture of the "double" originates as a means for primitive people to resist the fear of death by dividing the world into body and soul, which is to say that metaphysics emerges as the suppression of a fear. But this primitive fear returns in civilization whenever the distinction between imagination (representation) and reality (presentation) based on that original division is "effaced." The double reverses to become the "uncanny harbinger of death,"[55] returning the civilized subject to the primitive fear and the adult to the childhood scene of violation. This return to the primal scene, this "return of the repressed," horrifies in a way that activates "the urge towards defence which has caused the ego to project the material outward as something foreign to itself."[56] Elsewhere, Freud argues that this defensive mechanism of repulsion is erected during the "latency" period in which the child/primitive is trained to sublimate its original perversions with feelings of "disgust, feelings of shame, and the claims of aesthetics and moral ideals."[57] In these terms, aesthetics is a defensive mechanism of repression that excludes whatever disgusts by forcing the effacement of the distinction between presentation and representation. As aesthetics operates in the service of metaphysics, which is nothing more than the maintenance of that distinction, it is unsurprising that Freud finds:

As good as nothing is to be found upon this subject [the uncanny] in comprehensive treatises on aesthetics, which in general prefer to concern themselves with what is beautiful, attractive and sublime—that is, with feelings of a positive nature—and with the circumstances and the objects that call them forth, rather than with the opposite feelings of repulsion and distress.[58]

The aesthetic exclusion of the disgusting resists the primitive fear of death revived by the uncanny. It is a certain coming to terms with death. Aesthetic pleasure is that of mourning which, for Freud, derives from systematically detaching and taking within oneself ("introjecting") all the parts of oneself contained in what has been lost. As he argues in "Mourning and Melancholia": "the ego, confronted as it were with the question whether it shall share [the] fate [of the lost object], is persuaded by the sum of the narcissistic satisfactions it derives from being alive to sever its attachment to the object that has been abolished."[59] As the detachment of all interest, all desire, from the object, mourning is the paradigm of aesthetic pleasure. That which forces one to desire to vomit is, as Derrida argues, that which prevents mourning: "let it be understood in all senses that what the word *disgusting* denominates is what one cannot resign oneself to mourn."[60] The tradition of reason, which, as Heidegger argues, depends on, rather than simply orchestrates, aesthetics,[61] can be displaced by demonstrating that this inability to mourn of the disgusting not only inhabits taste but makes it possible. Good taste cannot detach itself from the forbidden pleasure of the distasteful. It can only, indeed has to, conceal it.

Derrida offers a more detailed account of the disgusting in his reading of the psychoanalysis of the refusal to mourn by Nicholas Abraham and Maria Torok, who reread Freud by arguing that the pathological condition of this refusal is a fantasy of "incorporation," of taking into the body the lost object itself, literally consuming the object but doing so precisely to preserve it, to deny its loss: "It is to avoid 'swallowing' the loss, that one imagines swallowing, or having swallowed, what is lost, in the form of an object."[62] As Derrida notes, the object is appropriated to keep it as other, as foreign, as a foreign body within one's own body, taken into the body precisely to stop it from contaminating and disfiguring the body by keeping it withdrawn in indefinite quarantine: "retaining the object within itself but as something excluded, as a foreign body which is impossible to assimilate and must be rejected."[63] Unable to simply expel the object, "the fantasy involves eating the object (through the mouth or otherwise) in order *not* to introject it, in order to vomit it, in a way, into the inside, into the pocket of a cyst."[64] The forbidden object is thrown up into some folds in the body's limit, hidden in a space that is neither inside nor outside.

Such a fantasy is necessary when normal mourning would expose and destroy the pleasure of a shameful experience with an indispensable object. To preserve this secret pleasure, the subject preserves and protects the object, keeping it alive. Or, more precisely, allowing it to survive, to live on, neither alive nor dead, as some kind of phantom. The original trauma of the illegitimate experience transformed the subject's psychic topography, and this transformation has been hidden ever since. The fantasy of incorporation maintains this hidden topography in the face of the reality of a loss that, if acknowledged, would make the transformation visible and compel an unbearable topological change. It does so by maintaining the illusion that the illegitimate experience never occurred. To do so requires an "act of vomiting to the inside,"[65] which defines a secret vault within the subject, what Abraham and Torok call a "crypt," constructed by the libidinal forces of the traumatic scene which, as Derrida argues, "through their contradiction, through their very opposition, support the internal resistance of the vault like pillars, beams, studs, and retaining walls, leaning the powers of intolerable pain against an ineffable, forbidden pleasure."[66]

As both the hiding of a secret and the hiding of that hiding, the crypt cannot simply take its place in the topography it preserves. The traditional demarcations between inside and outside, the closure established by the drawing of a line, the division of a space by a wall, is disturbed by the internal fracturing of the walls by the crypt. The crypt organizes the space in which it can never simply be placed, sustaining the very topography it fractures. However, these fractures are not new. They have been present in the topography ever since the original traumatic scene, organizing the self and making the illusion that the scene never occurred possible. The fantasy of incorporation maintains a crypt that was already secreted within a pocket in the topography.

Not having been taken back inside the self, digested, assimilated as in all "normal" mourning, the dead object remains like a living dead abscessed in a specific spot in the ego. It has its place, just like a crypt in a cemetery or temple, surrounded by walls and all the rest. The dead object is incorporated in this crypt—the term "incorporated" signalling precisely that one has failed to digest or assimilate it totally, so that it remains there, forming a pocket in the mourning body . . . By contrast, in normal mourning, if such a thing exists, I take the dead upon myself, I digest it, assimilate it, idealize it, and interiorize it . . .[67]

By resisting consumption, this cryptic "architecture" disturbs the operation of language that Abraham and Torok argue is acquired through mourning: the substitution of signs for the absence of objects, which "makes up for that absence by *representing* presence."[68] In orthodox terms, this substitution begins with the absence of the mother's breast within the mouth: "First the empty mouth, then the absence of objects become words, and finally experiences with words themselves are converted into other words."[69] The crypt is constructed because of the impossibility of using language in the normal way (by exchanging words for certain objects in voicing grief for their absence) without revealing a shameful secret: "the impossibility of expressing, of placing words onto the market."[70] Nevertheless, it hides itself within the marketplace as another kind of contract, organizing another operation of language. Even while keeping its secret, the crypt leaks. It does so through convoluted transformations of the word as a material object, which displaces words that cannot be spoken without giving away the secret into words that can be safely uttered.[71] Through these displacements, in which, as Derrida puts it, "a certain foreign body is here working over our household words,"[72] the crypt is secreted within the visible space of the house.[73]

This cryptic language can be decoded by "procedures that are far from classical in psychoanalysis."[74] As the crypt (de)constructs itself in a way that displaces traditional architectural thinking, its analysis can neither simply enter nor violently fracture the crypt to find its secret. Rather, it involves a double play that patiently locates the cracks through which the crypt is already leaking and then forces entry. In this way, the analyst violates that which is already violated, that which is actually "*built* by violence."[75]

To track down the path to the tomb, then to violate a sepulchre: that is what the analysis of a cryptic incorporation is like. The idea of violation [*viol*] might imply some kind of transgression of a right, the forced entry of a penetrating, digging, force, but the violated sepulchre *itself* was never "legal." It is the very tombstone of the illicit, and marks the spot of an extreme pleasure [*jouissance*], a pleasure entirely *real* though walled up, buried alive in its own prohibition.[76]

It is in this sense that Derrida tacitly associates Abraham and Torok's work with his own. Deconstructive readings involve the kind of strategic violence advocated by Heidegger when reading Kant: "Certainly, in order to wring from what the words say, what it is that they want to say, every interpretation must necessarily use violence. Such violence, however, cannot be roving arbitrariness."[77] The violence is not that of an external force applied to an innocent victim. On the contrary, it is an exploitation of the covert violence of the very tradition it disturbs.[78] The appearance of innocence is maintained by an ongoing violence, a double violence. The sanctity of the domestic enclosure is maintained by the repression of both these forms of domestic violence. The overtly forced entry of deconstructive readings rehearses the violence of both the regime that polices domestic space and its ongoing subversion, what *Of Grammatology* describes as the covert "forced entry" of the representations that secretly infiltrate and constitute the domain of presence that supposedly excludes them, the "archetypal violence: eruption of the *outside* within the *inside*,"[79] which the tradition can mask but not eradicate without collapsing its own space. Violent transgression has always already begun within the very site privileged for its innocence.[80] The alien has always already improperly "violated the interior of the system."[81] The interior is, in the end, but an effect of this violation. Deconstructive discourse is therefore at once violent and faithful, faithful in its very violence.

[V]iolently inscribing within the text that which attempted to govern it from without, I try to respect as rigorously as possible the internal, regulated play of philosophemes by making them slide—without mistreating them—to the point of their non-pertinence, their exhaustion, their closure. To "deconstruct" philosophy, thus, would be to think—in the most faithful, interior way—the structured genealogy of philosophy's concepts, but at the same time to determine—from a certain exterior that is unqualifiable or unnameable by philosophy—what this history has been able to dissimulate or forbid, making itself into a history by means of this somewhere motivated repression. By means of this simultaneously faithful and violent circulation between the inside and the outside of philosophy—that is of the West—there is produced a certain textual work that gives great pleasure.[82]

This gesture, whose very pleasure interrupts and embarrasses, if not disgusts, the philosophical tradition, does not simply violate spaces but traces the entangled violences of those spaces and the spacing embedded within them, the economy of violence inscribed into spaces that constitutes them as such. Derrida's reading of the crypt does not direct attention to some new kind of architectural figure that might supplant the traditional architectural rhetoric and could be appropriated by architectural discourse. Rather, it directs attention to the implicit violence of architecture by identifying the subtle mechanisms with which a space can conceal, the precise but elusive geometry of concealment that produces the effect of space by orchestrating a sustained double violence.

6

Doing the Twist

The critical architectural condition of the crypt is that both the illicit pleasure it buries and the burial site are illegal. The crypt hides the forbidden act within the very space in which it is forbidden. It breaks the law merely by occupying that space, and this violation must itself be concealed. To locate this spacing that disrupts space and is itself hidden, Derrida too must break the law by rupturing the space in some way.

Violence is not simply addressed by deconstructive discourse, but is enacted by it, though not in the sense of an external force exerted upon a preexisting space. The violence of deconstructive discourse, like that of the tradition, is already bound into both space and spacing. The discourse engages with their respective and interrelated forms of violence. A sense of this engagement can be gained here by even more slowly tracking the intermittent traces of a particular argument about the violence of space embedded within Derrida's texts. It is only by somewhat mechanically accumulating these traces here, multiplying them, or rather, showing the way in which they are already multiplying themselves in his writing and overdetermining its overt trajectory, that the architectural force of deconstructive discourse can be felt.

One way of beginning such a reading is by following a line of argument that can be found running through the extended chain of essays in which Derrida addresses the question of law. The question of the law of the house is, after all, that of the status of law itself. The law is never more than domestic.

Building a Case against the Law

In "Title (To Be Specified)," a reading of Maurice Blanchot's short story "La Folie du Jour," Derrida looks at the curious architectonic role of any title. The title appears to be a supplementary label attached to a text, a supplement that can easily be detached and drift away from it (to a table of contents or the cover of a book or a catalogue, and so on). The title obviously comes before the space of the text to which it refers, divided from that space by what seems to be a clear border. But even though it is over the border, it can only perform its role by entering the space, violating it in a way that produces the sense of the border in the first place—which is to say the sense of the interior, the text's definition, its rule, its law. The title's transgressive "spacing" actually produces the sense of space it disrupts: "No title without spacing, of course, and also without the rigorous determination of a topological code defining borderlines."[1] Space is but an effect of spacing. Neither inside nor outside the text, the title's spacing is "a violence, an illegality which founds the law and the right of its procedure"[2] such that "it only makes the law right from a violence before the law."[3] The foundation of the law, that which comes before it and secures it, is the very violence it legislates against. Security is made possible by that which threatens it. The law is based on insecurity, and it is not distinct from the space it polices. Rather, it is the space, a topology produced by systems of lines that demarcate territory by dividing insides from outsides. As Derrida puts it, "topology poses the law." More than simply defining or maintaining a space, the law is a space, a kind of interior, such that to break the law is to be "outside" it, an outlaw. And if the space of the text is produced by the spacing of the title that illegally violates it, it is the very violence that effects the production. There is no space without violence. But this violence is hidden by the space it institutes, buried within the very sense that there is a space.

Any space, in turn, is a regime of overt violence, the always violent enforcement of the law. There is no space without police action and no police action that is not the maintenance of a space. Derrida's reading of Benjamin's "Critique of Violence," in

"Force of Law: The 'Mystical Foundation of Authority'," looks at the relationship between this overt violence and the covert violence that founds the law it enforces, the relationship between legal and illegal violence. Again, the law is understood, and understood to understand itself, as a space. It is an institution that makes decisions, drawing lines when it "cuts" and "divides" the terrain it monitors. Any legal system is a spatial system, a definition of space that continually redraws itself. Laws are endlessly reinscribed in, or, rather, as, space. Derrida argues that the institutional violence of this space cannot be separated from the violence that makes it possible in the first place. Legal violence cannot be separated from illegal. The originary violence is not a singular historical act that puts the institution in place and then submits to the authority of that institution, which would immediately and forever attempt to banish it. Unable to be evicted, it can only be repressed. It withdraws from the space, as distinct from leaves, by secreting itself within the very structure of the space and endlessly calls for its repetition in the regime that represses it. Legal violence is produced by illegal violence. The regime of violently enforced legal decisions is but an unwitting extension of the violent movements of the undecidability that occupies it, that about which a decision can never be made but upon which all decisions depend. The overt violence of space remains indebted to the violence of spacing that it cannot control, even while it derives its authority from everywhere announcing its ability to do so.

Deconstructive discourse reenacts rather than simply addresses this doubly violent scene, directing itself against institutional spaces in a way that those spaces cannot control, violating them according to a complicated and unstable protocol, which does not collapse a space but articulates the violence involved in its construction. In "Living On: *Border Lines*," for example, which gives an extended reading of the same story by Blanchot, the "law of the text" sustained by the suppression of the violence that put it in place "calls for a violence that matches it in intensity, a violence different in intention, perhaps, but one that exerts itself against the first law only in order to attempt a commitment, an involvement, with that law. To move, yieldingly, towards it, to draw close to it fictively. The violent truth of 'reading.'"[4] Derrida's concern is not the demolition of the law but its construction, the ruses by which it establishes authority and exercises its force. To trace these complications, he proceeds to read Blanchot's text "with great violence," focusing on the questions of spacing in it. Which is to say, both the forms of spacing with which Blanchot undermines the tradition and those embedded in his own text, making its own law, its own space, possible. Derrida traces the heterogeneous effects of violence before the law, effects that are always spatial.

This oblique argument about spatial effects that is embedded in Derrida's essays, which is, in the end, about the very effect of space, becomes clearer in "Before the Law," his reading of Kafka's story with the same title. In the story, the law is even more explicitly a space, literally an interior accessible through a door, and the "before" [*devant*] is again both spatial and temporal, or, more precisely, in Derrida's reading, it is the spacing that comes before the space of the law. The "before" is like that of the title positioned before the text: neither inside nor outside it (such that Kafka's title reproduces what it describes). As Derrida points out, the space in the story turns out to be "empty." The law cannot be found beyond the door. It is not simply "in" the space but is encrypted by its markers. The essence of the law, which is to say, of the space, turns out to be its violation by spacing, a violation that is always hidden, "always cryptic." The door is therefore "an internal boundary opening on nothing."[5] The space it marks is no more than the maintenance of this "secret." The origin of the law is "safeguarded" by the space, not by being hidden within it but by being hidden by the space itself, which is to say, by the representation of a space. It is the very idea that there is an interior that encloses the secret. The most secure hiding place is the representation of interior made possible by an ongoing repression.

The way in which the representation of space necessarily harbors a secret is elaborated further within the essay "Shibboleth," which pays attention to one of the markers of a text's place in space and time: the date. The date ostensibly positions the text, not only in the place and time of its origin, but also in the institutional space of a literary category (in the case of the texts by Celan being read, the category of "poetry"). The date is *"marked off,"* "detached," from the space it marks and yet it makes a "cut or incision" in that space, violating its ostensible limits. This violation is concealed. It is necessary that the marker "encrypt itself," effacing itself precisely in order to mark. Defying the logic of traditional space, there is no simple access to this crypt, no passage through any door: "If there is indeed a door, it does not present itself in this way."[6] But while there is no access to the crypt, it is the crypt that provides access to the space of the text. Occupation of the space is made possible by that which defies it. It is necessary to read this strange mark, the mark of a secret that does not appear "in" the space, in order "to get over the border of a place or the threshold of a poem, to see oneself granted asylum or the legitimate habitation of a language."[7] The space cannot be inhabited without the spacing of the crypt. To inhabit the space is to share its secret.

The sense that the inhabitation of a space depends on the maintenance of a secret, the secret of that which defies the space, is always, at least, political. The politics of space turn on that which exceeds it. If spaces are always institutional and institutions always spatial, it is the maintenance of their secret, the secret of the space's constitutional violation, that is the basis of their power. In Derrida's essay, the membership of an institution that gives access to its power requires knowledge of the crypt. The key to the space is a secret code shared by the members. A similar argument is made in "How to Avoid Speaking: Denials" when it describes the "politopology" in which the maintenance of a secret produces at once a space and a community which claims it as its own. The visible sense of place is bound to the concealed place of the secret. Cryptic figures are not simply exchanged by the members of that community, but act as "political stratagems" inasmuch as they establish "the solid barrier of a social division."[8] The solidity of this socio-spatial division is a product of the spacings the figures conceal, the unspeakable complications that precede space. And this enigmatic production of space as political space is not simply a unique condition described by the particular texts of negative theology that the essay is reading. It goes on to locate precisely such "an irreducible spacing interior to (but hence also exterior to, once the interior is placed outside)" the ongoing tradition of philosophy inaugurated by Plato.[9]

This, in turn, recalls another of Derrida's lesser known essays, "Scribble (Writing-Power)," which also addresses the role of crypts in the establishment of political institutions. It does so in reading Warbuton's *Essay on Hieroglyphs*, which argues that the original function of writing as the transmission of natural law, the "communication of laws and the order of the city," is "perverted" by another kind of writing that violently poses another order, an unnatural structure that benefits an elite through the operations of a crypt that only they share. In this "cryptopolitics of writing," as Derrida describes it, writing "becomes the instrument of an abusive power."[10] Acting in the name of nature, that which is supposedly "at home" with itself, but actually violating natural order, it becomes "like the exteriority of the alien, the parasite: the necessity, at once natural and unnatural, of the crypt."[11] The official law encrypts its own violence. It is the crypt that gives the institution, which is to say the space constructed by and as a political body or corporation, a certain natural authority. The institution is able to assume power inasmuch the crypt enables it to represent its unnatural force as natural.[12] It is precisely by defying space that the crypt gives space its force, a force that is always aligned with a certain systemic brutality.

This line of argument about law that binds violence and space in addressing the organization of institutions can be traced throughout Derrida's writing, but becomes most explicit when he addresses the relatively recent institution of law itself as a discipline, which he argues is symptomatically contemporary with those of literature, art, and the university. In "Title (To Be Specified)," the constitutional role of the title in relationship to the space of the text it appears to supplement is also understood to be that of literature and the other arts in relationship to the space of the university that they supplement. Their various spacings "before" the law of that space, which actually institute that law and, in so doing, that space, are then immediately subordinated by that law and excluded from the space it makes possible under names like "literature" and "art," before being eventually domesticated within it by disciplines apparently devoted to their study. These disciplines conceal rather than study the ruses of space on which they are "built."[13] Derrida notes the key role that "literary and artistic forms in general" played in the production of the "structure" of the university, which immediately claims to be concerned only with "higher" things. Which is to say, the constitutional role of their spacing in the production of its space, the originary and ongoing violation of the space that produces the institution as such and then is effaced within it, even, if not especially, within those recently admitted departments ostensibly dedicated to them.

To elaborate Derrida's argument, it can be argued that the emergence of these disciplines marks the continuation of the attempt to discipline their respective forms of spacing that began with the assigning of proper names. Such categories are already mechanisms of domestication before they are used to mark an institutional space.[14] The disciplinary spaces are only a certain repetition of the conceptual space, a monument to a domestication achieved long before. To name something is always to locate it within a space. The sense of the proper name is that of the proper place. Names are always place names. By designating something as "art" or "law," for example, is already to resist its subversive qualities and to make a place for it in a conceptual scheme, marking its site, delimiting its domain. And this resistance, which takes the form of systemic repression, doesn't just make space available. Rather, it is what makes space in the first place. There is no space without resistance.

In Derrida's texts, these repressive institutional spaces are again tacitly associated with the space of a building. If "Title (To Be Specified)" speaks of the "structure" of the institution, "Living On: *Border Lines*" speaks of the institution "built on" the judicial framing of the "law of the text," and "Force of Law" speaks of the law as a "standing" that is "constructed" on the "ground" through an originary act of "foundation," which establishes a "structure" and "superstructure."[15] And it must be noted yet again that this architectural rhetoric most explicitly surfaces in Derrida's writing when the question is most explicitly political and more than ever when it is a question of the politics of deconstruction itself. The essay "Force of Law," for example, elaborates its argument to show that deconstructive discourse only "apparently" fails to address politics, ethics, and justice, asserting that it has not only addressed them from the beginning, but has done nothing but address them, even though such an address, if it is to be rigorous, must often be "oblique."[16] Again, it would seem that it is when the stakes are highest for deconstructive discourse that architecture comes to the surface.

The repression of the originary violence of spacing that empowers institutional violence must therefore be, in this sense, architectural or, at least, bear upon the structure or status of architecture. It does so by way of the quasi figure of the crypt. In the erection of law, the originary violence is "buried, dissimulated, repressed"[17] only to return in a displaced form. Its burial takes the form of an incorporation. As Derrida puts it at one point, "carnivorous sacrifice" founds the law. Both the burial and the return are made possible by the strange anarchitecture of the crypt. The incorporation of the undecidables into the structure, as the very possibility of its law, suppresses them through a "silence" that "is walled up in the violent structure of the founding act. Walled up, walled in"[18] in an act of "forgetfulness." The structure does not simply forget. It is a structure only inasmuch as it forgets. Structure is forgetting and the crypt is nothing more than the structure of forgetting, the perverse structure of structure. The forbidden violence is hidden within the walls themselves that it makes possible, encrypted within the sense of space its effacement produces. There is "nothing" in the space beyond that violence. Only spacing is secreted in space, which is only to repeat that the secret of space is spacing.

Such a reading in no way calls into question the capacity of institutions to define space and thereby institute regimes of suppressive and repressive violence. On the contrary, it identifies the inevitably violent ruses of space. Spaces cannot be cleansed of violence. Institutions are not collapsed by demonstrating that their architecture does not obey the very laws they enforce (and all laws are, in the end, arguably architectural). On the contrary, architecture is seen to derive its force from the way its own violation of the law is violently concealed. Architecture is an effect of this concealment.

When deconstructive discourse deploys a strategic violence against institutional spaces, it does so to trace the workings of the ongoing but hidden violence that makes those spaces and their overt violence possible. The violence of deconstruction sometimes appears to be that of the law itself and other times appears to be that of an abuse of the law. In each space it reads, it passes from an extremely, if not obsessively, strict application of the particular institutional codes that define that space to what seems to be a flagrant disruption of those codes. But its own force derives from problematizing this distinction, demonstrating that the most strict adherence to a law ends up violating that very law and vice versa. In these terms, the double violence of deconstructive discourse reproduces that which founds an edifice. Such a discourse teases an architecture, exploiting all its visible and hidden resources in a way that explores the strange economy that makes it possible, the strange space of architecture itself, a space that is precisely not architectural.

The Deconstructive Dance

Although deconstructive discourse has read many heterogeneous architectures in this way, they are always domestic. Each structure masks its own structural violence in order to produce the effect of a space, an interior governed by a legal system that has the power to include or exclude. Inasmuch as institutions are always "interior spaces"[19] of domination, as "Before the Law" puts it, their regimes of violence are mechanisms of domestication. The edifice is always a house, the law can only ever be the law of the house.

While Derrida's essays on law only once explicitly and momentarily touch the question of "the law of *oikos*" that punctuates so much of the rest of his work, their analysis is critically marked by the effect of that punctuation. The way they call the space of the law into question transforms the sense of domestic space. It is not just that each particular space is made strange. Rather, space itself becomes a strange effect. The encrypted spacing that makes the institutional space of the law possible also makes the law "even more frightening and fantastic, *unheimlich* or uncanny."[20] All legal decisions, all definitions of space, become, like the one made in Kafka's story, "uncanny, *unheimlich*."[21] Spatial markers, like the date in "Shibboleth," for example, are uncanny inasmuch as they install a covert spatiality "within the habitation" of the domestic space they supposedly mark. Such an installation "takes on the strange, coincident, *unheimlich* dimensions of a cryptic predestination" by marking a "secret configuration of places"[22] within the visible space, the very space that only becomes visible as such because of the covert operations of the mark. In a thoroughly Heideggerian gesture, the familiar sense of a space becomes one of "strangeness, estrangement in one's own home, not being at home, being called away from one's homeland or away from home in one's homeland."[23] In such terms, deconstructive discourse at once traces and reenacts the violence of the hidden spacings that establish domestic space, or, rather, establish space as domestic. Its gestures do not simply identify the strange things that uncannily occupy familiar spaces, but the uncanniness of space itself.

When reading Heidegger in "The Ends of Man," Derrida describes the "simultaneously faithful and violent" double play of deconstruction, what he elsewhere calls its "violent fidelity,"[24] as an oscillation between two gestures toward the house, one that remains inside it and another that goes outside:

a. To attempt an exit and a deconstruction without changing terrain, by repeating what is implicit in the founding concepts and the original problematic, by using against the edifice the instruments or stones available in the house . . .
b. To decide to change terrain, in a continuous and irruptive fashion, by brutally placing oneself outside, and by affirming an absolute break and difference.[25]

Either gesture alone fails to disturb metaphysics. In the end, both are forms of "inhabiting" the house, the latter doing so "more naively and more strictly than ever."[26] To resist such inhabitation, "a new writing must weave and interlace these two motifs of deconstruction" in a Nietzschean "dance, outside the house" which is not the "outside" defined by philosophy since, as we have seen, whatever philosophy places outside is still inside precisely because it is "placed," enclosed by the house in the very gesture of being excluded from it. Deconstructive discourse seeks an uninhabitable outside on the inside. As Derrida puts it in "Dissemination," "the absolute outside is not outside and cannot be inhabited as such."[27] The dance that resists the logic of inhabitation is a form of "affirmation" inasmuch it occupies the house, running the risk of consolidating its force, but without nostalgia for it and its associated "myths" (family, homeland, primal language, proximity, and so on) as "Différance" argues: "we must *affirm* this, in the sense in which Nietzsche puts affirmation into play in a certain laughter and a certain step of the dance."[28] The dance displaces the house in its own terms. When "Choreographies" addresses the insidious but pervasive logic of the *oikos,* or "house arrest" [*assignation à résidence*] with which metaphysics institutes itself by defining the "place" for woman as a place of confinement, it is the dance, with its "multiplicities of rhythm and steps" that subverts this violent logic of placement: "The most innocent of dances would thwart the *assignation à résidence,* escape those residences under surveillance."[29] The dance disrupts the spatial regime by locating something aspatial within it.

A similar argument can be found embedded within "Aphorism Countertime." Again, it is a question of "rhythm," and the ongoing but always unsuccessful attempt of the law to "arrest" its movements by defining space with social conventions like "place-names," "property registers," and "topographical marks," which are "cast like nets over time and space."[30] These institutional codes constitute a "marked spacing," a visible space whose spatial logic attempts to resist the spacing of rhythm by effacing it. But in constituting itself to repress that unmarked spacing (which is actually the spacing of the mark itself) the space is, in the end, shaped by the very thing that it is designed to conceal. The spatial regime depends on the very "disjunction, dislocation, separation of places, deployment or spacing of a story"[31] that it blocks. Spacing is involved in the institution of the spaces that conceal it. Spatial order (and order can only be spatial) is made possible by a certain ongoing disorder. House arrest, the visible use of space as a mechanism of subordination (which is perhaps the only visible use of space, the way in which space makes objects visible, even producing the effect of objects as such) is made possible by forces it cannot arrest, restless subterranean movements that occasionally erupt sideways across its surface, perforating any spatial division. In this sense, deconstructive discourse is concerned with that which cannot be pinned down, that without a fixed place or home, which is not quite yet to say the homeless. It is not a question of that which is without a house, but that evasion of presence within the very structure of the house that makes the house possible.

In these terms, the deconstructive dance is not a particular kind of movement through an already constituted space, but is itself a spacing that at once subverts and produces a space, one that cannot simply be subjected to the logic of the house that depends upon it. Deconstructive discourse occupies an already constituted space in ways that raise the question of the space's constitution. It is in this sense that the discourse is always concerned with institutions. It does not take them apart or critique them, but endlessly rehearses the event of institution to reveal its structural enigmas. The kind of Nietzschean dance Derrida calls for does not simply defeat house arrest. Rather, it affirms its logic but in the very terms that logic appears to resist. It is therefore not just a question of producing a new theory of space, a new way of representing space as an alternative to the traditional policing of space. A space is never independent of the systems of representation that appear to monitor it. House arrest is not the policing of the space of the house but the house itself as police action or, more precisely, police action as housing. To arrest, after all, is to domesticate by restricting movement, defining its limits, drawing a line. The dance does more than twist such lines. It shows that they are already twisted and that this twisting cannot be regulated. No line can never be straightened out. Loopholes are the law.

The paradoxes of this affirmative dance can be found within Derrida's early reading of Artaud's critique of traditional theater. Artaud theorized the necessity of what he called a "dance" in order to subvert the classical space of theater, which he saw as subservient to the theological and metaphysical authority of the voice. In "The Theater of Cruelty and the Closure of Representation," Derrida argues that Artaud's sense of dance "inhabits or rather *produces* a nontheological space"[32] through a new regime of movements whose spacing eludes the classical space: "an experience which produces its own space. *Spacing* [*espacement*], that is to say, the production of a space that no speech could condense or comprehend (since speech primarily presupposes this spacing)."[33] This transformation, which Artaud calls "a new notion of space," does not simply abandon the old space but exploits its "undersides." The new space, "opened by transgression" of the old, constitutes an "irruptive force fissuring the space of the stage."[34] And not only is the violent force of this dance exerted within and against the traditional space, but it also participates in the overt violence of that space. The violence of the dance is already written into the tradition and can only be traced through the very force that suppresses it and yet unwittingly depends on it. It is only by enforcing the law ever more vigilantly than the tradition that claims to uphold it that the space it produces can be displaced.

This enigma, which is central to any thinking of deconstruction, was explored in Derrida's even earlier essay "La Parole Soufflée," which argues that Artaud's "raising of the repressed" sense of spacing is paradoxically achieved with an obsessive commitment to institutional violence, the "totalitarian codification and rhetoric of forces" of a "cruelty" that establishes a space by suppressing spacing: "this new theatrical arrangement sutures all the gaps, all the openings, all the differences. Their origin and active movement—differing, deferral—are *enclosed*," thereby establishing "*the law of the house,* the initial organization of a dwelling space."[35] Artaud reconstructs the house of the tradition even more vigilantly than the tradition itself and it is precisely in so doing that he disturbs it. Citing Nietzsche on the need "to dance with the pen,"[36] Derrida argues that, in the end, Artaud's "dance of cruelty"[37] admits into this domestic space what it at first appears to exclude: the parasitic alien, the illegitimate stranger that is always the agent of ruin. Echoing Heidegger, Derrida argues that Artaud's simultaneous commitment to both metaphysics and its subversion marks "a necessary dependency of all destructive discourses: they must inhabit the structures they demolish, and within them they must shelter an indestructible desire for full presence."[38] It is not a question of simply occupying the house as some kind of irritant that will always in the end be domesticated but of reproducing the space, endlessly retracing its supposed limits to identify the strange logic that produces the effect of limits in the first place, making the very sense of enclosure uncanny. The deconstructive dance reconstitutes the domestic space it subverts, subverting it only by faithfully constituting it, and in so doing, registering the irreducible uncanniness of space.

To dance here, when talking of deconstruction and architecture, would be to look for what is buried in the space of the house that allows space to bury in the first place. The rhythm of this dance must be somehow built into the structure of the house that locks things up merely by placing them either inside or outside, by placing them, that is, "in" space. This apparently simple sense that things can be put "in" space, which is to say the sense that space is itself a kind of interior, is no more than the sense of the house. The idea of the house is not so much that of an interior space but that of space as interior, space as that which can be inhabited. The rhythm of the dance calls into question the house by inhabiting space in a way that frustrates inhabitation.

Haunted Houses

The particular sense of this frustration can be elaborated in terms of the way in which Derrida's essay "Desistence" at one point reads Lacoue-Labarthe's sense of "rhythm" as the spacing that "haunts" the space of the tradition. This haunting is understood as domestic, an uncanny internal displacement of the "law of the *oikos*."[39] Derrida appreciates the way in which Lacoue-Labarthe does nōt simply look at the tradition's attempt to enforce this law by policing the interior of the space and violently excluding the other, but pays attention to the "domesticity" of the other, the way in which the tradition is "regularly visited, haunted, inhabited by"[40] what it thinks it has excluded. Inasmuch as the institutional spaces that are haunted by strange rhythms are always domestic, Derrida seems to be tacitly describing institutions as haunted houses.

While the question of haunting often comes up in his texts, Derrida never talks about haunted houses. Indeed his most explicit description of ghosts involves transferring the alogic of haunting from its classical site in the house to the contemporary technologies of representation:

> Contrary to what we might believe, the experience of ghosts is not tied to a bygone historical period, like the landscape of Scottish manors, etc., but on the contrary, is accentuated, accelerated by modern technologies like film, television, the telephone. These technologies inhabit, as it were, a phantom structure. . . . When the very *first* perception of an image is linked to a structure of reproduction, then we are dealing with the realm of phantoms.[41]

But this transference also works in the other direction. The house is itself, first and foremost, a system of representation. Indeed, the traditional sense of the haunting of a house is precisely the sense that the house is not simply an object that may be represented, but is itself a mechanism of representation. Likewise, it can be argued that contemporary systems of representation can only be understood as haunted inasmuch as, like the house, they are understood to be mechanisms that define space. By definition, only space can be haunted, and space is understood as that which houses. After all, the word "haunting" is etymologically bound to that of "house." Haunting is always the haunting of a house. And it is not just that some houses are haunted. A house is only a house inasmuch as it is haunted.

The sense of haunting that can be traced in so many of Derrida's texts, from the very first one on, cannot be separated from the sense of architecture they sustain, the architecture of the edifice as a tomb, and, specifically the house as tomb. It is the sense of haunting that links the idea of edifice to that of tomb. Indeed, it can be argued that this subterranean argument about haunted houses, like the haunting it describes, structures the spaces of all the texts of Derrida within which its traces can be found.

When Derrida's first book, published in 1962, identifies the way in which, for Husserl's *Origin of Geometry,* the apparently subordinate spatial marks of writing and drawing turn out to be the very possibility of the ideal objectivity they supposedly merely supplement and register, it does so in terms of the way in which a text can be "haunted," "the entombment of lost intentions and guarded secrets" and the "transcendental sense of death" inscribed in those spatial marks.[42] Truth is "no longer *simply* exiled" in this spatiality, but finds its "primordial habitat" there. The question of architecture is already raised in this first text when it follows Husserl in asking whether what is true of writing is also "the same for the ideality of the plastic arts, of architecture?"[43] And, more significantly, the text goes on to examine the complications of Husserl's dominant architectonic metaphor of *level* or *stratum:* "the image of the concealed presence that an activity of excavation can always re-produce above ground as the foundation, that is itself grounded, of higher stratifications. It brings all this together in the structural and *internal* unity of a system, of a "region" in which all deposits, interrelated but distinct, are originally prescribed by an *archi-tectonics.*"[44] This architectural image is crucial inasmuch as its rereading would form the basis of Heidegger's sense of "*Destruktion*" and, therefore, in turn, Derrida's sense of "deconstruction." In his first text's sustained reworking of this image, all the main arguments of his later work have already been put in place.

This passage from the question of haunting to that of architecture is not coincidental, just as it is not when Derrida's detailed discussion of the way Paul De Man's account of allegory uses the architectural metaphor for deconstruction is immediately followed by a description of the rhetorical categories that surround allegory as "ghostly figures" that produce a "ghost-effect" inasmuch as they:

speak like phantoms in the text, certainly, but above all they phantomize the text itself. It remains to be seen what the phantom means or—this can have still other meanings—what the word "phantom," the "*word*" phantom means. In a phantom-text, these distinctions, these quotation marks, references, or citations become irremediably precarious; they leave only traces, and we shall never define the trace or the phantom without, ironically or allegorically, appealing from one to the other.[45]

If the phantom allegory that haunts Derrida's own text is architecture, it does so precisely as haunted architecture. More precisely, what haunts all of his work is the sense of a haunted house that never simply appears as such, but whose phantomlike traces can be found throughout the space of his texts.

These traces are even marked in *Cinders,* the book in which Derrida rereads all his previous texts in order to trace the theme of ashes, to trace the trace of the trace, that has repeatedly marked them without ever becoming their ostensible subject. For Derrida, this theme is a ghost that haunts his texts: "For nearly ten years, this spector's comings and goings, unforeseen visits of the ghost."[46] But more than this, the specter that haunts his texts is itself a "ghost story," a story marked by architecture. Although it does not appear to be about architecture, a particular sense of architecture is put in place by a chain of associations mobilized by it. The ghost story is that of a "feminine phantom" hidden within a "sheltered" place, a strange kind of shelter produced by the mechanisms of incorporation that resist mourning by keeping the other in the inaccessible reserve of a crypt, a convoluted anarchitecture produced as "the monument of an impossible tomb," a crypt that prevents the kind of mourning that shelters by constructing a visible monument, blocking "the slow decomposition that shelters, locates, lodges" by establishing the "tomb of a tomb,"[47] the tomb, that is, of architecture. This ghost, "trembling deep within the word," seems to prevent any traditional building, any "erection that stands—or falls."[48] Derrida's text moves relentlessly, seemingly inevitably, toward the image, taken from a story by Virginia Woolf, of empowered women neither rebuilding the patriarchal university on an old plan nor constructing an entirely different one but setting fire to the traditional architecture and dancing around it as it burns. The cinders that haunt Derrida's texts turn out to be those of a building. More precisely, it is a house: "There are cinders only insofar as there is the hearth, the fireplace, some fire or place. Cinder as the house of being."[49] The force of Derrida's text comes from suggesting that the cinders are not simply produced by the burning down of a structure. The cinders are the possibility of the house. It is the fire that builds.[50] The visible structure, like the structure of Derrida's own work, is made possible by that which resists it, that which is only evident as an oblique trace within it, the trace of its own disruption, if not consumption, the elusive phantom "camouflaged" within it. The dance that deconstructs architecture, interrogating the sense of building and enclosure, making them tremble in order to see what is already trembling within them, within and as their very structure, is at least doubly bound to the sense of the haunted house.

This sense is only ever obliquely inscribed into Derrida's texts, and it is precisely in this obliqueness that it attains its greatest, if not brutal, force. It underwrites his essay "Ulysses Gramophone: Hear Say Yes in Joyce," for example, in the form of a gradual slippage that can be traced from the initial question of institution, to that of foundation, to family, to domestication, to domestic interiority, to place, to guests, to strangers, to parasites. And each term in this chain is mediated by the image of an institution haunted by spacing such that, if we violently extract the terms from their context and crudely piece them together here: the "domestic interiority" of the "structure" of the university institution is "*haunted*—joyously ventriloquized by a completely different music" of "telephonic spacing," which "acts like a parasite" that interrupts "the cycle of reappropriation and domestication" with a "laughter" that "always betrays some kind of mourning."[51]

This ghostly laughter is the same Nietzschean laughter that Bataille argues is the only thing that resists being "domesticated" by Hegel's philosophical system, "*inserted* into a sphere, *like children in a house*,"[52] as he puts it. It resists precisely by being a form of affirmation of that house rather than an overt form of subversion. In his "From Restricted to General Economy: A Hegelianism without Reserve," Derrida argues, as he did of Artaud, that Bataille displaces Hegel's work by affirming it, repeating it in a way that disturbs its structure even while rebuilding it, gradually and almost imperceptibly forcing open, with each repetition, all of its joints but never quite collapsing what they assemble.[53] The "laughter" that "bursts out" when the joints are shaken open from within makes Hegelian discourse "dislocate *itself*"[54] rather than be broken by some external force. By inhabiting the discourse, it is possible to exploit "a certain strategic twist" that "with a violent and sliding, furtive movement must inflect the old corpus,"[55] interfering with its capacity to "assimilate" its other. This twist resists the generic law of the house by disrupting the repressive economy of consumption. It is a dance step that exposes the specter of a certain indigestion in the structure, the haunting of the house by that which it always fails to consume and which threatens to disorder, if not collapse, it.

Since the haunted house is, for Freud, "the most striking of all" "examples" of the uncanny,[56] it is unsurprising that the tacit sense of the haunted house produced by the anarchitecture of the crypt that can be found in Derrida's work is repeatedly linked to the sense of the uncanny. In "Living On: *Border Lines*" for example, Derrida describes the cryptic logic of incorporation as the production of an "exceedingly strange space"[57] that enables something to be "living on" [*survivre*] as a "ghost." In reading Blanchot's text, he is concerned with "the entire enigma of this supplementary logic. Survival and *revenance* [haunting], living on and returning from the dead,"[58] reading not only what that text says about ghosts but also the sense in which its own structure is that of haunting, that there are "only relationships of cryptic haunting from mark to mark."[59] Yet again, this sense of the strange topology by which visible space is haunted is bound to the sense that the "law of the *oikos* (house, room, tomb, crypt)" is that of "*Heimlichkeit/ Unheimlichkeit.*"[60]

This bond between ghosts, incorporation, and the uncanny is even clearer in "Cartouches," which again concerns a quasi-architectural scene and describes the role of haunting as structural, as the possibility of visible structure rather than something that happens to it. In reading the design and construction of a miniature coffin and a series of drawings that appear to be based on it by the artist Gérard Titus-Camel, Derrida describes the "paradigm," or architectural model, "built like a crypt, so as jealously to keep its secret at the moment of greatest exhibition,"[61] as itself a "ghost": "Necessarily the dead takes his revenge. And the paradigm returns, it gets its own back. The 'model' is always the dreamed-of ghost [*le revenant rêvé*]. Haunting does not befall it, but takes the first step."[62] The text immediately goes on to refer to the ghost story in Freud's *Das Unheimliche* essay, of which he says "it would all need to be quoted," but symptomatically, given the always strange role that essay plays in Derrida's work, he does not do. The text then explores all the complications of such ghostly returns, passing again through the question of fire, specifically, the fire of the house—the hearth, the hearth of the family, the crematorium as the hearth of such hearths—whose *unheimlich* condition can only be marked by the ashes in a family tomb, before declaring at the end that "above all *haunting* lays down the law."[63] As always, the law of the house is made possible by that which always occupies the house but cannot be domesticated by it.

The same gestures can be seen in Derrida's rethinking of the house in "To Speculate—on Freud," which describes the "law of the *oikos,* of the proper as the domestico-familiar and even, by the same token, as we will verify, as the domestico-funerary."[64] Exploring in detail the endless "return to the house, to the home" of the dead in Freud's thinking, the text argues that "whatever becomes *too* familiar can always be suspected of jealously keeping a secret, of standing guard over the unexpected."[65] At two key moments, Freud's essay on the uncanny is quickly invoked, but not read "again," as if it has been done so in depth elsewhere: "Here, I cannot take up again what was set in place elsewhere."[66] Instead, yet another of his passing, if not cryptic, references to the essay (in "The Double Session") is pointed to. Likewise, Derrida's "Telepathy" makes a passing reference to the "essential" argument of Freud's *Das Unheimliche* essay in another discussion of ghosts and incorporation revolving around a patient of Freud who is "haunted by her dream 'as by a ghost'" and the ghosts incorporated in psychoanalysis itself as it attempts to read such dreams.[67] The essential argument is once again invoked at a key moment but not pursued, although the question of the uncanny clearly underwrites the whole text.

Derrida's repeated hesitation around the uncanny parallels his hesitation around architecture, which is likewise invoked at strategic points and not pursued although its effects can be everywhere traced in his texts. Indeed, the two gestures are related. The uncanny is, in the end, no more than the sense that a house is a house only inasmuch as it is haunted. If architecture is withdrawn from the most explicit surface of Derrida's texts in order to return in a highly displaced form as a key subtext that organizes the very texts from which it has been withdrawn, it returns, precisely, in the equally displaced theme of haunting. The architecture of deconstruction is not only haunted. It is also that which haunts deconstruction, organizing its space without simply appearing within it. If haunting is what produces space rather than simply occurs to it or within it, the sense of haunted architecture, of architecture as that which is haunted, that itself haunts deconstructive discourse actually produces the space of that discourse.

In laying down the law it appears to disturb, the uncanniness of haunting is the very possibility of space and its politics.[68] Consequently, the sense of the haunted house is bound to that of violence. It is always a violence that haunts. The architecture of deconstruction is violent. When "Force of Law," in following Benjamin's "Critique of Violence," speaks of the founding violence repressed by an institution, it is a "phantom violence." Buried alive, it becomes a "ghost" in the space that appears to exclude it. The space is haunted by the "ghost of undecidability," the illegal aspatial violence that institutes it. The law of the house is the "law of the phantom" whereby "the undecidable remains caught, lodged, at least as a ghost—but an essential ghost—in every decision, in every event of decision. Its ghostliness deconstructs from within any assurance of presence."[69] The house, as the very figure of presence, is disrupted from within by that which it incorporates, that whose "survival" is made possible by the complex folds of the crypt.[70]

It is not that the violence of spacing simply haunts space like a brutal stranger. The haunting is itself the product of a double, uncanny violence. The burial of the violence that founds any institution, which is not an isolated event but an ongoing action that conserves the institution, is itself necessarily violent. The official violence that sustains the institution can never detach itself from what it buries. It is "as if one violence haunted the other"[71] such that "what today bears witness in an even more "spectral" (*gespenstiche*) way in mixing the two forms of violence (conserving and founding), is the modern institution of the

police."[72] The police—and there is no institution without police—acts as a hinge between the two forms of violence that
constitute any space. Even while marking the overt violence of a
space, police force also marks the covert violence that haunts it.
Deconstructive discourse does not simply oppose the force of the
police, but attempts to insert itself between these violences, tracing the elaborate folds that knot them together and in so doing
rethinks space in a way that displaces the house.

In tracing the "absence of a frontier" between the forms of
violence, such a discourse calls into question the general effect
of frontier, which is to say, the effect of space sustained by the
architecture of the institution. It "ruins" the frontier by identifying a "disgusting ambiguity," an indigestible undecidability that
forever distorts the line. Again, this ruining of institutions, which
itself involves a sustained violence, is affirmative rather than
destructive: "One cannot love a monument, a work of architecture, an institution as such except in an experience itself precarious in its fragility" of the structure's "fragility."[73] Just as a
structure can only be radically threatened by being affirmed, it
can only be appreciated inasmuch as it is weakened. But what
exactly is love here?[74] Exactly what kind of relationship does
deconstructive discourse want with architecture?

The force of deconstruction comes from its claim that an
institutional structure's vulnerability, its Achilles' heel, is the possibility of its very strength, that insecurity is the possibility of
stability, that institutional violence is formidable precisely because it is unsecured. If, as Derrida argues, the violence enacted
in the name of reason is never reasonable, it will not be disturbed
by any demonstration that this is the case. If the very possibility
of the institution is a sustained violation of its own law, then no
simple appeal to the law could dislodge it. Legal recourse must
be replaced by a quasi-ethical injunction, a call to some sense of
responsibility. Such a call is repeatedly marked in Derrida's texts
but usually neglected by his readers.

It needs to be remembered that the sense of ethics written into
Derrida's argument that deconstructive discourse violates that
which is already violent is indebted to the writings of Emmanuel
Levinas. As his early reading of Levinas in "Violence and Meta-

physics" puts it: "acknowledging and practicing the violence within it. Violence against violence. *Economy* of violence. . . . one must combat light with a certain other light, in order to avoid the worst violence, the violence of the night which precedes or represses discourse. This *vigilance* is a violence chosen as the least violence."[75] The necessity of this doubling of violence is related to the inevitable haunting of space. This can be seen by looking at the tacit argument about the haunted house in Derrida's later reading of Levinas in "At This Very Moment in Whose Work I Am," which opposes inhabiting to haunting by looking at the way Levinas's interventions violently "tear" familiar language in a way that locates another language, the language of the other, within it that "doesn't inhabit it, but haunts it."[76] The familiar "is there, but dislodged so as to leave room for (though not to establish residence in)"[77] the other, which produces the sense that "as if from now on we didn't dwell there any longer, and to tell the truth, as if we had never been at home."[78] When its walls are forced to reveal what they hide, even, if not especially, if what they hide is a certain emptiness, the capacity of the space to house is frustrated and, furthermore, revealed to always be frustrated. A house never simply houses.

Again, this disruption of the house's image of itself as secure involves indigestion. Through Levinas's violent forcing of the familiar text, the house of language "disassimilates"[79] the other, throwing it up into the space, making visible in the space that which the space always attempts to conceal, the indigestible that is normally thrown up into an internal pocket in the lining of the walls. The haunting of the space of the house that can be exposed by a violent and yet vigilant reading is sustained by the encrypting movements of incorporation.

The indigestible other that haunts the space is not simply at odds with the law that governs that space. On the contrary, it is its very possibility. There is no official text or institutional practice that is not marked by the faint traces of the convoluted folds that encrypt the indigestible. Equally, such traces can be found within those practices that appear to undermine institutional authority, no matter how sophisticated or effective they are. Derrida goes on, for example, to read Levinas's own texts "violently" to show what they themselves encrypt even while they break open a number of vaults. Specifically, he argues that they encrypt feminine mastery within the house by making sexual alterity secondary and thereby reproducing the familiar domestic regime, the closed economy that is the law of the house.

Because the relationship between the law and its subversion is not a simple opposition but an entangled structural complication, what is indigested by the space is, in the end, never simply a subversive other. The law must itself be encrypted. The mastery *of* the feminine, for example, must be situated in the house, as its law, but in such a way that it is not subjected to that law: "The aneconomical, that must not have been *economized*, situated in the house, *within* or *as* the law of the *oikos*" is nevertheless incorporated, encrypted within it "retained, as other, within the economic zone of the same. Included in the same, it is by the same stroke excluded: enclosed within, foreclosed within, foreclosed within the immanence of a crypt, incorporated."[80] In the always strange logic of the house, that which is domesticated as "other," officially labeled as such, is thereby admitted into the space while that which is not other, the "same," cannot be subjected to the law, the force of the space. Only the other can be admitted in order to be controlled. In the end, it is the law of the house itself that is neither inside nor outside the space of the house. What is really indigestible is the law itself. Which is to say that spacing, in the end, is the law. The spatial logic of the house is not in itself spatial. No inside is ever simply severed from an outside. Space is but an elaborate effect of the spacing that appears to haunt it.

This possibility had already been raised in passing by Derrida's earlier reading of Levinas, when it parenthetically asks whether the inside/outside pair that organizes all the operations of metaphysics is itself spatial: "the spatial pair inside-outside (but is this, in all its aspects, a *spatial* pair?)."[81] The traditional opposition that organizes all other conceptual oppositions in the tradition of philosophy is able to produce the effect of space, the effect of interior, only by repressing spacing. And inasmuch as space is made possible by spacing, spacing must somehow be involved in its own repression. The indigestible is not an object that is hidden at a certain moment. Rather it is an ongoing double movement of hiding. What is hidden is precisely that which cannot be transformed into an object, the elusive phantom.

Such a sense of the haunting of space by spacing can also be found in Derrida's "The Deaths of Roland Barthes," an essay devoted to the question of mourning. It speaks of the central role that Barthes assigns to a certain supplement to the photograph, the "*punctum*" that violates the space of the image (*"studium"*), the singular point that "rends space" by puncturing it without ever becoming visible within it: "It belongs to it without belonging to it and is unlocatable in it; it never inscribes itself in the homogenous objectivity of the framed space but instead inhabits, or rather haunts it."[82] And yet again, it is "rhythm," which is to say, the twisting dance of spacing, that haunts: the "supplement parasiting the haunted space of the *studium*, the *punctum* gives rhythm to the *studium*."[83] The space of the photograph is organized by that which enigmatically violates it. The external violence of the photographic frame that defines the space in isolating the image depends on this internal violence. Like the crypt, the *punctum* occupies the space but cannot be placed within it. It is a point, that which takes up no space, that which has no space, an unlocatable nonplace that exceeds the frame it occupies.

This constitutional haunting of space by spacing is not just understood as a property of photographs or their analysis by particular "conceptual oppositions" that define certain logics of reading. Rather, "it traces a relationship of haunting which perhaps is constitutive of all logics."[84] It is the haunting of a space that organizes the conceptual structure of the institutional codes of reading (and institutions are never more than codes for reading, culturally enfranchised systems of representation) that are applied to that space but cannot recognize its phantoms. If, as Derrida argues elsewhere, all the binary oppositions that structure the Western tradition are organized by the spatial opposition between inside and outside, or, rather, the opposition ostensibly concerned with space, they are, in the end, organized by the haunting that produces this effect of space in the first place. Inasmuch as deconstructive discourse is always a "reading" of institutional space, it must disturb the institutions of reading sustained by, and in the end, indistinguishable from, that space.

To raise the question of deconstruction and architecture is therefore not only a matter of identifying a certain reading of space as a key subtext within Derrida's readings, it is also a question of the spatiality of reading. In particular, it is a question of the point at which the two are conflated, the point at which Derrida's reading of space addresses the space of reading.

The Subject of Vomit

Such an intersection can be found in *Glas*, which is everywhere concerned with the intersection between the house and mourning, hence its ongoing subtext of houses and burial, the *oikos* as tomb, the domestic economy as an economy of death governed by haunting. Following the psychoanalytic account of mourning as eating, it reads the question of digestion in Hegel and Genet in a convoluted and elaborately spaced-out text that passes through "the work of mourning, anthropophagy, cannibalism, all the processes of incorporation and introjection"[85] in their work to focus on "the strange word (and mode) disgust [*écoeurement*]"[86] and the elusive crypt that configures it. Derrida's concern is with the space, or, rather, spacing, of indigestion. As he points out in the interview "Ja, ou le faux-bond," *Glas* asks of multiple institutional structures the question: "out of what exclusion is it constructed? What does it desire to vomit? . . . The neither-swallowed-nor-rejected, that which remains stuck in the throat as other."[87] Which is to say that the text is concerned with the enigmatic spacing of the crypt. But the crypt is not simply the subject of that text, it is also its effect, or, at least, desired effect:

When I say that *Glas* is also working on the "reading effect," what I mean in particular is that it has as one of its principal themes reception (assimilation, digestion, absorption, introjection, *incorporation*) or non-reception (exclusion, foreclosure, rejection and once again, but this time as internal expulsion, *incorporation*), thus the theme of internal or external vomiting, of mourning-work and everything that gets around to or comes down to *throwing up*. But *Glas* does not only treat these themes; in a certain way, it offers itself up to all these operations.[88]

The text opens itself to the convoluted operations of the crypt by opening its space to the effects of spacing. It engages with the cryptic logic, or, rather, subversion of logic, through its own spacing, reproducing the operations it describes. Derrida refers to the "reading effect" of his writing in spatial terms, identifying it with the spacing of rhythm: "one would have to add or rather identify the question of the 'rhythm,' the rhythmed delays, etc."[89] It is only through the multiple and heterogeneous interactions between this spacing of the text and its concern with spacing that the question of the crypt can be raised.

A reference to these interactions can be found early on in *Glas* where a small and, at first glance, surprisingly autobiographical fragment on the outer edge of one page describes the text as "the interminable analysis of vomit, of a nausea [*écoeurement*] rather, by which I am affected and which causes me to write."[90] Derrida is not simply contrasting the institution's need to encrypt what it desires to vomit and his own desire to resist the institution by throwing it up. The point here is precisely that his desire, which is to say his nausea or disgust, is no different from that of the institutions that constitute themselves by veiling that desire and its object. Furthermore, he is not simply speaking of his "own" desire here, that which supposedly belongs only to him as an individual subject, but rather the desire that structures the subject as such. It is not a question of his choice to write about the spacing that the institution represses, but the sense in which the institution is that which represses writing understood as a certain spacing. Spacing is the possibility of both the institution and the subject; the subject being, in the end, which is really to say, from the beginning, an institution.[91]

The indigestion institutions experience in the face of spacing is not something they can choose to address or repress. Indigestion is their structural condition. The subject, for example, does not simply experience indigestion. It is never anything more than indigestion, as can be seen in the interview "'Eating Well,' or the Calculation of the Subject," which speaks of digestive movements (assimilation, ingestion, incorporation, introjection, eating as an interiorization that effects an identification, and so on) as conditions that produce the subject, rather than being its actions.[92] In Derrida's use of Abraham and Torok's arguments, incorporation becomes the possibility of the subject rather than one of its contingent pathologies. The subject is constructed as such by the spacing of the crypt. Its therefore not just that the crypt is the desired effect of Derrida's texts or even that the crypt is always an effect of desire. More than the maintenance of a forbidden desire, the crypt is the very figure of desire. Desire is by definition cryptic. It is never straightforward. It's all in the detour.

The question of deconstruction and architecture must therefore involve a rethinking of the subject. The subject is not just housed within space or detached from it as a kind of reader of the space, but is produced by that which violates space and is concealed to produce the effect of space in the first place. The subject is neither violently controlled by space nor exercises control over it. It is the concealment of spacing in the name of space, which is to say the image of space, that makes the idea of a subject detached from space possible. The logic of the subject is bound to a certain representation that cannot be separated from architecture and is sustained by an array of disciplinary structures that need to be interrogated.

Inasmuch as the traditional idea that the subject takes place is the idea that it can take a place, the possibility of the subject is the possibility of place. To rethink the subject must be to interrogate the idea of place. In "Eating Well," for example, Derrida argues that the cryptic indigestion of incorporation defines the "place" of the subject as a "non-place": "In the text or in writing, such as I have tried to analyze them at least, there is, I wouldn't say a place (and this is a whole question, this topology of a certain locatable non-place, at once necessary and undiscoverable) but an instance."[93] Likewise, "Ja, ou le faux-bond" speaks of a "non-place" when it addresses the question "Where does a "reading effect" take place, if it takes place?"[94] In both cases, the twisting of space by spacing unravels place. This unraveling is not limited to the specific question of the subject. Inasmuch as Derrida's work is, from the beginning, as is being argued here, a disruption of the architecture of the house, it is everywhere concerned with the question of place, exploring the critical slippage between having a place, making a place, taking a place and taking place. In the end, the elusive architecture of deconstruction is produced in its engagement with place.

7

Dislocating Space

The irrepressible haunting of space, the spectral economy of the haunted house that underpins Derrida's work without ever being its apparent subject, is first and foremost the enigmatic movements of displacement or dislocation. Derrida explicitly identifies the tradition of metaphysics that sustains itself by sustaining a certain image of space with the constitution of place. When speaking of the deconstructive dance that disrupts the house by subverting the logic of house arrest that domesticates by transforming movements into objects and assigning them places, "Choreographies" asserts: "the dance changes place and above all changes *places*. In its wake they can no longer be recognized."[1] The dance's twisting of space is at once a subversion of both particular places and the institutional logic of place, which is to say, the logic of the institutions that orchestrate them. A dance step is only a step "on the condition that it challenge a certain idea of the *locus* [*lieu*] and the place [*place*] (the entire history of the West and of its metaphysics)."[2] Furthermore, inasmuch as the dance traces an exterior hidden inside the house, something foreign to the space, foreign to space itself and yet uncannily part of its very constitution, the dance does not simply take place. To dance is to displace the house and the whole regime of placement based upon it. Dance is that which displaces place.

Derrida's essays are everywhere concerned with this question of place, or, rather, as he once put it, "the question of the enigma of place."[3] There is no essay that doesn't at some point raise it, almost always literally as a question. In fact, it is usually two questions. Of each of his texts' ostensible subjects, Derrida asks: "where does it take place?" and "does it take place?" In a sense, deconstructive discourse can be understood as a protracted yet always incomplete response to these interrelated questions.[4] Yet this almost never becomes the explicit focus of Derrida's writing and has received almost no commentary. The question of place is always worked through indirectly even if, in every case, the intermittent responses to it usually act as signals that critically redirect each text's line of argument. It is arguably this insistent indirectness that both gives the question such force in Derrida's work and also marks the point of its greatest vulnerability. His rethinking of place has to be followed in some detail here, especially because it involves a rethinking of architecture, even if it is not explicitly presented in architectural terms or, rather, especially if it is not; one of the first implications we have to draw from Derrida's argument about the crypt is that it is likely to be a certain withdrawal of architecture from the explicit surface of his own work that marks the point of its greatest dependence on a thinking of architecture, a dependence that only manifests itself as such in oblique and seemingly isolated moments in his discourse.

Household Pests

If the most forceful architecture is that which cannot be seen but returns to haunt the visible space in which it is buried, it actually leaves most traces in Derrida's sporadic references to haunting. It is not so much that his work is simply haunted by an architecture as it is that his sense of haunting involves, and is, perhaps, no more than a displacement of architecture. This displacement does not manifest itself so much in his repeated and explicit questioning of the traditional logic of spatial "position" (which, following Heidegger, is always understood as a discursive construction sustained by the millennial tradition of metaphysics[5]), as it does in his more elusive thinking around the question of place. It is marked there by the intermittent "figure" of haunting, a slippery figure that involves a rethinking of the house. The rethinking of place, like that of space, presupposes a rethinking of house.

The invisible anarchitecture of the crypt is always bound to a visible architecture. As Derrida puts it, there is "no crypt without edification,"[6] no secret without the defensive erection of a dissimulating "edifice" that veils its convoluted folds to produce the image of a unified structure, no invisible other without a building that renders space visible and defines place. Furthermore, there is no architecture without crypt. Every apparently stable building presupposes such a concealed and unstable spacing that is itself a mechanism of concealment, a strange mechanism that sustains a haunting that complicates space by disrupting place. The crypt is a "pocket" folded into space, a "no-place or non-place within space, a place as no-place"[7] that enables a "ghost" to "haunt [the subject] with all kinds of ventriloquism,"[8] complicating the visible architecture of the space by staging a "haunting return or *unheimlich* homecoming."[9] The rethinking of the house marked by the subtext of the uncanny that punctuates so much of Derrida's writing is bound into the theme of crypt and turns on the sense of place, which is to say that his extended questioning of place harbors within it a questioning of architecture.

One of the points in Derrida's writing where the question of architecture begins to emerge in the discussion of place, only to be symptomatically withdrawn, can be found in the essay "Limited Inc. a b c . . ." Repeatedly addressing the cryptic operations of incorporation and, having described undecidability as "calling into question the entire traditional philosophy of the *oikos*"[10] (understood as the domesticity of a legal system that acts as an ethico-political regime sustained by different kinds of institutionalized violence), the text identifies the simultaneously constructive and subversive role of parasites in the house. The logic of incorporation turns out to be that of the parasite, the foreigner occupying the domestic interior and unable to be expelled from it, by being thrown up and out, without ruining the space. This hidden logic of the domestic is again tacitly understood as a haunting of the house. The uncanniness of the parasite is that it "is never *simply* alien to and separable from the body to which it has been transplanted or which it already haunts [*hante*]."[11] The space is haunted by that which exceeds it: the para-site, that which is supplementary (para) to the site. The house, as the paradigm of place, is haunted by that which disrupts place but cannot be expelled from it. The parasite's uncanny quasi occupation of the house is seen to displace its law by disturbing the logic of place:

It should also be remembered that the parasite is by definition never simply *external*, never simply something that can be excluded from or kept outside of the body "proper," shut out from the "familial" table or house. Parasitism takes place when the parasite (called thus by the owner, jealously defending his own, his *oikos*) comes to live *off the life* of the body in which it resides—and when, reciprocally, the host incorporates the parasite to an extent, willy nilly offering it hospitality: providing it with a place. The parasite then "takes place." And, at bottom, whatever violently "takes place" or occupies a site is always *something* of a parasite. *Never quite* taking place is thus part of its performance, of its success as an event, of its taking place.[12]

This sense of the structural haunting of the house by the parasite, which at once installs and subverts the logic of place, is not just one analysis in Derrida's work alongside so many others. He goes on to argue that his work is "everywhere" concerned with it: "The parasitic structure is what I have tried to analyze everywhere, under the names of writing, mark, step [*marche*], margin, différance, graft, undecidable, supplement, *pharmakon*, hymen, *parergon*, etc."[13] To which we could add: the fetish, *khairein*, signature, title, poem, purloined letter, date, castration, shoe, circumcision, metaphor, translation, preface, and so on. While Derrida multiplies his terms to avoid turning any one of them into the basis of a new law, destabilizing them to avoid the illusory coherence of a conceptual system, he nevertheless reads them all in terms of the parasite, understood as a specific form of quasi occupation of the house. Of each he asks: "where does it take place?" and "does it takes place?"[14] And in each case, the respective reading at some point notes, and arguably turns on this point, that the undecidable in question has no legitimate place within the system it occupies. Each is understood as an illegal alien transgressing a house. To place is to house, whether inside or in the outside that is always, in the end, an inside. The parasite is that which is neither inside nor outside a house, that which is beyond, and yet essential to, the space. Every house has its parasites. Like an expert on household pests, each of Derrida's essays identifies the particular species embedded within a heterogeneous range of houses and demonstrates that each would collapse if its uninvited guests were exterminated, which, of course, they cannot be since they never simply occupy the space but elusively haunt it.

Each of the supplements Derrida interrogates turn out to have no proper place.[15] And yet a place is always forcibly assigned to them by specific institutional practices that attempt to contain them. Derrida tracks the way in which supplements elude the spatial regimes that attempt to domesticate them, even, if not especially, if that attempt involves assigning them the place of that which is without place. In "Le facteur de la vérité," for example, he shows how the missing letter in Poe's story eludes Lacan's sustained attempt to return it to "a proper place . . . a determinable place that is always the same and that is *its own*,"[16] even when that place is identified as the place where something is missing, a gap around which a psychic economy is organized. "By determining the place of the lack, the topos of that which is lacking from its place, and in constituting it as a fixed center," before organizing the psychoanalytic "topology" around that place, Lacan is seen to be returning the letter, along with all the other seemingly placeless fetishistic substitutes, "back into their *oikos,* their familiar dwelling, their proper place."[17] In so doing, he locates the spatial order maintained by psychoanalytic theory, the truth of the psyche sought by that theory, within the fictional space of Poe's story, a truth seen to inhabit that space "as the master of the house, as the law of the house."[18] The homeless letter becomes the law of the home. But, in being monumentalized in this way, it is given a home. Lacan's psychoanalysis consolidates rather than displaces the house. In the very gesture of analyzing that which has no place and moves uncontrollably through "*all* the places," Lacan domesticates it and restores the traditional sense of space, covering over the "*Unheimlichkeit*"[19] of Poe's story to produce a stable conceptual system within which, symptomatically for Derrida, "the problematic of [Freud's] *Das*

Unheimliche does not intervene."[20] All of the uncanny movements that produce anxiety for the theorist by disrupting the space are repressed.[21] Nevertheless, they return to interrupt the very theory that is instituted to repress them.

The labor of deconstructive discourse is to trace the way in which the unspeakable parasite eludes the institutionalized attempts to control it, returning to uncannily haunt the domestic space that appears to repress it. But it must be emphasized that this return, and the way it is traced by deconstructive discourse, does not produce a crisis for the house. The uncanny is only threatening to the institution, in fact it is only uncanny, inasmuch as it cannot be treated as a crisis, the sense of crisis being precisely, as Derrida's "Economies de la crise" argues, never more than an institutional resistance to a more radical threat to the integrity of the domestic space:

> The concept of crisis would be the signature of a last symptom, the convulsive effort to save a "world" that we no longer inhabit: no more *oikos,* economy, ecology, livable site in which we are "at home". . . ."The "representation" of crisis and the rhetoric it organizes always have at least this purpose: to determine, in order to limit it, a more serious and more formless threat, one which is in fact faceless and normless. A monstrous threat but that holds some desire in suspense: a threat to desire. By determining it as crisis, one tames it, domesticates it, neutralizes it—in short, one *economizes* it. One appropriates the Thing, the unthinkable becomes the unknown to be known, one begins to give it form, to inform, master, calculate, program.[22]

That which is threatening is that which cannot be localized, that which cannot be placed either inside or outside an enclosure. The sense of crisis is manufactured to cover over this deeper threat to the sense of place. Derrida argues elsewhere that even the concept of crisis now finds itself in crisis inasmuch as its symptoms cannot be localized: "Sparing no region, this ill-being and threat do indeed affect the destination of humanity, and, more than ever in the last fifty years, we are unable to localize them, assign them a proper place so as to contain them. It would be a matter, rather, of an illness of the place."[23] The "sickness of the home" described by *Of Grammatology* is equally the "illness of the place." The sense of place is always as infected as that of the house. But it is not lost with the disruptive return of what is buried within it. On the contrary, it is produced by that very return. Place is a side effect of the specter that disrupts it.

Taking Place

In each of Derrida's readings, such a return of the repressed that uncannily resists the law of the house, the form of resistance that is actually the possibility of that law, the law that is only a law inasmuch as it places, calls into question whether anything "takes place" in a particular space and even whether the space itself takes place. When Derrida speaks of the uncanniness of undecidability in "The Double Session," for example, he is speaking of the way the hymen doesn't take place inasmuch as its spacing subverts space: "*between* the inside and the outside . . . the hymen only takes place when it doesn't take place . . . located between present acts that don't take place. What takes place is only the *entre*, the place, the spacing, which is nothing."[24] In each essay, it is a question of such a nonplace that complicates the structure of the events that supposedly take place. A poem, for example, which "blurs" philosophy's limit, complicating its sense of space, "no longer has any place. This no-place . . . is the poem's taking place."[25] Any parasitic supplement, as *Of Grammatology* puts it, always "adds only to replace. It intervenes or insinuates itself *in-the-place-of . . . takes-(the)-place*"[26] such that, in the end, as the book later argues, it has not taken place.[27] The critical question asked at some point by each of Derrida's essays—"Does it take place?"—is always effectively answered "no and yes." Taking place, like place, becomes an institutional effect, a representation sustained by systemic repression. In unpicking the mechanisms of that repression, deconstructive discourse exposes the fragility of this effect.

Derrida contests every apparent event. His work is like, as he once put it, "a war over taking place."[28] It always looks for what "Living On: *Border Lines*" calls the "placeless place,"[29] that which "takes place without taking place,"[30] or "takes place, placelessly."[31] In all these enigmatic points, and examples could endlessly be multiplied here, place is understood as an institution, space is always constructed. As "Shibboleth," puts it, "a border is never natural." Furthermore, this "line—of the place, of the country, of the community, of what takes place in a language,"[32] which is constantly patrolled, monitored by some kind of police force, and scrutinized for intruders, is always constructed by an uncontrollable oscillation across it called for by the very institution that patrols it. The effects of place and taking place depend upon the parasitic ruses of the crypt, by which that which is officially expelled over the line is secretly appropriated in order to hold the line:

[The crypt] can only take on meaning in relation to a *place*. By place, I mean just as much the relation to a border, country, house, or threshold, as any site, any *situation* in general from within which, practically, pragmatically, alliances are formed, contracts, codes and conventions established which give meaning to the insignificant, institute passwords, bend language to what exceeds it, make of it a moment of gesture and of step, secondarize or "reject" it in order to find it again.[33]

Derrida everywhere looks for a certain "elsewhere," a "non-site," "non-place," or "atopos." There is no essay of his that does not raise the question of place and of taking place in this way. Although it never emerges as the ostensibly central theme of any particular deconstructive reading, one of his interviews does identify it as the "central" focus of those readings. Yet again, it is presented as a question: "the ultimate site (*lieu*) of my questioning discourse . . . would be a non-site . . . My central question is: from what site or non-site (*non-lieu*) can philosophy as such appear to itself as other than itself?"[34] To disturb the traditional construction of space, deconstructive discourse looks for another kind of spatiality to use as a lever to force open the tradition:

It is simply that our belonging to, and inherence in, the language of metaphysics is something that can only be rigorously and adequately thought about from *another* topos or space where our problematic rapport with the boundary of metaphysics can be seen in a more radical light. Hence my attempts to discover the non-place or *non-lieu* which would be the "other" of philosophy. This is the task of deconstruction.[35]

Similar appeals to the need to find another kind of space occur throughout Derrida's writing, but in each case the sense of the word "space" is fundamentally displaced. Rather than simply crossing the boundary of the particular space produced by the discourse of metaphysics in order to find another, it is a matter of interfering with the very sense of boundary produced by that discourse, the sense of space that is the dominant effect of the tradition. And this sense of boundary can only be threatened precisely by being affirmed rather than stepped across. The logic of boundary cannot be stepped over, or even broken, without reconstituting it. To be outside the law is to remain in its space. When Derrida's "Tympan" asks "can one, strictly speaking, determine a nonphilosophical place, a place of exteriority or alterity from which one might still treat *of philosophy?* . . . From philosophy—to separate oneself, in order to describe and decry its law, in the direction of the absolute exteriority of another place," the answer is "no" inasmuch as "exteriority and alterity are concepts which by themselves have never surprised philosophical discourse."[36] Indeed, they are the very basis of the construction of space. Rather than stepping outside, breaking the law by breaking the line, it is a question of "opening" a space within the old one, where opening is not understood as a new space that can be occupied but as an opening in the very idea of space, a loophole that is precisely not a hole with its own borders, but a kind of pocket secreted within the old sense of border.

Derrida repeatedly refers to this sense of "opening," arguing that "deconstruction, if such a thing exists, should open up."[37] This clearly follows Heidegger's equally repeated call for an "opening" of the philosophical tradition, the necessity of "disclosure" understood as the "opening of space,"[38] and his account of the fundamental condition of being as "openess."[39] For Heidegger, this opening of space is not just an opening "in" a space, but is the "pre-spatial" opening up that "provides the space in which space as we usually know it can unfold."[40] The opening of space is the opening that makes space possible. His destruction of the philosophical tradition does not simply break or rearrange the familiar "closed" "physically-technologically projected space"[41] that the tradition produces by maintaining a certain image of architecture, but attempts to expose that space to the openess that exceeds it and makes it possible. Derrida, who describes himself as working within and transforming the specific "opening of Heidegger's questions," understands deconstruction as the "opening of a space through a principle of dislocation,"[42] which is itself "inscribed in a space" no longer that of philosophy.[43] As with Heidegger, ostensibly nonphilosophical sites like "literature and the arts," the "spatial arts" which, while "never totally free from the marks of philosophical language," establish some kind of internal "distance" from those marks that "provides the necessary free space from which to interrogate philosophy anew,"[44] a subversive space from which to investigate the space protected by philosophy and demonstrate that despite this protection it is already inhabited by their disruptive spacing, that the protection takes the form of institutional denial or disavowal. Inasmuch as this interrogation is affirmative, it always returns to the tradition and "opens up the space for a *remarking*."[45]

Such an internal disruption and reinscription of space is, by definition, always the disruption of an institution. Deconstructive "theory," for instance, which is, in the end, neither strictly philosophical nor artistic, is described as "the opening of a space" in the university. Having developed in the "space" of literary studies, it moves on to a new kind of interdisciplinary work that previously met "nowhere."[46] Nowhere becomes the site of action. This seemingly contingent detour through the designated space of a "spatial art" toward some nonsite within a classical space is symptomatic. What Derrida locates in the unmappable territory that binds philosophy and the spatial arts in convoluted and surprising ways, the atopic spatiality in which one cannot "make a diagram . . . draw a sort of chart, or cartography of their positions," is "writing."[47]

Throughout his work, writing acts the figure of this other spatiality, the spacing that opens a traditional space and displaces the institutionalized logic of place. This can clearly be seen in "Freud and the Scene of Writing," which looks at the way Freud employs the "metaphor" of writing that "haunts" traditional discourse as his own metaphor for the haunting that is repression. Derrida argues that writing, for Freud, is a "breaching" in the sense of the "opening up of its own space"[48] through the "violent inscription of a form." In describing repression as a form of writing, Freud must dislodge the traditional understanding of

writing that attempts to repress its effects, the enforced placement of writing in space which conceals its spacings. He must
open a new space and does so by identifying writing itself as the
opening of a space: "a different writing space must be found, a
space which writing has always claimed for itself."[49] Writing is
invoked as the figure for opening.

This is, of course, also a description of Derrida's own practice.
Everywhere, his work appeals to "writing" as both a new space
and as the opening up of such a space, the new space being no
more than the opening of the old. In these terms, the space of
writing is spacing. Writing, in this transformed sense, acts as both
the persistent theme and quasi model of deconstructive discourse that everywhere attempts to insert itself into the knots
that bind this spacing to the very institutionalized sense of space
that represses it. The "distance" that the discourse takes from
traditional space is clearly not itself spatial. It is an internal
dislocation of space rather than a detachment from it, as can be
seen when Derrida's "Voice II . . ." describes the dislocating
"spacing" of telephony:

I do not know whether these voices must *pass through, across* or *in* some
space that pre-exists them, commands them, borders or supports them.
And even if it lets them pass, such a space would still threaten to submit
them to its law. . . . we should perhaps not rely too much on names
commonly attributed to that "space." It may not be a space, a locus,
even a "region," but a strange force of dislocation . . . without reference
to a fixed place in an objective topology . . . truly this madness of the
voice is without place or, better, it is atopical.[50]

But even then, this atopic writing is not so much a dislocation of
a stable space as it is an identification of the extent to which the
sense of space that the tradition constructs is always dislocated
and dislocating. The haunting of space by the unlocatable turns
out to be what produces the sense of space as such in the first
place. It is the opening in the structure that is the very possibility
of the sense of structure maintained by institutions like philosophy, which is to say that the unacknowledged opening is structural. Institutional space is necessarily built around its opening
to something other. As "Genesis and Structure" proposes, "the
structurality of an opening—such, perhaps, is the unlocatable
site in which philosophy takes root. Particularly when it speaks

of and describes structures."[51] Space is but an effect of dislocation, as are all the values associated with it—enclosure, presence,
immediacy, truth, law, stability, security, order, and so on—and
the multiplicity of institutions that privilege those values.

This argument is explicitly Heideggerian. The "Ends of Man,"
when speaking of Heidegger's deployment of the space of the
house as is the dominant and inescapable "metaphor" of these
values,[52] argues that Heidegger disrupts the traditional spatial
logic by rethinking it "according to the opening of a spacing
which *belongs* neither to time nor to space, and which dislocates,
while producing it, any presence of the present."[53] This spacing
of the tradition, this veiled force of dislocation that is "buried in
its *oikonomia*," is buried in the house precisely inasmuch as it is
unlocatable. It attains its force inasmuch as it cannot be placed
by the very mechanisms of place it inhabits. Just as the explicit
rethinking of place in Derrida's essays follows that of Heidegger,[54] the sense of the haunted house that pervades those essays,
without ever being described as such, is Heideggerian, even
though, if we follow Derrida's extended readings of Heidegger's
texts, those texts ultimately resist it.

Derrida's "Restitutions: The Truth of Pointing," for example,
begins its reading of Heidegger's "The Origin of the Work of
Art" by describing itself as a "ghost story."[55] Following Heidegger's identification of the architectonic logic of grounding,
founding, standing, erection, monument, and so on, with that of
the institution, it focuses on the question of place and institution,
institution as that which places. It reads Heidegger's attempt to
place two shoes, themselves understood as "an institute, a monument,"[56] in a painting by Van Gogh and thereby return them to
an owner from whom they are apparently detached. In the end,
the shoes cannot be placed. Like all supplementary ornaments,
they turn out to be neither attached to nor detached from any
of the structures that could be used to pin them down, whether
it be a peasant's feet, the space of the painting, the space of the
exhibition, the institutional spaces of art history and philosophy,
Heidegger's own argument, and so on. Derrida's "spectral analysis" exposes the point at which Heidegger's argument, which
itself complicates the relationship between structure and ornament, resists his own assertion that Being is fundamentally un-

canny. It does so by linking the idea of haunting to the uncanny.[57] The ghost is always an uncanny guest. Inasmuch as the "familiar (*heimlich*)" shoes are haunted, they are "*unheimlich.*" But so too is whatever they are supposedly detached from.[58] The shoes are both "haunted" and "haunting," as is Heidegger's discourse in its engagement with them. Haunting is never singular. If it involves the return of a "ghost," it is always a return to a ghost ["*revenant au revenant*"].[59] In the end, a space is not simply haunted. Rather, the space is itself haunting. Derrida follows this "accumulation of haunting" that disrupts the always institutional logic of structure/ornament and the familiar conceptions of space and place it sustains. The structure is as much haunted by the ornament as the ornament is by the structure, and this convoluted "relation of haunting" exceeds the institutional space produced by the system of philosophical oppositions, calling into question the always, at the least, political logic of place and identity. In showing that the institutional logic of space, the all-pervasive logic of the house, is made possible by the haunting that exceeds it, Derrida turns Heidegger's arguments upon themselves, tacitly extracting from them a diabolic scene of haunted space, the domesticity of space as that which is, and cannot be without it, haunted.

The spectral scene everywhere inscribed in Derrida's texts, albeit in oblique and dispersed traces, can never be isolated from this refolding of Heidegger's arguments. Derrida's ambivalent struggle with Heidegger continues in those texts that do not appear to address Heidegger, particularly where they, as is so often the case, raise the question of place.

The elusive sense of the house haunted by the spacing buried within it can be seen, for example, in "The Deaths of Roland Barthes," which argues that the massively overdetermined point Barthes calls the *punctum* "haunts" the space of the photograph by virtue of being unlocatable within it: "We are prey to the ghostly power of the supplement; it is this unlocatable site which gives rise to the specter."[60] The *punctum* punctures space and, inasmuch as it is unlocatable, it is not just a particular space that it punctures, but the very sense of space itself. It is heterogeneous to space and yet, at the same time, is not simply opposed to space. It leaves the definition of place behind, but it is only in being left behind, only in the wound that marks the puncture, that there is a sense of place: "a wound no doubt comes in (the) place of the point signed by singularity, in (the) place of its very instant (*stigmé*), of its point. But *in* (*the*) *place of* this event, the place is left."[61] What is left behind, the trace of the trace, is place. Place is an effect of the double withdrawal that encrypts spacing.

This argument draws on Derrida's early reading of Heidegger in "*Ousia* and *Grammé*," which notes that when *Being and Time* reads Hegel, the point is seen to mark the first of the successive stages (followed by the line then the surface) by which space constitutes itself by withdrawing its own conditions of possibility. As Derrida puts it: "The point is the space that does not take up space, the place that does not take place; it suppresses and replaces the place, it takes the place of the space that it negates and conserves. It spatially negates space."[62] What Heidegger often calls the "spatiality of space,"[63] is concealed by the point, the minimal marker in space, the spatial marker, as it is by all the visible manifestations of space that succeed the point. The apparent articulation of space actually marks the effacement of its basic condition: "Pure spatiality is determined by negating properly the indetermination that constitutes it, that is, by negating itself . . . Space, therefore, has become concrete in having retained the negative within itself. It has become space by losing itself."[64] The way in which Derrida describes spacing's implication in its own repression echoes the concept of "withdrawal" that organizes so much of Heidegger's writing. Indeed, the whole argument about space embedded within Derrida's writing that has been followed at length here remains deeply indebted to Heidegger even after exercising its sustained and rigorous criticism of Heidegger's use of it.

Displacing Discourse

It is crucial to remember that Derrida's extended reworking of Heidegger's argument about space is not simply a discourse "about" space and its dislocations. One of its first effects is to dismantle the simple opposition between discourse and space. A discourse is itself a space and spaces are produced by discourse.

At one point in the essay "Geschlecht, Sexual Difference, On-tological Difference," Derrida pays attention to Heidegger's argument that the spacing that is repressed within our familiar sense of space surfaces in language, the spatial rhetoric of language being the very mark of its origin rather than a contingent accident. The sense of being-there (*Dasein*) in the world "hides, shelters in itself"[65] the possibility of spatial "dispersion," a spacing that is "structural" rather than a disruption of an already established space, a spacing that is always "before" space, before, that is, the sense of space constructed by the philosophical tradition. Heidegger employs a number of terms for this dispersion, each of which "names a spacing . . .'before' the determination of space."[66] This spacing is not a dispersal "in" space, but is the dispersal that produces space as such. It is the possibility of anything taking place or time, establishing "the originary spatiality of *Dasein*, its *Räumlichkeit*. The spatial or spacing dispersion is manifested in language for instance. Every language is first of all determined by spatial significations (*Raumbedeutungen*)."[67] Spacing always inscribes itself, albeit obliquely, within the very space from which it withdraws. Any discourse necessarily carries within itself traces of a withdrawn spacing and can never detach itself from the particular effect of space produced by that withdrawal. Furthermore, that effect, the very construction of space as such, is always discursive. Space is only ever a discursive effect.

In these terms, Derrida is already engaging with spaces and with the question of space in ways that are themselves necessarily spatial inasmuch as he engages with the institutional structure of discourses, which he always does, whether he explicitly addresses space or not. Often his texts do address it, weaving backward and forward between what a discourse directly or indirectly says, or, as is often the case, will not say, about space and its own constitution of a space, articulating the convoluted but structural forms of transference between them. In the end, the question of deconstruction and architecture that we have been pursuing here turns on this transference.

The way in which architecture is written into Derrida's relentless binding of discourse and space can be seen in "Plato's Pharmacy," in which the dislocation of space is yet again understood as the dislocation of the domestic. The text rehearses the argument we have been following by looking at the role of the *pharmakoi* (wizards, magicians, poisoners) in Plato's *Phaedrus* who, through their subversive play with spacing, are seen as sources of evil that should be "cut off from the space of the city"[68] by being expelled across its borders and yet are invited back in and domesticated: "the representative of the outside is nonetheless *constituted*, regularly granted its place by the community, chosen, kept, fed, etc., in the very heart of the inside. These parasites were as a matter of course domesticated by the living organism that housed them at its expense."[69] That which is supposedly excluded from the domestic space nevertheless takes its place within it, kept inside in order to be symbolically excluded whenever there was a crisis, excluded in a way that determines the contours of "the boundary line" that marks the space. That which has no place is "granted its place" in order to define the place as such. Place, yet again, is an effect of the placeless.

Derrida uses this apparently literal example of dislocation employed by classical discourse to analyze the structure of that very discourse. The story is itself one of the myths [*khairein*] that Plato has supposedly banned from the space of his dialogue, a discursive space that, following the classical tradition, explicitly understands itself as a topology, a system of *topoi* or places that structures an argument: "The *topoi* of the dialogue are never indifferent. The themes, the topics, the (common-)places, in a rhetorical sense, are strictly inscribed, comprehended each time within a significant site. They are dramatically staged, and in this theatrical geography, unity of place corresponds to an infallible calculation or necessity."[70] And yet, having been banned from the topological regime of this spatial system, the myth returns into the space, violating its precisely calibrated and policed order. Furthermore, it returns precisely to tell the story of the inevitable return of the excluded. In both cases, the story and the *pharmakon* it describes, that which has no place in the space reenters it, takes an illegitimate place, but does so at the invitation of the police of the space, the representatives of its law. The illegal alien is recalled by the law, returning to cover over some kind of embarassing deficiency in the space, to shore it up and articulate the very borders it violates.

The myth, like the *pharmakon* it speaks about, not only takes a place in Plato's argument, it "takes *place*" in the name of truth. It returns to establish the truth of philosophy, which is to say, the space maintained by philosophical discourse. Each is a "house-breaker"[71] that establishes the structure of the "household of *logos*,"[72] constructing the very domestic law it breaks. Philosophy, that which determines the place of things, is itself determined by that which exceeds its law, that which disrupts domesticity inasmuch as it cannot be securely placed. The space of philosophy, the "house" of metaphysics that monumentalizes the distinction between inside and outside, which is to say the house that preserves the very idea of the house, is secretly inhabited and made possible by the spacings that are excluded from it and yet return to haunt it as a "ghost":

If one got to thinking that it can only be out of something like writing—or the *pharmakon*—that the strange difference between inside and outside can spring; if, consequently, one got to thinking that writing as a *pharmakon* cannot be assigned a site within what it situates, cannot be subsumed under concepts whose contours it draws, leaves only its ghost to a logic that can only seek to govern it insofar as logic arises from it—one would then have to *bend* [*plier*] into strange contortions what could no longer even simply be called logic or discourse.[73]

In identifying the contortions of the always haunted house, deconstructive discourse disturbs the space of discourse before it disturbs the discourse about space. This raises the question of philosophy's own place, the place of the discourse which places and polices, the question that Derrida most explicitly addresses in the essay "Languages and the Institutions of Philosophy." When looking at the "topological structure" of the university, its division of places understood to be, like all determinations of space, a political division, a "politology," the essay asks where is philosophy itself placed: "if it *takes place*, if it has *a place*, and if the philosopher himself takes place."[74] In the original thinking of the university, the philosopher has "two places: a circumscribed place and a non-place."[75] On the one hand, there is a department of philosophy located within the structure and, on the other hand, there is no part of the institution that is not philosophical. Philosophy is actually "at once everywhere and nowhere"[76] and the philosopher is figured as the "undiscoverable subject and as a non-place of the constructed institution or of the topology."[77] And inasmuch as the philosophical thinking that organizes the university has no place, it "never takes place anywhere" and, furthermore, even "the university itself doesn't take place."[78] The logic of place that governs the institutional topology is itself without place. In the end, the order of place is actually displacement, there is no location without dislocation. Each site is fragile, which is not to say vulnerable. On the contrary, each space, and the official discourse used to legitimate it, gains its force, one that is always political, from the way it exceeds, or even contradicts that very discourse.

This reading, like all readings of place, is bound to the architectural logic of the house, as can be seen when another of Derrida's essays returns to Kant's description of the "unlocalizable place" of philosophy in order to engage in the ongoing debate about the contemporary status of philosophy in the French university and argue against its "enclosure" or "house arrest" in any particular place.[79] The discipline traditionally devoted to the law of the house must not itself be subjected to that law by being "confined" to a "little cell" within the university. The "proper *home*" of philosophy, as he puts it in yet another essay from the same debate, must be put into question.[80] But, at the same time, the traditional space should not simply be abandoned by the contemporary thinking that has for "the last twenty years" undermined this domestic law and redefined the role of philosophy. Rather, there is an ongoing and irresolvable tension between the need for the "architecture of the discipline" to be gathered in a traditional site with a "localizable identity" and its need to be always "opening itself up to new objects in a way that knows no limit of principle . . . that exceeds all bounds," a contradiction that, among many others, produces an "incredible topology [*topologie incroyable*]."[81] This is to say that the enigmas of Kant's institutional architecture remain the enigmas of contemporary thinking in and about the institution.

In this way, the interrelated structural complications of both the place of the tradition of philosophy and the concept of place articulated within it also organizes those discourses that displace that tradition. The slippages between the theme of place and the discourse about place are multiplied, for example, in Derrida's "At This Very Moment in Whose Work I Am" when it addresses the crypt that Levinas locates within the familiar space of classical discourse by continuously dislocating that space, rupturing it in a way that produces a "fault" or "tear" that exposes what the space buries. Derrida argues that this "dislocation" does not collapse the space but, on the contrary, inaugurates it and continues to covertly structure it. Levinas is deconstructive inasmuch as he "opens" the space to something other by exploiting the opening that makes the space possible, the folds that endlessly complicate the lines that appear to define the space. As Derrida puts it, this dislocation of space "will have taken place—another place, in the place of the other—only on the condition of another topic."[82] The space of a discourse can only take place, constituting itself as a place, through such slippery atopic movements of dislocation. Its capacity to place things depends on this displacement. It can only take place by making a place, or rather, a certain nonplace, in its interior for that which officially has no place there.[83]

Derrida asks the same kind of questions of Levinas's own disruptive discourse, questions about its place, the very questions that Levinas asks of traditional discourse and appears to answer in a way that leaves the reader "no longer familiar with the places" where traditional questions "linger."[84] Noting that the questions might themselves already be "out of place," Derrida asks of Levinas's writing, "What would have taken place? . . . What would be the proper-place of this text, of this faulty body? Will it have properly taken place? . . . Does the body of a faulty text take place? . . . How does he manage to give a place there to what remains absolutely foreign to that medium?"[85] If Levinas locates the elusive crypt secreted within the home, where is his own discourse located? It clearly has no place outside the space it subverts, and that subversion takes the form of an ongoing displacement, a defamiliarization of the space that shows that it is haunted by the other, the elusive phantom that dislodges it from within, exposing the sense of place as but the fragile effect of systemic repression. It is only ever, and always, dislocation that takes place.

This, in turn, must lead to the question of the place and the taking place of Derrida's own work. He repeatedly warns against the "domestication" of deconstructive discourse, the risk of which becomes greater the more it carries out its work in any one site.[86] At one point, he portrays it as a restless "nomadic" discourse without a "home,"[87] while at another he argues that if it was to be "at home" anywhere, it would be in the kind of places (including architecture departments) that he elsewhere describes as "far from the places familiar to me,"[88] rather than those usually allocated to it:

> If, hypothetically, it had a proper place, which is precisely what cannot be the case, such a deconstructive "questioning" or meta-questioning would be more at home in law schools, perhaps also—this sometimes happens—in theology or architecture departments, than in philosophy departments and much more than in the literature departments where it has often been thought to belong.[89]

On another occasion, he asks whether there is a "proper place" for deconstruction, given that it can no longer be contained by the "classic architecture" of the academic disciplines it has transformed, and explores the possibility that "America would be the proper name of deconstruction in progress, its family name, its toponymy, its language and its place, its principal residence," since it has been "the most sensitive, receptive, or responsive space of all to the themes and effects of deconstruction,"[90] only to argue that the discourse cannot simply occupy such a space, as it is always a question of translation between languages, that is, between spaces.[91] In the end, it is only concerned with forms of "transference" and so has no place.

At the same time, deconstructive discourse always addresses the place it finds itself in. It is a strategy necessarily, as Derrida puts it elsewhere, "dictated by places . . . I write from the place—several places—in which I find myself."[92] Each of his essays explicitly engages with its own space, its spatio-institutional context, interrogating the various mechanisms that frame it and identifying the way their ruses and complications are actually folded into the ostensible subject of the text which usually appears to be detached from them. Each essay explores the ways its arguments are affected by the space in which it is placed, which is not to say that it simply occupies that space. In terms of the phenomenon of "deconstruction *in* America," for example, the symptomatic way in which deconstruction both seems to have found a place there, that it can take place there, seemingly able to occupy American institutions more successfully than anywhere else and at the same time be more violently resisted by them than anywhere else, is part of what produces the sense of that place: "the place itself is defined in this context on the basis of the symptom which is produced there."[93] Deconstruction is not simply imported into America from some "foreign" place.[94] Far from being simply "French,"[95] it is built into the very construction of America's identity as a place. While it has no place, it can never be detached from the spaces in which it can be found. The overt and violent resistance to deconstructive discourse is not a resistance to an outsider that could simply be expelled, but is a resistance to something internal, a resistance that was ongoing before the "arrival" of the discourse that articulates that internal discomfort, and was no less violent for being covert. On the contrary.

And following its own relentless logic, deconstruction, inasmuch as it doesn't have a place, doesn't take place. It "simply doesn't take place, doesn't have an exclusive place which could be attributed to it."[96] If it is anything, it is an "event."[97] Rather than taking place, it is the enigmatic movements of taking place, of becoming space. And if deconstruction is spacing in this sense, what about deconstructive discourse? If there is no discourse that is not a space and no space without spacing, what would be the space of a discourse about spacing? Is it even possible to have such a discourse? After all, spacing is precisely that which withdraws from discourse and opens it to something other. This opening can therefore never simply be the object of a discourse. As Derrida puts it in "The Time of a Thesis":

How is it that philosophy finds itself inscribed, rather than itself inscribing itself, within a space which it seeks but is unable to control, a space which opens onto another which is no longer even *its* other . . . How is one to name the structure of this space? I do not *know;* nor do I know whether there can even be what may be called *knowledge* of such a space.[98]

Deconstructive discourse cannot simply involve writers looking for nonsites within particular spaces, as the nonsite is precisely that which cannot simply be seen, that which cannot be located within space, the elusive dislocation that at once disrupts and produces the effect of the writer (as a subject detached from the objects of its discourse) in producing the effect of space. As Derrida argues, when speaking in an interview of the tremors of deconstructive movements, "I don't know where such tremors can be located. They situate us. These events don't have a place, they are looking for their place. Inside and out, their space is already foreign, in any case, to what is called the history of philosophy."[99] Deconstructive discourse is itself "situated," placed by the dislocations it attempts to indirectly articulate. Although the movements of deconstruction have no proper place, the deconstructive discourse that identifies this inevitably finds itself placed by those movements inasmuch as it is a discourse.

This enigma is explored further in "Some Statements and Truisms," which addresses the unstable "place" of deconstruction in the university, its "institutional place" in the system that both allocates places and protects the very logic of place: "But that which thus allows them to take place has no stable or theorizable place. It is in this non-place that the appearance of deconstruction can be situated, and I will later distinguish this process from a state, from a 'deconstructionist' theory, or an unlikely set of 'deconstructionist' theorems."[100] Although deconstructive discourse is nomadic, it is always given a space, institutionalized even, by the very dislocations it reads.

One of the consequences of this enigma is that the restless movements of deconstruction are arrested, domesticated, given place, located in space, as much by its ostensible supporters as by its critics: "I would say that even on the side where one in general tries to situate 'deconstruction,' . . . even there, 'deconstructionists' and 'deconstructionism' represent an effort to re-appropriate, tame, normalize this writing in order to reconstitute a new 'theory.'"[101] Although deconstructive discourse inevitably finds itself "situated" by what it reads in ways that are always surprising, any attempt it might make to actively situate deconstruction is already to domesticate it, to consume it in a way that resists its operations. Even then, it must also be noted that, as Derrida argues elsewhere, such a consumption could never be straightforward:

Deconstruction in the singular cannot be simply "appropriated" by anyone or by anything. Deconstructions are the movements of what I have called "exappropriation." Anyone who believes that they have appropriated or seen appropriated something like deconstruction in the singular is a priori mistaken, and something else is going on. But since deconstruction is always "something else," the error is never total or pure.[102]

Deconstruction can only be consumed inasmuch as it is an object, which it is not. Rather, it is the very movements of the spacing whose repression produces the effect of an object in producing the effect of a space. An object, like a subject, can only appear as such in space. The simple belief that deconstruction is something that can be either supported or criticized already marks the always frustrated attempt to domesticate its play. The question of space is therefore written into the whole debate around deconstruction, even though it is rarely raised as such. In their shared attempt to place deconstruction, the ostensibly warring factions in the debate attempt to efface its force by effacing spacing. The sustained collective silence around the question of space, which is actually the maintenance of the traditional account of space, and the particular sense of the political that this account maintains, is the first sign of this resistance.

Listening to the Silence about Space

The strategic role of this effacement can be seen, for instance, in the infamous exchange between Derrida and John Searle. In "Limited Inc. a b c . . ." Derrida addresses the "domestication"[103] of his work effected by what he sees as the systematic violence done to his essay "Signature, Event, Context" by Searle's published response to it. In documenting and interpreting this violence, Derrida, as always, argues in the terms that we have been exploring here. His counter-response begins by noting the "strange, uncanny familiarity" of Searle's reading and raising the usual questions of place and taking place: "What is the nature of the debate that seems to begin here? Where, here? Here? Is it a debate? Does it Take Place? Has it begun already? When? . . . If it takes place, what is its place?"[104] The text goes on to identify the multiple senses in which the debate between his essay and Searle's is "not quite taking place" and ends with the question "Will it have taken place, this time? Quite."[105] Derrida's argument is that it is actually the way in which a debate about deconstruction can never quite take place that disrupts the "topology" of traditional academic discourse, upsetting the "logic of its places"[106] and threatening its empowered guardians, its academic police. It is the impossibility of placing deconstruction that is its greatest threat.

It is not coincidental that the particular text that Searle has so violently "domesticated," by "assimilating" it in a way which produces a "comfortable" because reductive "digest," is one that explicitly raises the questions of space and place in a way that Searle ignores. It also begins with the question of what "takes place" (in this case, what takes place in communication) and explicitly addresses writing as an "opening" of the "space" of communication, a "spacing" which, like all "parasites," disrupts the traditional sense of being "at home."[107] In attempting to restore this very sense of domestic security by digesting deconstruction, Searle attempts to domesticate arguments about the spacing of writing but without addressing spacing as such, abruptly restoring and reasserting the traditional concept of writing being called into question. It is arguably this effacement of space and spacing that effects the domestication. Although Derrida does not point to this effacement, his reply restores the argument about space by describing the undecidability "calling into question the entire traditional philosophy of the *oikos*"[108] in terms of the parasitic incorporation of the crypt built into the structure of any house:

> The structure of the area in which we are operating here calls for a strategy that is complex and tortuous, involuted and full of artifice: for example, exploiting the target [the "classical concept" of writing] against itself by discovering it at times to be the "basis" of an operation directed against it; or even discovering "in it" the cryptic reserve of something utterly different.[109]

The space being interrogated is haunted and its parasitic phantom is uncanny inasmuch as it "is never *simply* alien to and separable from the body to which it has been transplanted or which it already haunts."[110] After all, if the crypt is built into the structure of the house, it is built in as the very structure of the space.

And, yet again, this argument about the haunting of space directly concerns the political. Derrida attempts to show how a supposedly neutral philosophical discourse reproduces "the founding categories of all ethical-political statements"[111] that are the possibility of the production of "law."[112] Searle's violence, sustained or, rather, produced, by the guise of scholarly neutrality, is the violence of the law, the violence that maintains the academic space, the house whose structure Derrida undermines. In Derrida's later reflection on the exchange, he argues that it "concerned above all our experience of violence and of our relation to the law—everywhere, to be sure, but most directly in the way we discuss 'among ourselves,' in the academic world," particularly in the university.[113] This violence, which can never simply be eradicated, needs to be taken account of and its analysis, the analysis of the violence of analysis, the violence of even, if not especially, the simplest form of question, constitutes a form of political action, indeed is one of the actions that "contribute most to transforming the legal-ethical-political rules: *in* the university and *outside* the university."[114] Furthermore, this interrogation turns out to concern the very effect of inside and outside, the establishment of a sense of space that is an effect of the systemic violence involved in the familiar assumption promoted by Searle that there is a politically neutral "space of theory" detached from "real life."[115] There is no space without police force. It is not that any sense of space is, by definition, politically suspect, but that it is always, but not only, political from the beginning:

There is a police that is brutally and *rather* "physically" repressive (but the police is never purely physical) and there are more sophisticated police that are more "cultural" or "spiritual," more noble. But every institution destined to enforce the law is a police. An academy is a police. . . . if the police as such is not politically suspect a priori, it is never neutral either, never apolitical.[116]

Furthermore, it would follow from Derrida's argument that all police are academic inasmuch as they are all, in the end, the guardians of theory. Theoretical assumptions are always at stake in every institution—assumptions that cannot be asserted, let alone maintained, without violence, the violence of a space. Searle is not simply incriminated because he promotes a particular sense of space and attempts to enforce its law, but because of the particular contradictions involved in that enforcement. Derrida draws an "indispensable" distinction between the implicit force of the police and the "unjust brutality of a force that most often violates the very law to which it appeals."[117] If there is a responsibility in the realm of theory to which Searle appeals, it is to identify the structural nature of this kind of "abuse" of the rules when it establishes those rules and thereby defines a space. In the end, although he does not say as much, Derrida is calling for a certain responsibility in the construction of space.

This indirect but insistent call is typically responded to with a strategic silence, a regulated series of absences in the discourse of both "supporters" and "critics" of deconstruction, a shared silence that establishes the most solid defense to the workings of deconstruction. In these terms, the extensive debate around the question of deconstruction needs to be re-read in detail to track the critical but rarely acknowledged role of space in it and to demonstrate that what is always everywhere at stake for everyone is the construction of space, a construction bound into a certain image of architecture. Such a reading becomes even more urgent now that the question of architecture has begun to be raised by the discourse in recent years but raised defensively in a way that actually maintains rather than breaks the silence around space, a silence whose very loudness marks how high the stakes in space are.

Before making such a reading, it is important to note that the tension between the violence of the law that constitutes a space and the violence of the deconstructive arguments that undermine that space is never simply between supporters and critics, conservatives and revolutionaries, old and new, and so on. It is built into those arguments, from the beginning, in the same way that deconstructive movements are built into the traditional discourse that attempts to resist them. A tension about space is endemic to discourse as such. Inasmuch as a discourse is a space, it can never fully take account of space, let alone spacing. The question of space necessarily exceeds discourse. Part of the silence about space can never be filled. The argument about space built into Derrida's work at so many different levels is not simply resisted by other discourses. His own discourse is also punctuated by certain silences about space. Some of them constrain his arguments and can be broken to open up the discourse, but others are systemic and cannot be broken without threatening it.

If space can only ever be uncanny and all discourses are marked and organized by its uncanniness, there can never be a discourse, in the traditional sense, about that uncanniness. It must be remembered that a discourse is only deconstructive inasmuch as its violation of the institutionalized codes of reading organizing a space does not simply break the law but exploits the break already inscribed into the law, constituting it as such. Which is probably to say that, in the end, there can be no such thing as a "deconstructive discourse" as such or, rather, that all discourses are already deconstructive, but in a way they cannot simply articulate.

It must also be remembered that the two forms of violence that constitute space (that of spacing and the institutional violence that represses it) are always entangled. This interdependence is underlined in Derrida's reading of Blanchot in "The Law of Genre," which argues that subversion "needs the law in order to take place"[118] because, to abruptly short-circuit the text's elaborate itinerary here, there is "lodged within the heart of the law itself, a law of impurity or a principle of contamination"[119] a "counter-law" or "parasitical economy" in which an "unsituable" "fold" disrupts the sense of "objective space," "normed space," "visible space," or "enclosure," by configuring "an internal pocket larger than the whole"[120] whose "excess" violates the very "boundaries" it installs. And this crucial argument about space, one that has been tracked through so many texts here, is itself seen to arise from "an act of unjustifiable violence" on Derrida's part: "A brutal and mercilessly depleting selectivity will obtrude upon me, upon us, in the name of a law that *La folie de jour* has, in its turn already reviewed, and with the foresight that a certain kind of police brutality is perhaps an inevitable accomplice to our concern for professional competence."[121] The apparent space of deconstructive discourse (which is precisely deconstructive only inasmuch as it is not a delimited discourse but a certain spatial excess, an exceeding of spatial limits) can only be produced by some kind of affirmative complicity with the very brutality it appears to displace.

To break the silence about space that establishes the (always domestic) law will therefore not simply involve breaking the law by speaking loudly in the institutionalized void about architecture. Rather, it will involve actively engaging with the silence, turning the law against itself, exploiting its force to interrogate the very silence it preserves. To deconstruct architecture is not to deconstruct a certain strategic effect of institutional discourse by simply constructing different kinds of argument about architecture. Before this, it involves articulating the ways in which architecture is routinely constructed by certain silences that constitute rather than interrupt discourse, silences whose ongoing violence can, by definition, only be addressed obliquely. The challenge for, and to, deconstructive discourse is to rethink architecture by locating such an oblique address.

In-Conclusion

In place of a conclusion (deconstruction being, of course, anything but conclusive), the specific brutality of the reading of Derrida's texts being made here has to be acknowledged and its effects taken into account. The question of architecture (edifice, space, house, *oikos*, spacing, interiority, structure, ornament, uncanny, parasite, place, and so on) has been obsessively and violently extracted from Derrida's writing, crudely isolated and reassembled in a way that forces the sense of a single, albeit convoluted, argument running through all his work. The overt trajectory of each text has largely been ignored and the specific effects of the oblique question of architecture have not been followed through in all the sites in which it does not register as such. And, if this was not enough, those texts that might at first seem to be the most relevant—Derrida's later writings about architecture—have been abruptly bracketed out, along with all the other texts in the debate they have occasioned. Furthermore, there is even a formidable violence involved in simply nominating architecture as a question, a systematic brutality in relentlessly interrogating Derrida's texts, repeatedly asking of them the simple question of "architecture," forcing an answer, if not a confession, and tacitly incriminating any silence. The simplest of questions, as Derrida has repeatedly argued, is violent,[1] even if the question is, as it has always been here, about violence, the violence of architecture and the architecture of violence.

Off the Threshold

The brutality of this narrow reading cannot be conveniently legitimized by the protocol of violent fidelity that Derrida insists on. It has been argued here, from the beginning, that an architectural reading of deconstructive discourse must be an abusive one. Much of the violence of the reading made here is therefore necessary—necessary precisely in order to raise the question of architecture, a question on whose quiet burial the tradition depends—but at a certain point the violence is simply the consequence of an incompleteness of the reading, a reading that may even, if pursued more rigorously, turn out to be insufficiently violent in other senses.

Not only will the precise location of this point always remain unclear, but it can never be removed. Derrida's texts cannot simply be called on to arbitrate between good and bad violence. On the contrary, they everywhere argue that nothing can be legalized or authorized without some illegal violence. They attain their force only inasmuch as they call into question such mechanisms of authority, including, especially, their own. To invoke certain aspects of Derrida's texts in order to authorize certain readings of the rest of those texts is therefore already to do considerable violence to them and to begin to resist their more oblique, and, therefore, ultimately more telling, force. The architectural reading of Derrida's work cannot simply be subjected to some generic and higher code of reading that could discriminate between violent and faithful readings.

Furthermore, there can be no such code that is not already dependant on a certain construction of architecture. What is at stake in architecture is the status of reading itself. It has been repeatedly argued here that architecture is precisely not an object awaiting a reading, or a theme within certain readings waiting to be addressed. Rather, a certain image of architecture (the image of the building as a material object that simply stands and encloses) acts as the basis of the traditional construction of the subject as a reader. The generic idea that architecture stands before a subject that might choose to read it veils architecture's role in the construction of that subject, which is also to say, architecture's role in the veiling of its constitutional role, the ongoing withdrawal of its enigmas in favor of an unambiguous demarcation of space from which a reading subject is seen to be detached. To explore these repressed enigmas is necessarily to disturb the traditional concept of reading that is bound to that of architecture. Derrida's displacement of reading, which is provocative for architectural discourse inasmuch as it presupposes a displacement of architecture and starts to uncover some of the enigmas of architecture, must itself be displaced to explore them further. The surfaces of Derrida's essays, like those of architecture, have to be disfigured, scratched rather than simply scrutinized, to see what they repress within (as distinct from behind or beneath) their very surface.

Having said this, detailed attention has to be paid to the particular ways in which the partial nature of this reading of Derrida's essays and the excessiveness of its violence have contributed to its construction of architecture. Such attention would transform or, at least, multiply the trajectories of the text. It is in the interest of a more nuanced understanding or mobilization of architecture (rather than a simple, and highly problematic, notion of fidelity to Derrida's texts) that the narrowness of this reading must be interrogated and dislodged.

At the same time, I would insist—and perhaps this is the only claim being made here—that what has been so brutally extracted from Derrida's work here is not one subtext among others. Its role is not like the others in the chain of arguments in which it may be placed. Indeed, it configures that chain and is to do with precisely what it is to be placed. To say the least, it concerns the spacing between the links in the chain, the conceptual trajectory marked by the ongoing production of such gaps, the strategic role of spatial forms like that of a chain, and so on. Derrida's dissemination of lines of overlapping and yet heterogeneous arguments is itself, first and foremost, a spacing.

There are, of course, many dangers in monumentalizing spacing, turning it into some kind of solid building and thereby effacing its strange movements, arresting and domesticating them by gathering them together and placing them at some mythical center of the space of an equally mythical "discourse" (deconstruction) produced by an equally mythical "author" (Derrida). As we have seen, violence is always the agent of construction. Part of the violence with which the question of architecture has been isolated here has to be understood as a form of resistance to the subversive rhythms of deconstructive discourse. It reconstitutes the identity of architecture in the face of those dimensions of the discourse that have tacitly begun to call that identity into question and therefore must itself be immediately placed into question. But it is equally the case that it is only possible to identify the other dimensions of deconstructive discourse that already tacitly consolidate the traditional image of architecture by forcing the question of architecture upon the discourse, insisting on the centrality of architecture in precisely the ways that it would want to resist, or rather, always resists in order to constitute itself.

In such a confrontation, both deconstructive discourse and the sense of what architecture is are dislodged. The crude question of architecture (one whose very crudity is precisely determined by a millennial tradition that constructs a certain image of architecture, the image of architecture as the crudest object, the most basic spatial form defined by its brute materiality, the minimum articulation of order) splinters in the face of deconstructive discourse and, equally, that discourse is itself dislodged. But, unlike architecture, it is not dislodged by simply being splintered because it so often represents itself as a form of splintering that fractures the traditional image of architecture. On the contrary, it is dislodged by identifying the secure architecture that its splintering movements actually consolidate. The splinter is, after all, not simply the result of a fracture. It is equally the means of the effacement of fracturing. As a splint, it is that which holds a fractured body together, that which props it up, maintaining an architecture. From the beginning, the question of deconstruction and architecture forces a confrontation between splintered architecture and the architecture of splinters.

This text, which only begins to stage such a confrontation, to rehearse, imagine, or image it, is inevitably as divided as the discourse it appears to read, only "appears" to inasmuch as the confrontation is actually an internal one. The apparent division between this text and the deconstructive discourse it frames as an object in order to be read is internal to each. This is not only unavoidable but has been a central theme here. It is precisely through such congenitally multiple internal divisions, and the particular institutional practices that mask them, that architecture is at once produced and assumes its strategic role in dominant Western discourse as the figure of that which is not itself divided inasmuch as it is the very figure of division, which is to say that architecture is represented as that which has no architecture. The tradition depends for its strength on this veiling of the extent to which architecture is, in the end, a certain effect of the pervasive, ongoing, and irresolvable internal conflict that covertly entangles all the lines it appears to so unproblematically draw. Architecture is no more than the strategic effect of the suppression of internal contradiction. It is not simply a mechanism that represses certain things. Rather, it is the very mark of repression.

The reading of the relationship between architecture and deconstruction (the "between" actually internal to each, which binds them together so repeatedly and tightly that neither can be considered without the other) obviously cannot end here, or even begin. It must be as restless as the movements it articulates. Shaking the question of architecture out of Derrida's writing is but one of many necessary but insufficient gestures. In the end, what is offered here is, at most, an introduction to Derrida's writing, a narrow reading of his texts that offers a certain form of leverage into the ongoing exchange between deconstructive discourse and the discourse of architecture, a way of engaging with the different arguments being deployed, including those of Derrida.

This text has read Derrida up to, around, and beyond the threshold of his overt entry into the space of architecture without ever simply crossing that threshold. The reading is an extended hesitation at the threshold, or, rather, an attempt to think about the nature of the threshold, to ask what would be the threshold of architecture. Would it be itself architectural? If a threshold is always, by definition, both inside and outside a space, the threshold to architecture must be both architectural and nonarchitectural. But this still presupposes that the threshold to architecture has the traditional architecture of the threshold. Because the space of architecture cannot simply be architectural, its threshold must be other or, and this is to say the same thing, the space itself is other inasmuch as it doesn't have a threshold. At the same time, the space of architecture is precisely that which sustains the idea of the threshold. Each of the multiple institutional practices that constitute that space contributes to the sense of threshold, the sense of a mechanism that allows a line to be crossed, a mechanism that temporarily breaks, suppresses, or neutralizes an otherwise secure line. In everywhere complicating the apparently clear line, deconstructive discourse necessarily displaces the sense of the threshold that traditionally negotiates passage across such lines. Far from abandoning the threshold, the discourse generalizes its condition. There are only ever always thresholds. If the lines that appear to define space are but the effect of the institutionalized suppression of their fundamental complications, the threshold is the mechanism of that suppression, which is to say that the sense of the line is actually produced by the threshold that appears to cross it.

If deconstructive discourse begins by problematizing the architecture of the threshold, to simply cross the overt threshold to architecture in Derrida's work would already be to suppress the complicated role of architecture in that work. The most obvious opening to the question of architecture is, by virtue of its very obviousness, actually some kind of closure (remembering that what is at stake here is precisely the buried discursive mechanisms that make available the always architectural sense of closure and openness). Rather, it is a matter of scanning the other texts, interrogating their surfaces for the traces of other openings, openings that do not simply offer some kind of access to architecture, but mark the degree to which Derrida's texts are routinely perforated by architecture and depend on this very perforation for their force. Of course, the recent texts of Derrida "about" architecture, which have been forcibly kept at a distance here in order to think about the covert architectural economy in his work, must be read but read in a way that maintains a certain resistance to their overt economy, an economy that is, for architectural discourse at least, all too familiar and that threatens to overwhelm that thinking by reconstituting the very institutions designed to mask it (the author-architect, the philosopher-theorist, the project, the program, the site, the plan, the fetish of material, architecture as a high art, and so on). When these texts are removed from the quarantine imposed here, the issue will be to what extent the operations of deconstructive discourse are disturbed or reinforced by their overt naming of architecture as a question, their apparent transformation of architecture from a given to a question, a transformation whose potential impact on traditional discourse cannot be underestimated.

As with any discourse, the relationship between the tacit roles of architecture in Derrida's work and what it may say about architecture will always be complex, enigmatic, and structural. These relationships need to be read in detail by carefully unpicking his texts on architecture. The same structural enigmas can also be traced in the work of other deconstructive writers who have started to address architecture and those architects who are now addressing deconstruction. The evolving discourse needs to be patiently rethought, and this rethinking will necessarily extend to discourses within which neither architecture nor deconstruction appear to surface. The reading of the discourse's preconditions offered here attempts to establish at least one trajectory with which to open such an analysis.

The Institution of Space

At the same time, such an architectural reading of deconstructive discourse could only open that discourse if it occurs in parallel to, and entangled with, a deconstructive reading of the sociopolitical institution of "architecture." All of the complications that have been followed here are at least doubled in the case of architectural discourse. If institutions are always spaces and space is always institutional, what about architectural discourse, ostensibly the institution of space, that is, the institutional formation "responsible" for the particular space that is used as the paradigm of space by other discourses? What about the space of space? If institutions are, by definition, architectural, the institution of architecture, and its deconstructive reading, must be something other. To rethink this institution would be more than simply a rigorous response to the specificity of architectural discourse, one response among so many others. Rather, it would, at the very least, reconfigure all the operations of deconstructive discourse by displacing the particular thinking of the institution that organizes them.

The institution of architecture is clearly more than buildings and the practices by which they are produced. Architecture is not simply a specific kind of object that is produced by a number of material practices and can be represented before, during, and after its construction and in itself exceeds, in its physical presence, any such representation. The building "itself" is no more than a specific mechanism of representation. In fact, there is no such thing as a building outside of a large number of overlapping mechanisms of representation: schools of architecture, professional codes of ethics, critical practices, historiographical methodologies, academic protocols, pedagogical techniques, curriculum structures, the strategic role of the author's signature and project credits, legalization of the word "architect," designated safety factors in structural calculations, standardized drawing techniques and conventions, building codes, aesthetic codes, zoning codes, clothing codes, school admission standards, faculty classifications, fee structures, hiring and firing practices, rhetorical conventions, examination structures, model-making techniques, various forms of etiquette, legal contracts, copyright law, the structure of the slide lecture, strategic control and dissemination of ideas through conferences and publications, ritualized master worship, theoretical and graphic commonplaces, copyediting protocols, interview and presentation formats, photographic techniques, the institution of the architectural jury, portfolio construction and circulation rituals, competition formats, official and unofficial club membership control, multiple advertising strategies, the standardized framing of images, the specific techniques of publication, editorial control, funding patterns, the structure of the architectural monograph, the biography and so on, to name only some of the most obvious ones. All of them are mechanical systems of reproduction whose ritualistic, if not fetishistic, repetition constantly affirms the presence of architecture rather than analyzes it. Indeed, the very intensity of their repetition seems to mark a nagging but suppressed doubt about that presence. They are the real mechanics of architecture. The building is literally constructed by these mechanisms of representation. Its very solidity, the sense that it has an irreducible materiality that precedes representation, is but a product of their complex interactions. Although the building is constructed by such systems of representation, they precisely construct it as something that precedes them.

Each of these disciplinary technologies needs to be carefully analyzed in its specificity and interrelationships with other such mechanisms (both those of other disciplines and those that orchestrate specific transactions in everyday cultural life) to determine its strategic role in the construction of architecture. Each has to be read deconstructively to determine what its operations attempt to prohibit and the ways in which this prohibited other returns to covertly orchestrate the very discourse that appears to exclude it. Equally, they have to be read in a way that produces a more nuanced, if not displaced, account of this strange architecture of prohibition/return, which has been articulated at length by deconstructive discourse. In a kind of internal struggle, the deconstruction of architecture must reconfigure the architecture of deconstruction, and so on, and on.

This struggle would immediately raise a series of specific questions that must be asked of the institutions of architecture, questions about their strategic role in the organization of diverse cultural transactions like the distinction between high and low culture, the construction of gender and sexual orientation, the micro structures of disciplinary control, the elusive form of the global economy, the twisted space of psychoanalytic theory, the interwoven spaces of the emerging technologies of communication, the ongoing performance of identity, digital imagery, the waging of war, the re-constitution of public space, the perverse geometry of power flows, and so on. Such questions have become increasingly urgent. While some of them may look like new questions or questions about apparently new phenomena, they are actually traditional questions that need to be re-asked in a different way. In fact, they are only urgent inasmuch as they are traditional. It is precisely the traditional questions that must be repeated yet again, but repeated in a way that takes account of the institutional role of that repetition. In the end, the question is always, in what way is architecture repeating itself? What is being repeated? What is the repetition we call architecture? And what does it at once mobilize and conceal?

Multiple trajectories of inquiry need to be opened up and obsessively pursued by patiently following all the different fault-lines that are already inscribed, however faintly, into the surface of architectural discourse in some kind of dense web, an intricate pattern of scars that mark that which is buried within the very surface, that which the discourse is unable to speak about but actually makes it possible. Such inquiries look for slippages in the tradition by questioning all its routine categories and strategies but not to simply overthrow them. On the contrary, they intensify them, ruthlessly respecting their specific rigor in order to see exactly what it is that their slippages organize. It is only possible to explore the senses in which architecture is always operating otherwise by forcing the discourse designed to conceal them to face its own operations. Each such operation has to be pushed to its limit. Under this kind of sustained pressure, all the traditional subjects of architectural discourse (architects, buildings, movements, details, typologies, ornamentation, structural analyses, architectural histories and their own history, regional formations, perceptual analysis of spaces, and so on) will be at once reinforced, supplemented, and displaced. Only by respecting the discourse, affirming it, even, if not especially, in its stunningly impoverished moments, treating each of its seemingly incidental, if not trivial, habits as a highly systematic construction that maintains certain unstated assumptions that have specific political consequences, can it be opened up to other possibilities.

To some extent, this heterogeneous and uncoordinated interrogation of architecture has already begun in the work of a small number of writers and designers, sometimes in the name of deconstruction but often without it, if not against it. Only a small part of the very public discourse about "deconstruction and architecture" participates in this rethinking and most of that discourse in the end resists it. Indeed, in such a deconstruction of the institution of architecture the word "deconstruction" is clearly superfluous.

Furthermore, this rethinking does not simply open architecture up to "new" possibilities. Rather, it identifies the multiple openings that already structure architecture and on whose veiling so many cultural transactions depend, including, especially (since the question of time can never be detached from that of space), the very sense of the "new." If nothing can be new without the sense of the old that is bound to architecture, the apparently simple idea of a "new architecture" is, at the very least, extraordinarily complicated; which is only to repeat that to deconstruct the tradition of architecture is first and foremost to try and comprehend its role in the constitution of the very sense of tradition, the way it constructs the sense of familiarity and the extent to which that sense depends on its routine, but routinely masked, violation.

To say that this obsessive repetition of old questions does not simply authorize or project something "new" is not to say everything remains unchanged, the dominant structures remain dominant, and so on. Rather, it is to displace the sense of what constitutes a transformation by suggesting that any simple avant-gardist sense of a new practice (whether it be a kind of essay or building) necessarily and immediately reconsolidates the traditional institution of architecture it claims to dislodge or critique. It veils the extent to which the tradition constitutes itself as such by repressing that which always dislodges it from within and thereby maintains that repression, constructing the tradition as stable in the very gesture of destabilizing it. Deconstructive discourse is different but not simply new. Its difference is actually internal to the traditions it appears to displace.

Exhuming Architecture

The impact of such readings of the multiple institutional practices that constitute architectural discourse would necessarily exceed that discourse inasmuch as those practices defend a certain account of architecture against investigation in order that it may circulate between, and covertly orchestrate, a heterogeneous range of cultural discourses that do not seem architectural. That which architectural discourse labors so hard to protect never simply becomes visible within it. It is protected by being concealed. Since only what is recognized within the discourse is officially designated as "architecture," the fundamental concern of architectural discourse, that which it is designed to protect, that which must be buried by it, cannot simply be architectural. Likewise, the institutional mechanisms that determine what is architectural and bury this other sense cannot themselves be architectural, which is to say again that neither the space of architecture, nor what is hidden within it, can be architectural. To forcibly interrogate the institutions of architecture to release what they hide will be, by definition, to locate things that seem to belong outside the discipline.

At the same time, the anarchitecture buried within the discourse, buried within the official account of architecture in order that it can circulate outside that discourse, can never be separated from the discourse that buries it. Although the space of architecture can never be architectural, the various institutional practices that maintain it bear a curious and strategic relationship to this anarchitectural sense they bury in order that it may haunt so many other discourses. It is the official account of architecture that enables it to haunt. This account visibly circulates outside of architectural discourse and can be easily located in diverse discourses. In each location, it carries within it an unspeakable sense of architecture. The mechanism by which this sense is concealed within architectural discourse is reproduced outside it.

It is not that this mechanism is constructed within architectural discourse and then disseminated to circulate outside. Indeed, architectural discourse as such is an extremely recent phenomenon given the millennial tradition in which a particular image of architecture has organized thinking, a tradition stretching at least back to Plato and everywhere operative in, if not as, contemporary life. The discipline of architecture poses a unique threat to that ancient tradition inasmuch as it ostensibly investigates the condition of architecture and could uncover and thereby undermine its operations. The whole discursive economy hangs on the maintenance of the mechanism that represses the slipperiness of architecture behind a benign image of disciplined space. Architectural discourse was only recently allowed to constitute itself as such by offering, as it were, a guarantee, a carefully worded promise that the wildness of space can be domesticated and, once tamed, protected as some kind of endangered primeval species in a highly legislated and inaccessible reserve. The provision of this guarantee remains its central cultural role. The institution of architecture is not concerned with the construction of buildings but with the maintenance of the idea of building, the maintenance of an ancient and slippery construction that is completely dependant on certain unspoken contracts that protect political structures apparently unrelated to it. The discipline of architecture is more than the disciplining of space. Before that, it is the disciplining of a certain thinking "about" space, or, more precisely, it is a set of institutional practices that maintain the idea that thinking can only ever be "about" space inasmuch as it is always detached from the spaces it addresses. Separating thinking from architecture in the very moment it appears to direct thinking toward architecture, the discourse suppresses the anarchitecture that makes thinking possible and, in so doing, blinds itself to the enigmas of the spaces it addresses.

To try and speak about the heavily guarded anarchitectural sense that allows discourses to speak is obviously not to simply speak of buildings, let alone houses, as they are commonly understood. But equally, it is not to leave buildings behind. On the contrary, it is to say that buildings can never be left behind, that the seemingly familiar sense of a building is actually an enormously complicated sense that is the product of a. massive tradition, or system of overlapping traditions, which is being constantly and violently enforced in the name of laws supposedly founded on that very sense. This ancient tradition projects building outside itself, isolating buildings from discourse, constructing building as that which comes before discourse, a privileged point of contact with prehistorical, transcultural order. To raise the question of deconstruction and architecture is therefore not to simply address space, the edifice, the house, and so on, but to think about the domestication of space itself, the housing of the house, the domestication of the house, the domestication of the mechanisms of domestication, the housing of that which makes the house possible, the elusive architecture of architecture itself.

If houses are all, from the beginning, haunted, what exactly is it that the institution of architecture, the house that supposedly houses the question of the house, haunted by? In the end, this is not a question of haunted houses, but the extent to which we are always haunted by houses—haunted, that is, by the institutional mechanisms that construct space. The uncanniness of space is not only the sense that any space is always occupied by what it ostensibly excludes, but equally the sense in which space itself cannot be excluded. Discourse is haunted by architecture, haunted by its strangeness in the very moment that this strangeness has apparently been bracketed out by the ritualized gestures employed by most discourses that repeatedly exclude the literal sense of a building only to immediately invite it in as a metaphor, supposedly the least mysterious outsider, the most familiar and reliable guest of all, a touchstone whose presence is reassuring and stabilizing. Traditional discourse splits architecture across the division between literal and metaphorical, finding the literal building threatening and the metaphorical building reassuring. It maintains its space by maintaining this line. But inasmuch as the distinction between literal and metaphorical is based on the very image of architecture it appears to include, the line is actually radically convoluted and the threatening conditions of architecture cannot be excluded. They return to haunt the space whose institutional practices can no longer resist them by holding the line. And what returns is precisely the sense that architecture itself does not hold the line, that a building doesn't simply figure the security of spatial divisions, but is rather the product of the institutionally enforced repression of their convolution.

A deconstructive reading of architecture is therefore not only concerned with showing that architecture has its parasites, but also with showing that it is itself a parasite, but a very particular form of parasite. If, as Derrida argues, the parasite is the unruly and unwelcome houseguest whose very disruption of the space actually provides its law, the figure of architecture is the all-too-welcome houseguest, the well-mannered visitor whose very guarantee of the space would somehow disorder it if its terms were to be examined in any detail. It is the outsider that "stands for" the constitution of space rather than its violation, but it always harbors within itself the rhythms of spacing, the subversive movements that at once constitute and violate the sense of space.

The question that has been so insistently asked here must finally become that of the spacing of architecture itself. On the one hand, it is the spacing that makes architecture possible even while, or, rather, only by, violating its apparent order. On the other hand, it is architecture's spacing of other discourses, the violation of diverse institutions by a certain architectural thinking of space that makes their own spaces possible; the way in which architecture haunts other discourses; the extent to which they cannot think of themselves as discourses without being haunted by a particular logic of space sustained by architectural images. And if architectural discourse guarantees the spatial laws that other institutions enforce, this all too familiar logic of enforceable space, space as enforcement, harbors within itself an unspeakable architecture, a prohibited but irresistible spacing. The image of the house that necessarily haunts institutions inasmuch as they are institutions, the image which is always their self image, the very image of institution, is itself haunted. While the architectural discourse that protects that image is the designated institutional space of space itself, it is precisely not the designated space of spacing. On the contrary, what it protects is the effacement of spacing by space. No space, by definition, has space for spacing. And yet it is the major achievement of Derrida's extraordinary work, one whose consequences cannot be overestimated, to show that there is no space without it, that architecture is always haunted.

At the same time, it must be remembered that this complication also necessarily affects the space of deconstructive discourse, and Derrida's work in particular. Those texts that appear to rigorously pursue the question of spacing, whether they address architecture or not, are invariably haunted by stable constructions of space that punctuate their arguments without being called into question by them. Architecture remains the Achilles' heel of deconstructive discourse. The strength of that discourse depends on the veiling of its systemic weakness for architecture, a traditional weakness that structures the discourse as such and needs to be interrogated, especially when the question of deconstruction and architecture is being explicitly raised. Not only has such an interrogation hardly even begun here, but this text must immediately be subjected to it.

Notes

Preface

1. Mark Wigley, "Heidegger's House: The Violence of the Domestic," *D: Columbia Documents in Architecture and Theory,* no. 1, 1992, 91–121.

The Translation of Architecture

1. Jacques Derrida, "Des Tours de Babel," trans. Joseph F. Graham, in Joseph F. Graham, ed., *Difference in Translation* (Ithaca: Cornell University Press, 1985).

2. "[A]nd for the notion of translation, we would have to substitute a notion of *transformation:* a regulated transformation of one language by another, of one text by another. We never will have, and in fact never have had, to do with some "transport" of pure signifieds from one language to another, or within one and the same language, that the signifying instrument would leave virgin and untouched." Jacques Derrida, "Semiology and Grammatology," trans. Alan Bass, in *Positions* (Chicago: University of Chicago Press, 1981), 20.

3. Walter Benjamin, "The Task of the Translator," trans. Harry Zohn, in Hannah Arendt, ed., *Illuminations* (New York: Schocken Books, 1968), 69–82, 80.

4. Ibid., 72.

5. Ibid., 75.

6. "A text lives only if it lives *on* [*sur-vit*], and it lives *on* only if it is *at once* translatable *and* untranslatable . . . Totally translatable, it disappears as a text, as writing, as a body of language [*langue*]. Totally untranslatable, even within what is believed to be one language, it dies immediately. Thus triumphant translation is neither the life nor the death of the text, only or already its living *on*, its life after life, its life after death." Jacques Derrida, "Living On: *Border Lines*," trans. James Hulbert, in *Deconstruction and Criticism* (New York: Seabury Press, 1979), 75–176, 102.

7. See Jacques Derrida, "Me—Psychoanalysis: An Introduction to *The Shell and the Kernel* by Nicolas Abraham," trans. Richard Klein, *Diacritics,* vol. 9, no. 1, Spring 1979, 4–12.

8. "For if the difficulties of translation can be anticipated . . . one should not begin by naively believing that the word 'deconstruction' corresponds in French to some clear and univocal signification. There is already in 'my' language a serious (*sombre*) problem of translation between what here or there can be envisaged for the word, and the usage itself, the reserves of the word." Jacques Derrida, "Letter to a Japanese Friend," trans. David Wood and Robert Bernasconi, in David Wood and Robert Bernasconi, eds., *Derrida and Differance* (Coventry: Parousia Press, 1985), 1–5, 1.

9. Martin Heidegger, "Building, Dwelling, Thinking," trans. Albert Hofstadter, in *Poetry, Language, Thought* (New York: Harper Colophon, 1971), 143–161.

10. Immanuel Kant, *Critique of Pure Reason,* trans. Norman Kemp Smith (London: MacMillan and Co., 1929), 47.

11. Ibid., 608.

12. Ibid., 14.

13. Martin Heidegger, *The Principle of Reason,* trans. Reginald Lilly (Bloomington: Indiana University Press, 1991), 127. "[T]hat upon which something rests, namely what lies present before us, supportive . . . the basis, the footing, that is, the ground." Ibid., 104. "In measuring itself up to that about which it thinks, true thinking seeks in the being itself that on which it supports and grounds itself. All true thinking finds grounds and has definite possibilities of grounding." Martin Heidegger, *The Metaphysical Foundations of Logic,* trans. Michael Heim (Bloomington: Indiana University Press, 1984), 20.

14. Martin Heidegger, *An Introduction to Metaphysics,* trans. Ralph Manheim (New Haven: Yale University Press, 1959), 2.

15. "[T]he foundation upon which traditional metaphysics is built is shaken and for this reason the proper edifice of *Metaphysica Specialis* begins to totter." Martin Heidegger, *Kant and the Problem of Metaphysics,* trans. Richard Taft (Bloomington: Indiana University Press, 1990), 85.

16. Immanuel Kant, *Critique of Pure Reason,* 60.

17. "To this end, the general meaning of the term "laying the ground" [*Grundlegung*] must first be clarified. The expression's meaning is best illustrated if we consider the building trade. It is true that metaphysics is not a building or structure [*Gebäude*] that is at hand, but is really in all human beings 'as a natural construction or arrangement.' As a consequence, laying the ground for metaphysics can mean to lay a foundation [*Fundament*] under this natural metaphysics, or rather to replace one which has already been laid with a new one through a process of substituting. However, it is precisely this representation which we must keep out of the idea of a ground-laying, namely, that it is a matter of the byproduct from the foundation [*Grundlagen*] of an already-constructed building. Ground-laying is rather the projecting of the building plan itself so that it agrees with the direction concerning on what and how the building will be grounded. Laying the ground for metaphysics as the projecting [*Entwerfen*] of the building plan, however, is again no empty producing of a system and its subdivisions. It is rather the architectonic circumscription and delineation of the inner possibility of metaphysics, that is, the

concrete determination of its essence. All determination of essence, however, is first achieved in the setting-free of the essential ground.

Laying the ground as the projection of the inner possibility of metaphysics is thus necessarily a matter of letting the supporting power of the already-laid ground become operative. Whether and how this takes place is the criterion of the originality and scope of a ground-laying." Martin Heidegger, *Kant and the Problem of Metaphysics*, 1.

18. Jacques Derrida, "Structure, Sign and Play in the Discourse of the Human Sciences," in *Writing and Difference*, trans. Alan Bass (Chicago: University of Chicago Press, 1978), 278–294, 278.

19. "In architecture the chief point is a certain *use* of the artistic object to which, as the condition, the aesthetic ideas are limited . . . adaption of the product to a particular use is the essential element in a *work of architecture*." Immanuel Kant, *The Critique of Judgement*, trans. James Creed Meredith (London: Oxford University Press, 1952), 186.

20. Ibid., 188.

21. "Much might be added to a building that would immediately please the eye, were it not intended for a church." Ibid., 73.

22. Jacques Derrida, "Force and Signification," trans. Alan Bass, in Jacques Derrida, *Writing and Difference* (Chicago: University of Chicago Press, 1978), 3–30, 17. The essay goes on to argue that metaphor "is the essential weight which anchors discourse in metaphysics."

23. Ibid., 16.

24. Ibid., 5.

25. Ibid., 15.

26. Jacques Derrida, "White Mythology: Metaphor in the Text of Philosophy," trans. Alan Bass, in Jacques Derrida, *Margins of Philosophy* (Chicago: University of Chicago Press, 1982), 207–271, 224.

27. Some of the multiple complications this unique status produces can be seen when Derrida invokes the architectural "metaphor" to describe his sustained attempt to undermine the distinction between the conceptual system of philosophy and its metaphors: "I try to deconstruct the opposition between concept and metaphor and to rebuild, to restructure this field." Jacques Derrida, "Jacques Derrida on Rhetoric and Composition: A Conversation," interview with Gary A. Olson, *Journal of Advanced Composition*, 10, 1990, 1–21. 16. Deconstruction redeploys and undermines the image of architecture that, among so many other things, subordinates that very image of architecture.

28. Jacques Derrida, "Letter to a Japanese Friend," 1.

29. "With this problem of translation we will thus be dealing with nothing less than the problem of the very passage into philosophy." Jacques Derrida. "Plato's Pharmacy," trans. Barbara Johnson, in Jacques Derrida, *Dissemination* (Chicago: University of Chicago Press, 1981), 61–172, 72.

30. "Had their enterprise succeeded, the universal tongue would have been a particular language imposed by violence, by force, by violent hegemony over the rest of the world.

It would not have been a universal language—for example in the Leibnizian sense—a transparent language to which everyone would have had access." Jacques Derrida, "Roundtable on Translation," trans. Peggy Kamuf, in Christie V. McDonald, ed., *The Ear of the Other: Otobiography, Transference, Translation* (New York: Schocken Books, 1985), 91–162, 101. On the violent imposition of language, see also Jacques Derrida, "Languages and the Institutions of Philosophy," trans. Sylvia Soderlind et. al., *Recherche et Semiotique/Semiotic Inquiry,* vol. 4, no. 2, 1984, 91–154.

31. Jacques Derrida, "Roundtable on Translation," 102.

32. Jacques Derrida, "Architecture Where the Desire May Live," *Domus,* vol. 671, 1986, 17–25, 25.

33. Jacques Derrida. "'Genesis and Structure' and Phenomenology," trans. Alan Bass, in Jacques Derrida, *Writing and Difference* (Chicago: University of Chicago Press, 1978), 154–168, 155.

34. Jacques Derrida, "Des Tours de Babel," 184.

35. Ibid., 182.

36. Jacques Derrida, "Deconstruction in America: An Interview with Jacques Derrida," interview with James Creech, Peggy Kamuf, and Jane Todd, *Critical Exchange,* no. 17, Winter 1985, 1–33, 13.

37. "[I]n spite of appearances, deconstruction is neither an *analysis* nor a *critique* and its translation would have to take that into consideration. It is not an analysis in particular because the dismantling of a structure is not a regression toward a *simple element,* toward an *indissoluble origin.* These values, like that of analysis, are themselves philosophemes subject to deconstruction." Jacques Derrida, "Letter to a Japanese Friend," 3.

38. Jacques Derrida, "Des Tours de Babel," 165.

39. Jacques Derrida, "On Colleges and Philosophy," interview with Geoff Bennington, *ICA Documents 4: Postmodernism,* 1986, 66–71, 70.

Unbuilding Architecture

1. Jacques Derrida, "Différance," trans. Alan Bass in Jacques Derrida, *Margins of Philosophy* (Chicago: University of Chicago Press, 1982), 1–27, 21.

2. Jacques Derrida, "Limited Inc., a b c . . . ," trans. Samuel Weber, in Jacques Derrida, *Limited Inc.* (Evanston: Northwestern University Press, 1988), 34.

3. Jacques Derrida, "Architecture Where the Desire May Live," 18.

4. Martin Heidegger, *What Is a Thing?* trans. W. B. Barton and Vera Deutsch (Chicago: Henry Regnery Company, 1967), 118–121.

5. Ibid., 123.

6. Martin Heidegger, *The Basic Problems of Phenomenology,* trans. Albert Hofstadter (Bloomington: Indiana University Press, 1982), 22.

225

7. Ibid.

8. "Philosophy can be characterized only from and in historical recollection. But this recollection is only what it is, is only living, in the moment of self-understanding, and that means in one's own free, productive grasp of the task harbored in philosophy. The ways of historical recollection and of reflection on the present are not two ways, but are both essential elements of every way toward the idea of philosophy. This idea is to be defined not by our devising, say, a so-called modern notion of philosophy, so that we may then consult the history of philosophy in retrospect to find out what has already been thought and intimated of our idea and what has not. Nor is it an appropriate procedure for us to pick out a philosophy from history, be it the philosophy of Plato or Aristotle, or of Leibniz or Kant, and simply install ourselves in it as in the presumptive truth, in order then to tailor and supplement it, as it were, for modern needs. There is not a historical definition of philosophy and next to it a so-called systematic definition, nor conversely. . . . the distinction is spurious and must be eliminated." Martin Heidegger, *The Metaphysical Foundations of Logic*, 8.

9. "But this destruction is just as far from having the *negative* sense of shaking off the ontological tradition. We must, on the contrary, stake out the positive possibilities of that tradition, and this always means keeping it within its *limits* . . ." Martin Heidegger, *Being and Time*, trans. John Macquarrie and Edward Robinson (New York: Harper and Row, 1962), 44.

10. Martin Heidegger, *An Introduction to Metaphysics*, 93. "We speak of an abyss where the ground falls away and a ground is lacking to us, where we seek the ground and set out to arrive at a ground, to get to the bottom of something." Martin Heidegger, "Language," trans. Albert Hofstadter, in Martin Heidegger, *Poetry, Language, Thought* (New York: Harper and Row, 1971), 187–210, 191.

11. "What the principle of reason states in its ordinary formulation has in some fashion always resounded in Western thought. Yet measured historiographically, two thousand three hundred years were needed until the principle of reason came to light and let itself be set up as a fundamental principle." Martin Heidegger, *The Principle of Reason*, 53.

12. Ibid., 13.

13. Ibid.

14. Ibid., 100.

15. Ibid., 9.

16. Ibid., 13.

17. This degenerate translation is based on a degeneration that already occurred within the original Greek, requiring a return to a more primordial origin: "But with this Latin translation the original meaning of the Greek word *physis* is thrust aside, the actual philosophical force of the Greek word is destroyed. This is true not only of the Latin translation of *this* word but of all other Roman translations of the Greek philosophical language. What happened in this translation from the Greek into the Latin is not accidental and harmless; it marks the first stage in the process by which we cut ourselves off and alienated ourselves from the original essence of Greek philosophy. . . . But it should be said in passing that even within Greek philosophy a narrowing of the word set in forthwith, although the original meaning did not vanish from the experience, knowl-

edge, and orientation of Greek philosophy." Martin Heidegger, *An Introduction to Metaphysics*, 13.

18. "The perfection of technology is only the echo of the demand for *perfectio*, which means, the completeness of a foundation. . . . Modern technology pushes toward the greatest possible perfection. Perfection is based on the thoroughgoing calculability of objects. The calculability of objects presupposes the unqualified validity of the *principium rationis*. It is in this way that the authority characteristic of the principle of ground determines the essence of the modern, technological age." Martin Heidegger, "The Principle of Reason," the 1956 address published in *The Principle of Reason*, 117–129, 121.

19. "Only what presents itself to our cognition, only what we en-counter such that it is posed and posited in its reasons, counts as something with secure standing, that means, as an object. Only what stands in this manner is something of which we can, with certainty, say 'it is.' Only what is brought to a stand in a founded representation counts as a being." Martin Heidegger, *The Principle of Reason*, 27.

20. Ibid., 49.

21. Ibid., 51.

22. Of the word "deconstruction," Derrida argues that "Among other things I wished to translate and adapt to my own ends the Heideggerian word *Destruktion* or *Abbau*." Jacques Derrida, "Letter to a Japanese Friend," 1.

23. Jacques Derrida, "Roundtable on Autobiography," trans. Peggy Kamuf, in Christie V. McDonald, ed., *The Ear of the Other: Otobiography, Transference, Translation* (New York: Schocken Books, 1985), 39–90, 86.

24. Jacques Derrida. "Letter to a Japanese Friend," 1.

25. "On the word 'deconstruction,' which in my mind was intended to translate a word such as *Abbau* in Heidegger—*Destruktion* in Heidegger is not a negative word either—it's a matter of gaining access to the mode in which a system or structure, or ensemble, is constructed or constituted, historically speaking. Not to destroy it, or demolish it, nor to purify it, but in order to accede to its possibilities and its meaning; to its construction and its history." "Jacques Derrida in Conversation," interview with Raul Mortley in Raul Mortley, ed., *French Philosophers in Conversation: Derrida, Irigary, Levinas, Le Doeuff, Schneider, Serres* (London: Routledge, 1990), 92–108, 97.

26. Jacques Derrida, "From Restricted to General Economy: A Hegelianism without Reserve," trans. Alan Bass, in Jacques Derrida, *Writing and Difference* (Chicago: University of Chicago Press, 1978), 251–277, 260.

27. "But we must not equate such a shaking of the foundations [of all of man's thinking] with revolution and collapse. The shaking of that which exists may be the way by which an equilibrium arises, a position of rest such as have never been—because that rest, that peace, is already present at the heart of the shock." Martin Heidegger, *What Is Called Thinking*, trans. J. Glenn Gray (New York: Harper and Row, 1968), 65.

28. Jacques Derrida, *Of Grammatology*, trans. Gayatri Chakravorty Spivak (Baltimore: Johns Hopkins University Press, 1976), 163.

29. Jacques Derrida, "Fors: The Anguish Words of Nicolas Abraham and Maria Torok," foreward to Nicolas Abraham and Maria Torok, *The Wolf Man's Magic Word*, trans. Nicolas Rand (Minneapolis: University of Minnesota Press, 1986), xi-xlviii, xxiii.

30. Jacques Derrida, *Glas*, trans. John P. Leavy, Jr. and Richard Rand (Lincoln: University of Nebraska Press, 1986), 200.

31. Ibid., 110.

32. Jacques Derrida, "Force and Signification," 6.

33. Jacques Derrida, "The Art of *Mémoires*," trans. Jonathan Culler, in Jacques Derrida, *Memoires for Paul De Man*. (New York: Columbia University Press, 1986), 45–88, 72.

34. Ibid., 73.

35. Ibid., 73.

36. "The 'de-' of *de*construction signifies not the demolition of what is constructing itself, but rather what remains to be thought beyond the constructivist or destructionist scheme." Jacques Derrida, "Afterword: Towards an Ethic of Discussion," trans. Samuel Weber, in Jacques Derrida, *Limited Inc.* (Evanston: Northwestern University Press, 1988), 111–160, 147.

37. "As a cornerstone, it supports it, however rickety it may be, and brings together at a single point all its forces and tensions. It does not do this from a central commanding point, like a *keystone;* but it also does it, laterally, in its corner." Jacques Derrida, "The Art of *Mémoires*," 74.

38. Jacques Derrida, "Architecture Where the Desire May Live," 18.

39. Jacques Derrida, "Force and Signification," 6.

40. "If deconstruction were to find itself faced with some objects, or an *object* (I leave aside for the moment the question about this word and this concept, because I am not sure that deconstruction is concerned with something like an *object* or objects), it would not be simply a constructum or a structure that would have to be undone in order to uncover its archeological ground, its original foundation (or as someone recently put it, with a barely disguised and triumphant ingenuity, a *radical* beginning). On the contrary, it has been clear from the beginning that deconstructive questioning takes aim at and *against* such a fundamental mytho-radicology. At the same time, the question bears upon the philosophical project insofar as it requires a foundation, an architectonics and a systematics . . . ["Si la déconstruction se trouvait devant des objets, ou un *object* (je laisse pour l'instant la question de ce mot et de ce concept, n'étant pas sûr que la déconstruction ait affaire à quelque chose comme un ou des *objets*), ce ne serait pas seulement un constructum ou une structure qu'il faudrait défaire pour dégager enfin son sol archéologique, son fondement originaire ou, comme on l'a écrit récemment avec une ingénuité triomphante et à peine feinte, un commencement *radical*. Il a été clair dés le départ, au contraire, que la mise en question déconstructrice porte avec insistance *sur* et *contre* une telle mytho-radicologie fondamentale. Du même coup, la question porte sur le projet philosophique en tant qu'il exige le fondement et l'architectonique, le systémique . . .]" Jacques Derrida, "Ja, ou le faux-bond," *Digraphe*, 11, March 1977, 83–121, 118.

41. "Une pratique déconstructice qui ne porterait pas sur 'des appareils institutionnels et des processus historiques' . . . qui se contenterait de travailler sur des philosophèmes

ou des signifiés conceptuels, des discours, etc., ne serait pas déconstructrice; elle reproduirait, quelle que soit son originalité, le mouvement autocritique de la philosophie dans sa tradition interne." Ibid., 117.

42. Jacques Derrida, "Parergon," trans. Geoff Bennington and Ian McLeod, in Jacques Derrida, *The Truth In Painting* (Chicago: University of Chicago Press, 1987), 15–147, 19.

43. Jacques Derrida, "The Principle of Reason: The University in the Eyes of its Pupils," trans. Catherine Porter and Edward P. Morris, *Diacritics*, vol. 13, no. 3, 1983, 3–20, 3.

44. Ibid., 16.

45. Jacques Derrida, "Languages and Institutions of Philosophy," 135.

46. Ibid., 135.

47. "If those of us here are aware of ourselves as belonging to the university, then we move on the basis upon which the university itself rests. That is the principle of reason. However, what remains astounding is that we who are here have still never encountered the principle of reason . . . If the university is not built upon a principle, then perhaps it is built upon that about which the principle speaks?" Martin Heidegger, *The Principle of Reason*, 28.

48. "Un événement de fondation ne peut être simplement compris dans la logique de ce qu'il fonde." Jacques Derrida, "Mochlos ou le conflit des facultés," *Philosophie*, 2, April 1984, 21–53, 50.

49. "Mais la responsabilité minimale aujourd'hui, et en tous cas la plus intéressante, la plus nouvelle, la plus forte, pour quiconque appartient à une institution de recherche ou d'enseignement, c'est peut-être de rendre aussi claires et aussi thématiques que possible une telle implication politique, son système ou ses apories." Ibid., 41.

50. "Le lisant aujourd'hui, je perçois son assurance et sa nécessité comme on peut admirer la rigueur d'un plan ou d'une structure à travers les brèches d'un édifice inhabitable et dont on ne saurait décider s'il est en ruines ou s'il n'a simplement jamais existé, n'ayant jamais pu qu'abriter le discours de son inachèvement." Ibid., 30.

51. "Toute l'architectonique." Ibid., 33.

52. See, particularly, Martin Heidegger, *The Essence of Reasons,* trans. Terrence Malick (Evanston: Northwestern University Press, 1969), 105–111.

53. "Un concept institutionnel est en jeu." Jacques Derrida, "Mochlos ou le conflit des facultés," 41.

54. "Certaines institutions artificielles, dit-il alors, ont pour fondement une idée de la raison." Ibid., 23.

55. "L'institution, ce ne sont pas seulement des murs et des murs et des structures extérieures qui entourent, protègent, garantissent ou contraignent la liberté de notre travail, c'est aussi et déjà la structure de notre interprétation. Dès lors, si elle prétend à quelque conséquence, ce qu'on appelle très vite *la* déconstruction n'est jamais un ensemble technique de procédures discursives, encore moins une nouvelle méthode herméneutique travaillant sur des archives ou des énoncés à l'abri d'une institution donnée et stable; c'est aussi, et au moins, une prise de position, dans le travail même, à l'égard

de structures politico-institutionnelles qui constituent et règlent notre pratique, nos compétences et nos perfomances. Précisément parce qu'elle n'a jamais concerné seulement des contenus de sens, la déconstruction devrait ne pas être séparable de cette problématique politico-institutionnelle et requérir un questionnement nouveau sur la responsabilité, un questionnement qui ne se fie plus nécessairement aux codes hérités du politique ou de l'éthique. Ce qui fait que, trop politique aux yeux des uns, elle puisse paraître démobilisante aux yeux de ceux qui ne reconnaissent le politique qu'à l'aide des panneaux de signalisation d'avant la guerre." Ibid, 41.

56. "But the available codes for taking such a political stance are not at all adequate to the radicality of deconstruction. And the absence of an adequate political code to translate or incorporate the radical implications of deconstruction has given many the impression that deconstruction is opposed to politics, or is at best apolitical. But this impression only prevails because all of our political codes and terminologies still remain fundamentally metaphysical, regardless of whether they originate from the right or the left." Jacques Derrida, "Deconstruction and the Other," in Richard Kearney, ed., *Dialogues with Contemporary Continental Thinkers* (Manchester: Manchester University Press, 1984), 105–126, 120. "The signs by which you recognize that a discourse is political: that's an enormous question, one that has always mattered to me. I think that my work, from that point of view, has always been preoccupied by the question of the political, of what was political. At the same time one has to avoid letting one's discourse be ruled by the signals that are the usual criteria on this subject." Jacques Derrida, "The Derridean View: An Inter-view with Jacques Derrida," interview with Edward Marx, trans. Mary Ann Caws, *BM104*, vol. 2, no. 1, Sept. 1988, 4–5, 5.

57. The political threat posed by deconstructive discourse is produced by its displacement of the condition of architecture, a displacement that transforms the political. When describing its analysis of the hidden assumptions on which institutional powers "are built," Derrida argues that "what is considered threatening is not a politically revolutionary position, if it is expressed in a coded and traditional way, rather, it is something which sometimes doesn't look political but disturbs the traditional ways of reading, understanding, discussing, writing, using rhetoric, etc.—because this undermines, or not necessarily undermines, but at least discovers, what was hidden in the institution." Jacques Derrida, "Some Questions and Responses," Nigel Fabb et al., eds., *The Linguistics of Writing: Arguments between Language and Literature* (Manchester: Manchester University Press, 1987), 252–264, 256.

58. Jacques Derrida, "On Colleges and Philosophy," 69.

59. "Hence the necessity for deconstruction to deal with texts in a different way than as discursive contents, themes or theses, but always as institutional structures, and, as is commonly said, as being political-juridical-sociohistorical—none of these last words being reliable enough to be used easily, hence their relative rare use in the most cautious texts called deconstructive." Jacques Derrida, "Some Statements and Truisms about Neo-logisms, Newisms, Postisms, Parasitisms, and Other Small Seismisms," trans. Anne Tomiche, in David Carroll, ed., *The States of "Theory": History, Art and Critical Discourse* (New York: Columbia University Press, 1990), 63–94, 86.

60. Ibid., 64.

61. Ibid., 67.

62. Ibid., 68.

63. Ibid., 93.

64. Ibid., 88.

65. This trembling movement that founds the structure of the university is not confined to that structure. On the contrary, it marks that structure's participation in all of those institutional structures its walls appear to isolate itself from: "What we call deconstruction is . . . How shall I say? Imagine a great earthquake throughout California. And then in a university somebody sees a crack appear. Well, deconstruction—deconstruction under that name, and in the form of the discourses we've been referring to in the last few minutes—is the Western, literary, philosophical academic form for the essential part of this great human earthquake which is rocking all the structures of humanity. The logical, economic, social structures, etc." Jacques Derrida, "Deconstruction in America: An Interview With Jacques Derrida," 18.

66. Jacques Derrida. "Du Tout," trans. Alan Bass, in Jacques Derrida, *The Post Card: From Socrates to Freud and Beyond* (Chicago: University of Chicago Press, 1987), 497–521, 508.

67. Ibid., 519.

68. When speaking of the "translation" of deconstruction in America, Derrida argues that "I don't know if there is an original of deconstruction," that, if anything, deconstruction is itself already a translation: "The word 'deconstruction' itself has a whole genealogy. It's an old French word which had fallen out of use, that I used for the first time, so to speak, in this particular sense. But I did so with the sense that I was translating and deforming a word of Freud's and a word of Heidegger's. In Heidegger the word is 'Abbau,' as well as 'Destruktion.' But deconstruction is neither Heidegger's *Abbau* nor *Destruktion*, although it is related, naturally. So already the 'first use' of the word deconstruction was a sort of deforming translation in which the schema of an original requiring a supplement and so forth, was made to point back towards *Abbau* and *Destruktion*." Jacques Derrida. "Deconstruction in America: An Interview with Jacques Derrida," 22.

The Slippery Art of Space

1. Martin Heidegger, "The Principle of Reason" [the 1956 address] *The Principle of Reason*, 123.

2. Martin Heidegger, "The Origin of the Work of Art," in *Poetry, Language, Thought*, trans. Albert Hofstadter (New York: Harper and Row, 1971), 41.

3. Ibid.

4. Ibid, 43.

5. The Greek temple is neither a representation of the ground nor even a presentation, but its very production: "Truth happens in the temple's standing where it is. This does not mean that something is correctly represented and rendered there, but that what is as a whole is brought into unconcealedness and held therein." Ibid., 56.

6. Martin Heidegger, *Nietzsche, Vol. III: The Will to Power as Knowledge and as Metaphysics*, trans. David Farrell Krell (San Francisco: Harper and Row, 1987), 143.

7. Martin Heidegger, *The Principle of Reason*, 49.

8. "Being 'is' in essence: ground/reason. Therefore being can never first have a ground/reason which would supposedly ground it. . . . Being 'is' the abyss in the sense

of such a remaining-apart of reason from being. To the extent that being as such grounds, it remains groundless." Ibid, 51. "Being is intrinsically groundlike, what gives ground, presences as the ground, has the character of ground. Precisely because it is groundlike, groundgiving, it cannot need a ground. The groundlike is groundless, what grounds, what presences as basis does not need the ground; that is, it is without something to which it could go back as something outside of it, there is no longer any back, no behind itself, but pure presencing itself: the primordial." Martin Heidegger, *Schelling's Treatise on the Essence of Human Freedom*, trans. Joan Stambaugh (Athens: Ohio University Press, 1985), 170.

9. Martin Heidegger, "The Origin of the Work of Art," 20.

10. Ibid., 41.

11. In these lectures, Heidegger defends his assertion of the "priority" of the word for the Greeks whereby "poetizing and thinking had the highest rank" against the traditional view that architecture and sculpture were of a "higher rank." He argues that this question of rank only emerged with the aesthetic conception of art that "commences precisely (by essential necessity) with the inception of metaphysics" in Plato's texts and is sustained by the everyday "erroneous" view that "Architecture and sculpture use as their matter the relatively stable material of wood, stone, steel. They are independent of the fleeting breath of the quickly fading and, moreover, ambiguous word." Martin Heidegger, *Parmenides*, trans. André Schuwer and Richard Rojcewicz (Bloomington: Indiana University Press, 1992), 114–6. Against this view, he goes on to argue that "Indeed architecture and sculpture do not use the word as their matter. But how could there ever be temples or statues, existing for what they are, without the word? . . . the circumstance that in a temple or a statue of Apollo there are no words as material to be worked upon and "formed" by no means proves that these "works," in what they are and how they are, do not still need the word in an essential way. The essence of the word does not at all consist in its vocal sound, nor in loquacity and noise, and not in its merely technical function in the communication of information. The statue and the temple stand in silent dialogue with man in the unconcealed. If there were not the *silent word*, then the looking god as sight of the statue and of the features of its figure could never appear. And a temple could never, without standing in the disclosive domain of the word, present itself as the house of a god. The fact that the Greeks did not describe and talk about their 'works of art' 'aesthetically' bears witness to the fact that these works stood well secured in the clarity of the word, without which a column would not be a column, a tympanum a tympanum, a frieze a frieze . . . These 'works' *exist* only in the medium of the word." Ibid., 116. But inasmuch as Heidegger assumes that the word is prior to architecture, that there can be word without architecture, he has restored the very sense of rank, as well as the tradition of metaphysics, he claims to resist. At the same time, as he does in "The Origin of the Work of Art," he tacitly thinks of the word in architectural terms by giving it a structuring role, in the sense that, for him, art is "secured" by the word. The very idea of rank as a vertical structure, which he at once employs and discredits, is bound to the image of architecture he is attempting to subordinate. In the end, the "priority" of the word over architecture is not established. Rather, it is radically complicated.

12. Jacques Derrida, "Restitutions of the Truth in Pointing [*pointure*]," trans. Geoff Bennington and Ian McLeod, in Jacques Derrida, *The Truth in Painting* (Chicago: University of Chicago Press, 1987), 255–382, 262.

13. Jacques Derrida, "Parergon," 22.

14. Jacques Derrida, "Implications," interview with Henri Rose, trans. Alan Bass, in Jacques Derrida, *Positions* (Chicago: University of Chicago Press, 1981), 1–14, 10.

15. Jacques Derrida, *Of Grammatology*, 15.

16. Ibid., 44.

17. Ibid., 24.

18. Ibid., 98.

19. Ibid., 196.

20. Ibid., 166.

21. "The ideal form of a written signifier, for example, is not in the world, and the distinction between the grapheme and the empirical body of the corresponding graphic sign separates an inside from an outside, phenomenological consciousness from the world. And this is true for every visual or spatial signifier. And yet every non-phonic signifier involves a spatial reference in its very 'phenomenon,' in the phenomenological (nonworldly) sphere of experience in which it is given. The sense of being 'outside,' 'in the world,' is an essential component of its phenomenon. Apparently there is nothing like this in the phenomenon of speech." Jacques Derrida, *Speech and Phenomena: Introduction to the Problem of Signs in Husserl's Phenomenology*, trans. David B. Allison (Evanston: Northwestern University Press, 1973), 76. "This is why hearing oneself speak [*s'entendre parler*] is experienced as an absolutely pure auto-affection, occurring in a self-proximity that would in fact be the absolute reduction of space in general." Ibid., 79.

22. Jacques Derrida, *Of Grammatology*, 166.

23. Ibid., 290.

24. Jacques Derrida, "Plato's Pharmacy," 109.

25. Jacques Derrida, *Speech and Phenomena: Introduction to the Problem of Signs in Husserl's Phenomenology*, 86.

26. Jacques Derrida, *Of Grammatology*, 69. "A voice may detach itself from the body, from the very first instant it may cease to belong to it. By which it traces, it is a trace, a spacing, a writing." Jacques Derrida, "Voice II . . .," trans. Verena Andermatt Conley. *Boundary II.* vol. 12, no. 2, 1984, 76–93, 79. This sense of "spacing" is precisely opposed to that occasionally employed by Heidegger for whom "spacing" [*Abstand*] is only the spatial distance between geometric points. Martin Heidegger, *History of the Concept of Time: Prolegomena*, trans. Theodore Kisiel (Bloomington: Indiana University Press, 1985), 228.

27. Jacques Derrida, *Of Grammatology*, 232. "Whether it be linked by its origin to the representations of things in space or whether it remains caught in a system of phonic differences or social classifications apparently released from ordinary space, the proper-ness of the name does not escape spacing." Therefore it must be "*situated.*" Ibid., 89.

28. Ibid., 290.

29. "This fissure is not one among others. It is *the* fissure: the necessity of interval, the harsh law of spacing." Ibid., 200.

30. Ibid., 203.

31. Ibid., 200. Writing is a "ciphered spacing," an "essential spacing" such that "Spatiali-zation does not surprise the time of speech or the ideality of meaning, it does not happen

to them like an accident. . . . every symbolic synthesis, even before it falls into a space 'exterior' to it, includes within itself spacing as difference." Jacques Derrida, "Freud and the Scene of Writing," trans. Alan Bass, in Jacques Derrida, *Writing and Difference* (Chicago: University of Chicago Press, 1978), 196–231, 219.

32. "An interval must separate the present from what it is not in order for the present to be itself, but this interval that constitutes it as present must, by the same token, divide the present in and of itself, thereby also dividing, along with the present, everything that is thought on the basis of the present, that is, in our metaphysical language, every being, and singularily substance or the subject. In constituting itself, in dividing itself dynamically, this interval is what might be called *spacing*, . . ." Jacques Derrida, "Différance," 13. This spacing is the basis of Derrida's quasi concept of "différance": "*Différer* in this sense is to temporize . . . this temporization is also temporalization and spacing, the becoming-time of space and becoming-space of time . . . The other sense of *différer* . . . is a question of dissimilar otherness or of allergic and polemical otherness, an interval, a distance, *spacing*, must be produced between the elements other, and be produced with a certain perseverance in repetition. . . . *Différance* as temporization, *différance* as spacing." Ibid., 8.

33. Jacques Derrida, *Of Grammatology*, 201.

34. Ibid., 280.

35. Ibid., 160.

36. Jacques Derrida, "Desistance," trans. Christopher Fynsk, introduction to Christopher Fynsk, ed., *Typography: Mimesis, Philosophy, Politics* (Cambridge: Harvard University Press, 1989), 1–42, 32–33.

37. Jacques Derrida, "Deconstruction and the Other," 109.

38. Jacques Derrida, "Semiology and Grammatology," 27.

39. Jacques Derrida, "Positions," interview with Jean-Louis Houdebine and Guy Scarpetta, trans. Alan Bass, In Jacques Derrida, *Positions* (Chicago: University of Chicago Press, 1981), 37–96, 106.

40. Ibid., 81.

41. Ibid., 94. "Since the trace is the intimate relation of the living present with its outside, the openness upon exteriority in general, upon the sphere of what is not 'one's own,' etc. *the temporalization of sense is, from the outset, a 'spacing.'* As soon as we admit spacing both as 'interval' or difference and as openness upon the outside, there can no longer be any absolute inside, for the 'outside' has insinuated itself into the movement by which the inside of the nonspatial, which is called 'time,' appears, is constituted, is 'presented.' Space is 'in' time." Jacques Derrida, *Speech and Phenomena: Introduction to the Problem of Signs in Husserl's Phenomenology*, 86.

42. "Le tout sans nouveauté / qu'un espacement / de la lecture." Jacques Derrida, *Writing and Difference* (Chicago: University of Chicago Press, 1978), v. The citation is from Mallarmé's preface to *Un Coup de dés*.

43. "It is evident that the concept of spacing, by itself, cannot account for anything, any more than any other concept. It cannot account for the differences—the different things—between which is opened the spacing which nevertheless delimits them. But it would be to accord a theological function to this concept to expect it to be an explicating

principle of all determined spaces, of all different things. Spacing certainly operates in all fields, but precisely as different fields. And its operation is different each time, articulated otherwise." Jacques Derrida, "Positions," 81. "Of course, if I had only endlessly repeated the unique word *spacing*, you would be completely right. But I have no less insisted on the *other* and on several others. Spacing also signifies, precisely, the impossibility of reducing the chain to one of its links or of absolutely privileging one—or the other." Ibid., 107.

44. Jacques Derrida, *Of Grammatology*, 101.

45. "We have now been brought quite naturally to the problem of the *composition* of the *Essay:* not only of the time of its writing, but of the space of its structure. Rousseau divided it into chapters belatedly. What scheme guided him? The architecture must find its justification in the deep intention of the *Essay.* It is for that reason that it interests us. Yet we must not confound the meaning of the architecture with the declared intention of the work." Ibid., 195.

46. Ibid., 216.

47. Derrida looks, for example, at the "spacings" of the preface ("A certain spacing between concept and being-there, between concept and existence, between thought and time, would thus constitute the rather unqualifiable lodging of the preface." [Jacques Derrida, "Outwork, Prefacing," trans. Barbara Johnson, in Jacques Derrida, *Dissemination* (Chicago: University of Chicago Press, 1981), 1–59, 12.]), the margins (which produce both "the inequality of the internal spacings" of the "space" of philosophy and the apparent "regularity of its borders." [Jacques Derrida, "Tymphan," trans. Alan Bass, in Jacques Derrida, *Margins of Philosophy* (Chicago: University of Chicago Press, 1982), ix–xxix, xxiv]), and the title (Jacques Derrida, "Title (To Be Specified)," trans. Tom Conley, *Sub-Stance*, 31, 1981, 5–22.).

48. "Heidegger seems almost never to speak about sexuality or sexual difference. And he seems almost never to speak about psychoanalysis, give or take an occasional negative allusion. This is neither negligence nor omission. The pauses coming from his silence on these questions punctuate or create the spacing out of a powerful discourse." Jacques Derrida, "Choreographies," trans. Christie V. McDonald, *Diacritics,* vol. 12, no. 2, 1982, 66–76, 74.

49. Jacques Derrida, "Mallarmé," trans. Christine Roulston, in Derek Attridge, ed., *Acts of Literature* (New York: Routledge, 1992), 110–126, 120.

50. Ibid., 116. "For example, the sign *blanc* ('white,' 'blank,' 'space'), with all that is associated with it from one thing to the next, is a huge reservoir of meaning . . . It permeates Mallarmé's entire text . . . And yet, the white also marks, through the intermediary of the white page, the place of the writing of those 'whites'; and first of all the spacing between the different significations (that of white among others), *the spacing of reading.*" Ibid., 115.

51. Jacques Derrida, "Ce que j'aurais dit . . . ," in *Le complexe de Léonard ou la Société de création* (Paris: Editions de Nouvel Observateur, 1984) 77–92, 92.

52. When Derrida elaborates Genet's description of the newspaper report of a trial ("only ten lines, widely enough spaced to let the air circulate between the over-violent words"), he argues that "In writing's spacing, during the trial of the narrative [*récit*], the vertical lines (necktie, rain, glaive, cane or umbrella tip [*éperon*]) cut the horizontal lines of the newspaper or the book, of the wings or the spokes of the umbrella. Language cuts,

decollates, unglues, decapitates. The sentences coil around a direction like liana along a truncated column." Jacques Derrida, *Glas,* 74.

53. Ibid., 75.

54. "Two unequal columns, they say distyle [*disent-ils*], each of which—envelop(e)(s) or sheath(es), incalculably reverses, turns inside out, replaces, remarks [*recoupe*] the other." Jacques Derrida, Ibid., 1. When Derrida writes about the translation of *Glas* into English, he elaborates this play that binds text to architecture while arguing that the status of the translation can never be secured for speakers of either language: "Not for this at once trivial and false reason, that both would be imprisoned in the house of their own tongue, as if in a house in the form of a closed cylinder they could not go out of in order to go round [*faire le tour*], from one turn (of phrase) [*d'un tour*] or tower [*d'une tour*] to the other, in order to see what is heard from the neighboring cylinder. Now this book *presents itself* as a volume *of* cylindric columns, writes *on* pierced, incrusted, breached, tattooed cylindric columns, on them then, but also *around* them, *against* them, *between* them that are, through and through, tongue and text. *Kulindros* always names a round body, a conveyor roller for displacing stones, for example in the construction of monuments, pyramids, or obelisks, of other columns . . . *Kulindros* is also occasionally a rolled manuscript, a parchment scroll. So one is never enclosed in the column of one single tongue." Jacques Derrida, "Proverb: 'He that would pun . . . ,'" trans. John P. Leavy, Jr. in John P. Leavy, Jr., *Glassary* (Lincoln: University of Nebraska Press, 1986), 17–21, 17.

55. Jacques Derrida, "Implications," 14.

56. Jacques Derrida, "The Pit and the Pyramid: Introduction to Hegel's Semiology," trans. Alan Bass, in Jacques Derrida, *Margins of Philosophy* (Chicago: University of Chicago Press, 1982), 69–108, 105.

57. Ibid., 94.

58. Derrida describes each of the chain of terms he coins as having the "strange status" of "an aconceptual concept or another kind of concept, heterogeneous to the philosophical concept of the concept, a "concept" that marks both the possibility and the limit of all idealization and hence of all conceptualization." Jacques Derrida, "Afterword: Toward an Ethic of Discussion," 118.

59. Jacques Derrida, "How to Avoid Speaking: Denials," trans. Ken Frieden; Sandford Budick and Wolfgang Iser, eds., *Languages of the Unsayable: The Play of Negativity in Literature and Literary Theory* (New York: Columbia University Press, 1989), 3–70, 27.

60. On the "space of the classroom" and "auditorium," see Martin Heidegger, *What Is a Thing?*, 18–19; Martin Heidegger, *History of the Concept of Time,* 157–158; and Martin Heidegger, *The Basic Problems of Phenomenology,* 162–164.

61. Immanuel Kant, *The Critique of Judgement,* 68.

62. Ibid., 67.

63. Jacques Derrida, "Parergon," 59.

64. Jacques Derrida, *Of Grammatology,* 245.

65. Ibid., 167.

66. By no coincidence, the supplement in *Of Grammatology* is the "keystone . . . destined to reconstitute Nature's edifice." Ibid., 145.

67. See Mark Wigley, "Architecture after Philosophy: Le Corbusier and the Emperor's New Paint," *Journal of Philosophy and the Visual Arts*, no. 2, 1990, 84–95.

68. Jacques Derrida, "Parergon," 49.

69. Ibid., 59.

70. Immanuel Kant, *The Critique of Judgement*, 5.

71. Ibid., 159.

72. Jacques Derrida, "Parergon," 39.

73. Immanuel Kant, *The Critique of Judgement*, Part II, 33.

74. Ibid., Part I, 185.

75. Ibid., 160.

76. Ibid., Part II, 67.

77. Jacques Derrida, "Parergon," 40.

78. Martin Heidegger, "Building, Dwelling, Thinking," 159.

79. The text, which at one points examines and discredits the common association between the structure of scholastic philosophy and that of gothic cathedrals, addresses at length the "architectonic" idea of philosophical "system" ("*the* task of philosophy") as a building, before concluding by describing "construction as knowledge." In so doing, he locates philosophy in the "uneasy" domain between "the inner jointure giving things their foundation and support" and "mere external manipulation." He describes the endless slippage between these poles: "This fact points out that this inner possibility of wavering between jointure and manipulation and framework always belongs to system, that every genuine system always remains threatened by the decline into what is spurious, that every spurious system can always give the appearance of being genuine." Martin Heidegger, *Schelling's Treatise on the Essence of Human Freedom*, 26 "This strife between freedom as the beginning which needs no ground and system as a closed foundational context is, understood correctly, the inmost motive and law of motion of philosophy itself. Not only the object, but the state of philosophy." Ibid., 62.

80. Jacques Derrida, "Restitutions of the Truth in Pointing," 288.

81. Ibid., 290.

82. Note how Derrida argues that the university is "built" on the ideal of translation (Jacques Derrida, "Living On: *Border Lines*," 93–94) in the same way that he argues that it is "built" on the ideal of ground-as-support (Jacques Derrida, "The Principle of Reason: The University in the Eyes of Reason.").

83. "*Beneath* [emphasis added] the seemingly literal and thus faithful translation there is concealed, rather, a *trans*lation of Greek experience into a different way of thinking . . . *without a corresponding, equally authentic experience of what they say* . . . The rootlessness of

Western thought begins with this translation." Martin Heidegger, "The Origin of the Work of Art," 23. "We are not merely taking refuge in a more literal translation of a Greek word. We are reminding ourselves of what, unexperienced and unthought, *underlies* our familiar and therefore outworn nature of truth in the sense of correctness." Ibid., 52 [emphasis added].

84. Jacques Derrida, "Restitutions of the Truth in Pointing," 290.

The Domestication of the House

1. Martin Heidegger, "Letter on Humanism," trans. David Farrell Krell, in *Martin Heidegger: Basic Writings* (New York: Harper and Row, 1977), 193–242, 193.

2. Jacques Derrida, "*Ousia* and *Grammé*: Note on a Note from *Being and Time*," trans. Alan Bass, in *Margins of Philosophy* (Chicago: University of Chicago Press, 1982), 29–68, 48.

3. Jacques Derrida, "Deconstruction and the Other," 109.

4. Jacques Derrida, "The *Retrait* of Metaphor," trans. by editors, *Enclitic*, vol. 2, no. 2, 1978, 5–34, 12.

5. Jacques Derrida, "Positions," 54.

6. Jacques Derrida, "The Ends of Man," trans. Alan Bass, in Jacques Derrida, *Margins of Philosophy* (Chicago: University of Chicago Press, 1982), 109–136, 130.

7. Ibid., 135.

8. Jacques Derrida, *Of Grammatology*, 22.

9. Jacques Derrida, "The *Retrait* of Metaphor," 25. "This hearth is the heart of all metaphoricity." Jacques Derrida, "Plato's Pharmacy," 88.

10. Jacques Derrida, "Le facteur de la vérité," trans. Alan Bass, in Jacques Derrida, *The Postcard: From Socrates to Freud and Beyond*, (Chicago: University of Chicago Press, 1987), 411–496, 441.

11. Jacques Derrida, *Glas*, 134.

12. Jacques Derrida, "The Ends of Man," 129.

13. Appropriation is "poetizing building." Martin Heidegger. "Overcoming Metaphysics," trans. Joan Stambaugh, in Martin Heidegger, *The End of Philosophy* (New York: Harper and Row, 1973), 84–110, 110. "Appropriation assembles the design of Saying and unfolds it into the structure of manifold showing. . . . Appropriation grants to mortals their abode within their nature, so that they may be capable of being those who speak." Ibid, 128. "In the event of appropriation vibrates the active nature of what speaks as language, which at one time was called the house of being." Martin Heidegger, *Identity and Difference*, trans. Joan Stambaugh (Harper and Row, New York, 1969), 39.

14. To cite but one of the multiple examples of this association: Language "is the keeper of being present, in that its coming to light remains entrusted to the appropriating show of Saying. Language is the house of Being because language, as Saying, is the mode of

Appropriation." Martin Heidegger. "The Way to Language," trans. Peter D. Hertz, In Martin Heidegger, *On the Way to Language* (New York: Harper and Row, 1971), 111–136, 135.

15. Jacques Derrida, "The *Retrait* of Metaphor," 7. Derrida everywhere attempts to "explode" the opposition between the metaphoric and the proper. See particularly, "White Mythology: Metaphor in the Text of Philosophy," 217.

16. Ibid., 253.

17. Marsilio Ficino, "Commentary on the Symposium," chapter 5, cited in Erin Panofsky, *Idea: A Concept in Art Theory* (New York: Harper and Row, 1968), 137.

18. Martin Heidegger, "The Question Concerning Technology," trans. David Farrell Krell, *Martin Heidegger: Basic Writings* (New York: Harper and Row, 1977), 283–317, 294.

19. Jacques Derrida, "Plato's Pharmacy," 103.

20. Jacques Derrida, "Freud and the Scene of Writing," 215.

21. Jacques Derrida, "Violence and Metaphysics: An Essay on the Thought of Emmanuel Levinas," 113.

22. Ibid., 112.

23. Martin Heidegger, *Being and Time*, 209. "Both Dasein's interpretation of itself and the whole stock of significations which belong to language in general are dominated through and through by 'spatial representations'." Ibid., 421. Derrida also refers to this argument when he says "language can determine things only by spatializing them." Jacques Derrida, "Force and Signification," 16.

24. Jacques Derrida, "Geschlecht: Sexual Difference, Ontological Difference," *Research in Phenomenology*, XIII, 1983, 65–84, 78.

25. Jacques Derrida, "Plato's Pharmacy," 144.

26. Ibid., 124.

27. Jacques Derrida, "Tympam," xvii.

28. Jacques Derrida, "La Parole Soufflée," trans. Alan Bass, in Jacques Derrida, *Writing and Difference* (Chicago: University of Chicago Press, 1978), 169–195, 192.

29. Jacques Derrida, *Of Grammatology*, 157.

30. Jacques Derrida, "Entre crochets: entretien avec Jacques Derrida, première partie," *Digraphe* 8, April 1976, 97–114.

31. "This philosophical, dialectical mastery . . . is constantly put into question by a family scene that constitutes and undermines at once the passage between the pharmacy and the house. "Platonism" is both the general *rehearsal* of this family scene and the most powerful effort to master it, to prevent anyone's ever hearing of it, to conceal it by drawing the curtains over the dawning of the West." Jacques Derrida, "Plato's Pharmacy," 167.

32. Ibid.

33. Jacques Derrida, "Deconstruction and the Other," 117.

34. Sigmund Freud, "The Uncanny," *The Standard Edition*, vol. 17, 217–56, 222.

35. Jacques Derrida, "Double Session," trans. Barbara Johnson, in Jacques Derrida, *Dissemination* (Chicago: University of Chicago Press, 1981), 173–285, 220.

36. This becomes particularly striking in Derrida's "Le facteur de la vérité," which notes that Lacan's work never addresses Freud's essay on "The Uncanny" and that it systematically resists uncanny effects in order to establish a particular conceptual order. Derrida's essay, while identifying the specific uncanny effects effaced by one of Lacan's essays and obliquely comparing the way in which that essay bases a psychoanalytic theory on a reading of a work of fiction to the way Freud's essay does the same thing, never itself addresses Freud's text directly. Even Derrida's only citation of the text, in "Cartouches," is brief, only a citation of Freud's citation, and punctuated by a parenthetical deferral ("it would all need to be quoted"), which points to the necessity of further citations that are not made: "At the end of *Das Unheimliche* (it would all need to be quoted, as with the choice of the caskets), Freud recalls Nestroy's *Der Zerrissene;* the man who takes himself to be a murderer lifts up (*aufhebt*) the cover of each trap and sees rise up each time the supposed ghost (*vermeintliche Gespenst*) of the victim. He is scared: 'but I only killed one of them!'" Jacques Derrida, "Cartouches," trans. Geoff Bennington and Ian McLeod, in Jacques Derrida, *The Truth in Painting* (Chicago: University of Chicago Press, 1987), 183–253, 217.

37. Jacques Derrida, "Living On: *Border Lines,*" 121.

38. Jacques Derrida, *Of Grammatology*, 313.

39. Martin Heidegger, *Being and Time*, 321.

40. "Indeed, what threatens in this indefinite way is now quite near and can be so close that it is oppressive. It can be so near and yet not present as this or that, not something fearful, something to be feared by way of a definite reference of the environing world in its meaningfulness. Dread can 'befall' us right in the midst of the most familiar environment. Oftentimes it does not even have to involve the phenomenon of darkness or of being alone which frequently accompanies dread. We then say: one feels *uncanny*. One no longer feels at home in his most familiar environment, the one closest to him; but this does not come about in such a way that a definite region in the hitherto known and familiar world breaks down in its orientation, nor such that one is not at home in the surroundings in which one now finds himself, but instead in other surroundings. On the contrary, in dread, being-in-the-world is totally transformed into a 'not at home' purely and simply." Martin Heidegger, *History of the Concept of Time*, 289.

41. "Uncanniness is the basic kind of Being-in-the-world, even though in an everyday way, it has been covered up." Martin Heidegger, *Being and Time*, 322.

42. Heidegger's 1942–43 lectures on Parmenides elaborate his specific use of the word uncanny in the most detail: "But where, on the contrary, Being comes into focus, there the extraordinary announces itself, the excessive that strays 'beyond' the ordinary, that which is not to be explained by explanations on the basis of beings. This is the uncanny, literally understood and not in the otherwise usual sense according to which it rather means the immense and what has never yet been. For the uncanny, correctly understood,

is neither immense nor tiny, since it is not to be measured at all with the measure of a so-called 'standard.' The uncanny is also not what has never yet been present; it is what comes into presence always already and in advance prior to all 'uncanninesses.'. . . it surrounds, and insofar as it everywhere surrounds, the present ordinary state of things and presents itself in everything ordinary, though without being the ordinary. The uncanny understood in this way is, with regard to what is ordinary or natural, not the exception but the 'most natural,' in the sense of 'nature' as thought by the Greeks, i.e., in the sense of Φύσις. The uncanny is that out of which all that is ordinary emerges, that in which all that is ordinary is suspended without surmising it ever in the least, and that into which everything ordinary falls back. . . . For those who came later and for us, to who the primordial Greek experience of Being is denied, the uncanny has to be the exception, in principle explainable, to the ordinary; we put the uncanny next to the ordinary, but, to be sure, only as the extraordinary. For us it is difficult to attain the fundamental Greek experience, whereby the ordinary itself, and only insofar as it is ordinary, is the uncanny. . . . We are divesting from the word any representation of the gigantic, the overpowering, the exaggerated, the weird. Of course the uncanny can also, in its excessiveness, hide behind such figures. But it itself in its essence is the inconspicuous, the simple, the insignificant, which nevertheless shines in all beings." Martin Heidegger, *Parmenides*, 101.

43. Martin Heidegger, *Being and Time*, 214.

44. Ibid., 233–234.

45. Martin Heidegger, *What Is Called Thinking?*, 154.

46. Significantly, Heidegger's explicit use of the figure of the house begins with his "official" withdrawal from the Nazi regime and even acts as his figure for that withdrawal. It emerges out of the first lectures on Holderlin in 1934 and then is retained and emphasized in the postwar publications, beginning with the "Letter on Humanism." It arguably became explicit precisely to cover up his personal association with the violence of the regime. In the late essays, his argument that the familiar sense of the house is a cover of a double violence acts as his own cover. Just as the figure maintains his allegiance to the tradition of metaphysics it is supposedly deployed to displace, it also maintains his allegiance to what he still referred to in the 1935 *Introduction to Metaphysics* as the "inner truth" of the party, the truth from which the party itself is seen to have fallen. See Mark Wigley, "Heidegger's House: The Violence of the Domestic."

47. Martin Heidegger, "The Origin of the Work of Art," 54.

48. On the sexuality of *Dasein* for Heidegger, see Derrida's "Geschlecht: Sexual Difference, Ontological Difference."

49. Martin Heidegger, *An Introduction to Metaphysics*, 155.

50. Ibid., 157.

51. Ibid.

52. In the middle of Heidegger's lectures at the University of Marburg in 1925, he rejected the idea that to be "in" refers to a "spatial container (room, building)" and refers to an etymological study by Grimm (which compares the archaic German words meaning *domus*, or "house," that have the same form as the English word "inn") to argue that "in" primarily refers to "dwelling" rather than the occupation of space: "'In' comes from *innan*, which means to dwell, *habitare*; '*ann*' means: I am accustomed, I am familiar with, I take care of something—the Latin *colo* in the sense of *habito* and *diligo*. Dwelling is also

taken here as taking care of something in intimate familiarity, being-involved with [*Sein-bei*]. . . . 'in' primarily does not signify anything spatial at all but means primarily *being familiar with.*" Martin Heidegger, *History of the Concept of Time*, 158. He then employed this key argument in the same form at the beginning of *Being and Time* in a way that organizes the whole text that follows. Martin Heidegger, *Being and Time*, 80.

53. Martin Heidegger, *An Introduction to Metaphysics*, 163.

54. Ibid., 161.

55. Ibid.

56. Ibid., 150.

57. "The Greeks had no word for 'space.' This is no accident; for they experienced the spatial on the basis not of extension but of place (*topos*); they experienced it as *chōra*, which signifies neither place nor space but that which is occupied by what stands there. The place belongs to the thing itself. Each of the various things has its place. That which becomes is placed in this local 'space' and emerges from it. . . . the transformation of the barely apprehended essence of place (*topos*) and of *chōra* into a 'space' defined by extension was initiated by Platonic philosophy, i.e. in the interpretation of being as *idea*. Might *chōra* not mean: that which abstracts itself from every particular, that which withdraws, and in such a way precisely admits and "makes place" for something else?" Ibid., 66.

58. Martin Heidegger, *Nietzsche Vol. 1: The Will to Power as Art*, trans. David Farrell Krell (San Francisco: Harper and Row, 1979), 180.

59. Ibid., 173.

60. Martin Heidegger, "Language," 191.

61. Martin Heidegger, "Remembrance of the Poet," trans. Douglas Scott, in *Existence and Being* (Washington: Gateway, 1949), 233–269, 267.

62. Ibid., 259.

63. Heidegger argues that poets need to go into the abyss "To see this danger and point it out, there must be mortals who reach sooner into the abyss." Martin Heidegger, "What Are Poets For?," trans. Albert Hofstadter, in Martin Heidegger, *Poetry, Language, Thought* (New York: Harper and Row, 1971), 89–142, 117.

64. Martin Heidegger, *An Introduction to Metaphysics*, 167. "In the familiar appearance the poet calls the alien." Martin Heidegger, ". . . Poetically Man Dwells . . .," trans. Albert Hofstadter, in Martin Heidegger, *Poetry, Language, Thought* (New York: Harper and Row, 1971), 211–229, 225.

65. Martin Heidegger, "The Origin of the Work of Art," 76.

66. Martin Heidegger, *An Introduction to Metaphysics*, 169.

67. Ibid.

68. "All this merely conceals the uncanniness of language, of the passions, the powers by which man is ordained [*gefügt*] as a historical being, while it seems to him that it is *he* who disposes [*verfügt*] of them: The strangeness, the uncanniness of these powers resides

in their seeming familiarity. Directly they yield themselves to man only in their nonessence [*Unwesen*], so driving him and holding him out of his essence. In this way he comes to regard what is fundamentally more remote and overpowering than sea and earth as closest of all to him. How far man is from being at home in his essence is revealed by his opinion of himself as he who invented language and understanding, building and poetry." Ibid., 156.

69. Of the usual interpretation of the modern atomic age as a crisis of violence perpetuated by modern science that alienates man, Heidegger notes that the interpretation is itself "alienating and uncanny." Martin Heidegger, "The Principle of Reason," the 1953 address, 122. It is "uncanny" because it identifies the violence of atomic energy as foreign to man and a recent historical event rather than a mark of the way the "entire history of Western thought" has always been organized around the architectonic principle of ground. It is the veiling of the originary violence of architectonic thinking that is uncanny.

70. "Only if we understand that the use of power in language, in understanding, in forming and building helps to create . . . the violent act [*Gewalttat*] of laying out paths in to the environing power of the essent, only then shall we understand the strangeness, the uncanniness of all violence." *An Introduction to Metaphysics*, 157.

71. Martin Heidegger, *What Is a Thing?*, 121.

72. Martin Heidegger, "Letter on Humanism," 236.

73. Jacques Derrida, "The *Retrait* of Metaphor," 24.

74. "The father is always father to a speaking/living being. In other words, it is precisely *logos* that enables us to perceive and investigate something like paternity. If there were a simple metaphor in the expression 'father of logos,' the first word, which seemed the more *familiar*, would nevertheless receive more meaning *from* the second than it would transmit *to* it. The first familiarity is always involved in a relation of cohabitation with *logos*. Living-beings, father and son, are announced to us and related to each other within the household of *logos*." Jacques Derrida, "Plato's Pharmacy," 80. In *Glas*, Derrida looks at the way the concept of family "very rigorously inscribes itself in the system" of Hegel's philosophy (p. 5) and asks, "Will one rashly say that the finite family furnishes a metaphoric model or a convenient figuration for the language of philosophical exposition? A pedagogical ease? A good way to speak of abstract things to the student [*élève*] while playing with the familiarity of family significations? Even then what the absolute familiarity of a signification is must be known. If that can be thought and named without the family. Then one needs to ascertain that the finite family in question is not infinite already, in which case what the alleged metaphor would come to figure would be already in the metaphor." Ibid., 21. "In fact it seems necessary here to invert this order and recognize what I have elsewhere proposed to call the 'metaphoric catastrophe': far from knowing first what 'life' or 'family' mean whenever we use these familiar values to talk about language and translation; it is rather starting from the notion of a language and its 'sur-vival' in translation that we could have access to the notion of what life and family mean." Jacques Derrida, "Des Tours de Babel," 178. Likewise, the concept of economy is not used as a metaphor of metaphysics but is defined by it, produced by the very system of metaphysics it appears to illustrate: "all the major concepts which constitute the discourse of economics are philosophical." Jacques Derrida, "Deconstruction and the Other," 115.

75. Martin Heidegger, *What Is a Thing?*, 123.

76. Martin Heidegger, *Being and Time*, 44.

77. Jacques Derrida, *Of Grammatology*, 24.

Throwing Up Architecture

1. Immanuel Kant, *The Critique of Judgement*, 188.

2. Ibid., 162.

3. Ibid., 185.

4. Ibid., 186.

5. Jacques Derrida, "Psyche: Inventions of the Other," trans. Catherine Porter, in Lindsay Waters and Wlad Godzich, eds., *Reading De Man Reading* (Minneapolis: University of Minnesota Press, 1989), 25–65, 56.

6. Jacques Derrida, "To Speculate—on "Freud," trans. Alan Bass, in Jacques Derrida, *The Post Card: From Socrates to Freud and Beyond.* (Chicago: University of Chicago Press, 1987), 257–409, 280.

7. Immanuel Kant, *The Critique of Judgement*, 160.

8. Jacques Derrida, "Tympan," xvi.

9. Jacques Derrida. "Outwork, Prefacing," 5.

10. Jacques Derrida, "Cogito and the History of Madness," trans. Alan Bass, in Jacques Derrida, *Writing and Difference* (Chicago: University of Chicago Press, 1978), 31–63, 40.

11. Jacques Derrida, "Violence and Metaphysics: An Essay on the Thought of Emmanuel Levinas," 91.

12. Jacques Derrida, "Economimesis," trans. R. Klein, *Diacritics*, vol. 11, no. 2, 1981, 3–25, 20.

13. Immanuel Kant, *The Critique of Judgement*, 67.

14. Jacques Derrida, "From a Restricted To a General Economy: A Hegelianism without Reserve," 272.

15. "D'exclusion renfermant ce qu'elle veut neutraliser ou mettre dehors . . ." Jacques Derrida, "Ja, ou le faux-bond," 113.

16. Jacques Derrida, "Desistance," 16.

17. Immanuel Kant, *The Critique of Judgement*, 43.

18. Ibid., 65.

19. Ibid., 151.

20. Ibid., 155.

21. Jean-Jacques Rousseau. "A Discourse on the Origin of Inequality," trans. G. D. H. Cole, in Jean-Jacques Rousseau, *The Social Contract and Discourses* (London: Dent, 1973), 27–113, 50.

22. Jean-Jacques Rousseau, "A Discourse on the Moral Effects of the Arts and Sciences," trans. G. D. H. Cole, in Jean-Jacques Rousseau, *The Social Contract and Discourses*, 1–26, 5 [translation modified].

23. Ibid., 18 [translation modified].

24. Jean-Jacques Rousseau, "The Social Contract," trans. G. D. H. Cole, in Jean-Jacques Rousseau, *The Social Contract and Discourses*. 164–278, 197.

25. Jean-Jacques Rousseau, "A Discourse on the Origin of Inequality," 42.

26. "How could it have happened that modern languages, especially, have come to designate the power of aesthetic judgement by a term (*gustus, sapor*) that refers merely to a certain sense organ (the inside of the mouth) and to the way we use this organ to distinguish, as well as to choose, things we can enjoy [*geniessbarer Dinge*—'edible things']? A good meal in good company is unsurpassed as a situation in which sensibility and understanding unite in one enjoyment that lasts a long time and can be repeated with pleasure so frequently. But the meal is considered only the instrument for keeping the company together. The host shows his aesthetic taste by his skill in choosing with universal validity. This he cannot do by his own sense [of taste], because his guests might choose other foods or drinks, each according to his own private sense. So he arranges for a *variety* that enables each guest to find something that suits his sense, and in this way his choice has a relative universal validity . . . And this is how the organic feeling that comes through a particular sense could give its name to an ideal feeling: the feeling, namely, of a sensuous choice that is universally valid." Immanuel Kant, *Anthropology from a Pragmatic Point of View,* trans. Mary J. Gregor (The Hague: Martinus Nijhoff, 1974), 110.

27. "The philosopher should therefore consider whether it is possible for him to write the laws of dining socially for those whose way of life commits them to concern for the mind rather than the body in whatever they undertake." Immanuel Kant, "On Philosopher's Medicine of the Body," in Lewis White Beck, ed., *Kant's Latin Writings* (New York: Peter Lang, 1986), 217–243, 235.

28. To "gorge oneself with food" is "to violate a duty to oneself . . . in gluttony man more closely approximates animal enjoyment . . . a feast is always a temptation to what is immoral." Immanuel Kant, *The Metaphysical Principles of Virtue. II. The Metaphysics of Morals,* trans. James Ellington (Indianapolis: Bobbs-Merrill, 1964), 88–89.

29. Jean-Jacques Rousseau, "Essay on the Origin of Languages," trans. John H. Moran and Alexander Gode, in *On the Origin of Language* (New York: Frederick Ungar, 1966), 1–74, 53.

30. Immanuel Kant, *The Critique of Judgement,* 123.

31. Jean-Jacques Rousseau, "Discourse on the Origin of Inequality," 80.

32. Jean-Jacques Rousseau, "Essay on the Origin of Languages," 31.

33. Immanuel Kant, *The Philosophy of Law,* trans. W. Hastie (Edinburgh: T. T. Clark, 1887), 112.

34. "The only qualification required by a citizen (apart, of course, from being an adult male) is that he must be his *own master* (*sui iuris*), and must have some *property* (which can include any skill, trade, fine art or science) to support himself." Immanuel Kant, "On the Common Saying: 'This May be True in Theory, But it Does Not Apply in Practice,'" trans. H. B. Nisbet, in Hans Reiss, ed., *Kant's Political Writings* (Cambridge: Cambridge University Press, 1970), 61–92, 78. Although the wife must "obey" the husband "Nevertheless, they are all equal as subjects *before the law* . . ." Ibid., 75.

35. "A *woman*, regardless of her age, is under civil tutelage [or incompetent to speak for herself (*unmundig*)]; her husband is her natural curator, though if a married woman has property of her own, it is another man. It is true that when it comes to talking, woman, by her nature, is sufficiently glib [*Mundwerk genug hat*] to represent both herself and her husband, even in court (where it is a question of the Mine and Thine), and so could be literally described as more than competent to speak for herself [*bermundig*]. But just as it is not woman's role to go to war, so she cannot personally defend her representative. And this legal tutelage with regard to public transactions makes her all the more powerful where her domestic welfare is concerned; for the right of the weaker enters into this, and man's very nature calls on him to respect it and defend it." Immanuel Kant, *Anthropology from a Pragmatic Point of View*, trans. Mary J. Gregor (The Hague: Martinus Nijhoff, 1974), section 48, 79. The question of the domestic can be followed in many other texts by Kant. See, for example, "An Answer to Question: 'What is Enlightenment?',", which, in opposing the political control of people like "domesticated animals," turns on a distinction between the "private" domain of civil institutions, like teaching, as "never any more than a domestic gathering" and the "public" realm exemplified by publications. Immanuel Kant, "An Answer to Question: 'What is Enlightenment?'" *Kant's Political Writings* (Cambridge: Cambridge University Press, 1970), 54–60. This image of domesticity is sustained, at another level, in the concept of "hospitality" in "Perpetual Peace: A Philosophical Sketch," trans. H. B. Nisbet, in Hans Reiss, ed., *Kant's Political Writings*, 93–130, 105.

36. Jacques Derrida, *Of Grammatology*, 176–178. On the necessity for an "ethico-political" reading of the philosophical discourses "that reserve politics and public space for man, domestic and private space for woman," see Jacques Derrida, "The Politics of Friendship," *Journal of Philosophy*, vol. 75, no. 11, 1988, 632–645, 642–643.

37. Jacques Derrida, *Of Grammatology*, 157.

38. Jacques Derrida, "Interpretations at War: Kant, the Jew, the German," *New Literary History*, vol. 22, no. 1, 1991, 39–95, 60.

39. Jacques Derrida, *Glas*, 133.

40. Jean-Jacques Rousseau, "A Discourse on Political Economy," trans. G. D. H. Cole, in Jean-Jacques Rousseau, *The Social Contract and Discourses*, 115–153, 117.

41. Immanuel Kant, *Critique of Pure Reason*, 573. The phallogocentrism of metaphysics is not that of a tower that excludes, but that of a house that includes. The idea of the house is bound to that of grounded structure: "Throughout my writings I have made it clear that my method imitates that of the architect. When an architect wants to build a house which is stable on ground where there is a sandy topsoil over underlying rock, or clay, or some over firm base, he begins by digging out a set of trenches from which he removes the sand, and anything resting on or mixed in with the sand, so that he can lay his foundations on firm soil. In the same way, I began by taking everything that was doubtful and throwing it out, like sand; and then, when I noticed that it is impossible to doubt

that a doubting or thinking substance exists, I took this as the bedrock on which I could lay the foundations of my philosophy." René Descartes, "Seventh Set of Objections with the Author's Replies," trans. John Cottingham et al., *The Philosophical Writings of Descartes Vol. II,* (Cambridge: Cambridge University Press, 1984), 366–383.

42. Jacques Derrida, "Economimesis," 21.

43. Immanuel Kant, *The Critique of Judgement,* 173.

44. Immanuel Kant, *Anthropology from a Pragmatic Point of View,* 53.

45. Immanuel Kant, *Observations on the Feeling of the Beautiful and the Sublime,* trans. John T. Goldthwait (Berkeley: University of California Press, 1965), 83.

46. Ibid., 79.

47. Ibid., 83.

48. Jacques Derrida, "Economimesis," 25.

49. Ibid.

50. Jacques Derrida, "Otobiographies: The Teaching of Nietzsche and the Politics of the Proper Name," trans. Avital Ronell, in Christie V. McDonald, ed., *The Ear of the Other: Otobiography, Transference, Translation* (New York: Schocken Books, 1985), 1–38, 23. To give just one example of the structural role of indigestion in Nietzsche: "What changes the general taste? The fact that some individuals who are powerful and influential announce without any shame, *hoc est ridiculum, hoc est absurdum* [this is ridiculous, this is absurd], in short, the judgement of their taste and nausea; and then they enforce it tyrannically. Thus they coerce many, and gradually still more develop a new habit, and eventually *all* a new *need.* The reason why these individuals have different feelings and tastes is usually to be found in some oddity of their life style, nutrition or digestion . . ." Friedrich Nietzsche, *The Gay Science,* trans. Walter Kaufman (New York: Vintage Books, 1974), 106.

51. Jacques Derrida, "Structure, Sign and Play in the Discourse of the Human Sciences," 284.

52. Jean-Jacques Rousseau, *Emile,* trans. Barbara Foxley (New York: Dent, 1973), 120.

53. Immanuel Kant, *Education* (Ann Arbor: University of Michigan Press, 1960), 35.

54. Ibid., 241.

55. Sigmund Freud, "The Uncanny," 235.

56. Ibid., 236.

57. Sigmund Freud, "Three Essays on the Theory of Sexuality," trans. James Strachey, *The Standard Edition of the Complete Psychological Works of Sigmund Freud,* vol. 7, 1959, 125–243, 177.

58. Sigmund Freud, "The Uncanny," 219.

59. Sigmund Freud, "Mourning and Melancholia," trans. James Strachey, *The Standard Edition of the Complete Psychological Works of Sigmund Freud,* vol. 14, 243–258, 255.

60. Jacques Derrida, "Economimesis," 23.

61. "Pure Reason . . . is a faculty of judging according to a priori Principles. That is why a critique of judgement belongs to a complete critique of pure (theoretical as well as practical) Reason. Even in the [Kant's] third *Critique*, Reason is the real theme." Martin Heidegger, *The Principle of Reason*, 71.

62. Nicolas Abraham and Maria Torok, "Introjection-Incorporation: Mourning or Melancholia," in Serge Lebovici and Daniel Widlander, eds., *Psychoanalysis in France* (New York: International University Press, 1980), 3–16, 5.

63. Jacques Derrida, "Limited Inc., a b c . . . ," 77.

64. Jacques Derrida, "*Fors:* The Anguish Words of Nicolas Abraham and Maria Torok," xxxviii.

65. Ibid.

66. Ibid., xv. "a memory he buried *without legal burial place*, the memory of an idyll experienced with a prestigious object that for some reason has become unspeakable, a memory thus entombed in a fast and secure place, awaiting its resurrection. . . . both the fact that the idyll has taken place and its subsequent loss will have to be disguised and denied. Such a situation leads to the setting up within the ego of a closed-off place, a *crypt* . . ." Nicolas Abraham and Maria Torok. "A Poetics of Psychoanalysis: The Lost Object—Me," *Substance*, vol. 13, no. 2, 1984, 3–18, 4.

67. Jacques Derrida, "Roundtable on Autobiography," 57.

68. Nicolas Abraham and Maria Torok, "Introjection-Incorporation: Mourning or Melancholia," 6.

69. Ibid.

70. Jacques Derrida, "*Fors:* The Anguish Words of Nicolas Abraham and Maria Torok," xlii.

71. "Cryptonymy would thus not consist in representing—hiding one word by another, one thing by another, a thing by a word or a word by a thing, but in picking out from the extended series of allosemes, a term that then (in a second-degree distancing) is translated into a synonym." Ibid., xli.

72. Ibid., xxv.

73. This cryptic structure, which parasitically occupies the domestic space of language, should be compared to Hegel's account of language as mourning through the construction of tombs, exemplified by family crypts, monuments to the life of the family, monuments to domestic life, to the domesticity of life: "Hegel knew that this proper and animated body of the signifier was also a *tomb*. The association *sōma/sēma* is also at work in this semiology, which is in no way surprising. The tomb is the life of the body as the sign of death, the body as the other of the soul, the other of the animate psyche, of the living breath. But the tomb also shelters, maintains in reserve, capitalizes on life by marking that life continues elsewhere. The family crypt: *oikēsis*. It consecrates the disappearance of life by attesting to the perseverance of life. Thus, the tomb also shelters life from death. It *warns* the soul of possible death, warns (of) death of the soul, turns away (from) death. This double warning function belongs to the funerary monument. The

body of the sign thus becomes the monument in which the soul will be enclosed, preserved, maintained, kept in maintenance, present, signified. At the heart of the monument the soul keeps itself alive, but it needs the monument only to the extent that it is exposed—to death—in its living relation to its own body." Jacques Derrida, "The Pit and the Pyramid: Introduction to Hegel's Semiology," 82.

74. Jacques Derrida, "Roundtable on Autobiography," 59. compare with: "Despite appearances, the deconstruction of logocentrism is not a psychoanalysis of philosophy." Jacques Derrida, "Freud and the Scene of Writing," 196.

75. Jacques Derrida, *"Fors:* The Anguish Words of Nicolas Abraham and Maria Torok," xv.

76. Ibid., xxxiv.

77. Martin Heidegger, *Kant and the Problem of Metaphysics,* 138. "The actual interpretation must show what does not stand in the works and is nevertheless said. To accomplish this the exegete must use violence." Martin Heidegger, *An Introduction to Metaphysics,* 162. Compare to Derrida's "I slice things up somewhat barbarously and illegitimately as we always do." Jacques Derrida, "Living On: *Border Lines,*" 117.

78. "The present, the presence of the present, and the present of the present of presence, are all originally and forever violent. The living present is originally marked by death." Jacques Derrida, "Violence and Metaphysics: An Essay on the Thought of Emmanuel Levinas," 133. "Therefore, the thought of Being, in its unveiling is never foreign to a certain violence." Ibid., 147. "Moreover, the rapport of self-identity is itself always a rapport of violence with the other." Jacques Derrida, "Deconstruction and the Other," 117. "The violent relationship of the whole of the West to its other." Jacques Derrida, "The Ends of Man," 134.

79. Jacques Derrida, *Of Grammatology,* 34.

80. "The violence of writing does not *befall* an innocent language. There is an originary violence of writing because language is first . . . writing." Ibid., 37.

81. Jacques Derrida, "Parergon," 69.

82. Jacques Derrida, "Implications," 6.

Doing the Twist

1. Jacques Derrida, "Title (To Be Specified)," 8.

2. Ibid., 7.

3. Ibid., 11.

4. Jacques Derrida, "Living On: *Border Lines,*" 152.

5. Jacques Derrida, "Before the Law," trans. Avital Ronell and Christine Roulston, in Derek Attridge, ed., *Acts of Literature* (New York: Routledge, 1992), 181–220, 212.

6. Jacques Derrida, "Shibboleth," trans. Joshua Wilner, in Derek Attridge, ed., *Acts of Literature* (New York: Routledge, 1992) 370–413, 413. "The crypt remains, the *shibboleth* remains secret, the passage uncertain, and the poem only unveils this secret to confirm that there is something secret there, withdrawn." Ibid., 404.

7. Ibid.

8. Jacques Derrida, "How to Avoid Speaking: Denials," 23.

9. Ibid., 36.

10. Jacques Derrida, "Scribble (Writing-Power)," trans. Cary Plotkin, *Yale French Studies*, 59, 1979, 116–147, 124.

11. Ibid., 129.

12. See also Derrida's account of the undecidable "coup of force" with which the political space defined by the Declaration of Independence is necessarily instituted, a performative violence covered by portraying its institutional laws as founded on natural laws. Jacques Derrida, "Declarations of Independence," trans. Tom Keenan and Tom Pepper, *New Political Science*, no. 15, Summer 1986, 7–15.

13. In "Living On: *Border Lines*," Derrida points to the inability of the university discourse about art to examine the role of art in its own construction by again linking the strange role of the title on the border and the institution of literary studies: "What is a title? What borderline questions are posed here? I am here seeking merely to establish the necessity of this whole problematic of judicial framing and of the jurisdiction of frames. This problematic, I feel, has not been explored, at least not adequately, by the institution of literary studies in the university. And there are essential reasons for that: this is an institution built on that very system of framing." Jacques Derrida, "Living On: *Border Lines*," 88.

14. "Every time philosophy determines art, masters it and encloses it in the history of meaning or in the ontological encyclopedia, it assigns it a job as medium . . . By giving it the philosophical name *art*, one has, it would seem, domesticated it in onto-encyclopedic economy and the history of truth." Jacques Derrida, "Parergon," 34.

15. As Derrida points out elsewhere, "the vocabulary of foundation is always, already, a juridical vocabulary [*le vocabulaire du fondement est toujours, déjà, un vocabulaire juridique*]." "Popularitiés: Du droit à la philosophie du droit," in Jacques Derrida, *Du droit à la philosophie* (Paris: Galilée, 1990), 512, 525–553.

16. Jacques Derrida, "Force of Law: The 'Mystical Foundation of Authority'," trans. Mary Quaintance, *Cardozo Law Review*, vol. 11, no. 5/6, July/August 1990, 919–1046, 929.

17. Ibid., 963.

18. Ibid., 943.

19. Jacques Derrida, "Before the Law," 203.

20. Ibid., 199.

21. Ibid., 195.

22. Jacques Derrida, "Shibboleth," 402.

23. Ibid., 410. Derrida's whole argument here is an elaboration of a single stanza in a poem by Celan that invokes the uncanniness the date: "(Heart: / make yourself known even here, / here, in the midst of the market. / Call it out, the shibboleth, / into the alien homeland strangeness: / February. No passerán."

24. Jacques Derrida, "The *Retrait* of Metaphor," 19. "It means that we must remain faithful, even if it implies a certain violence, to the injunctions of the text." Jacques Derrida, "Deconstruction and the Other," 124.

25. Jacques Derrida, "The Ends of Man," 135.

26. Changing terrain risks "inhabiting more naively and more strictly than ever the inside one declares one has deserted, the simple practice of language ceaselessly reinstates the new terrain on the oldest ground." Ibid. Deconstruction is therefore "never on a totally, or simply, exterior terrain." Jacques Derrida, "Positions," 77.

27. Jacques Derrida, "Dissemination," trans. Barbara Johnson, in Jacques Derrida, *Dissemination* (Chicago: University of Chicago Press, 1981), 287–366, 358.

28. "And we must think this without *nostalgia*, that is, outside the myth of a purely maternal or paternal language, a lost native country of thought. On the contrary, we must *affirm* this, in the sense in which Nietzsche puts affirmation into play in a certain laughter and a certain step of the dance." Jacques Derrida, "Différance," 27.

29. Jacques Derrida, "Choreographies," 69.

30. Jacques Derrida, "Aphorism Countertime," trans. Nicholas Royle, in Derek Attridge, ed., *Acts of Literature* (New York: Routledge, 1992), 414–433, 419.

31. Ibid.

32. Jacques Derrida, "The Theater of Cruelty and the Closure of Representation," trans. Alan Bass, in Jacques Derrida, *Writing and Difference* (Chicago: University of Chicago Press, 1978), 232–250, 235.

33. Ibid., 237.

34. Ibid., 244.

35. Jacques Derrida, "La Parole Souflée," trans. Alan Bass, in Jacques Derrida, *Writing and Difference* (Chicago: University of Chicago Press, 1978), 169–195, 192.

36. Ibid., 184.

37. Ibid., 187.

38. Ibid., 194.

39. Jacques Derrida, "Desistence," 27.

40. Ibid., 16.

41. Jacques Derrida, "The Ghost Dance: An Interview with Jacques Derrida," interview with Mark Lewis and Andrew Payne, trans. Jean-Luc Svoboda, *Public*, 2, 1989, 60–73, 61.

42. Jacques Derrida, *"Edmund Husserl's 'Origin of Geometry': An Introduction,"* trans. John P. Leavy, Jr. (Brighten: Harvester Press, 1978), 88.

43. Ibid., 91.

44. Ibid., 99.

45. Jacques Derrida, "The Art of *Mémoires,"* 80.

46. Jacques Derrida, *Cinders,* trans. Ned Lukacher (Lincoln: University of Nebraska Press, 1991), 22.

47. Ibid., 53.

48. Ibid., 61.

49. Ibid., 41.

50. "She plays with words as one plays with fire, I would denounce her as a pyromaniac who wants to make us forget that in Sicily churches are built with the stone of lava." Ibid., 61.

51. Jacques Derrida, "Ulysses Gramophone: Hear Say Yes in Joyce," trans. Tina Kendall and Shari Benstock, in Derek Attridge, ed., *Acts of Literature* (New York: Routledge, 1992), 253–309, 272–294.

52. Bataille, *L'expérience intérieuré.* Cited in Jacques Derrida. "From Restricted to General Economy: A Hegelianism without Reserve," 261.

53. Ibid., 260.

54. Ibid., 253.

55. Ibid., 264.

56. Sigmund Freud, "The Uncanny," 241. Significantly, the example only comes up in the moment of its rejection: "We might indeed have begun our investigation with this example, perhaps the most striking of all, of something uncanny, but we refrained from doing so because the uncanny in it is too much intermixed with what is purely gruesome and is in part overlaid by it." Ibid. This simultaneous affirmation and rejection of the most explicitly architectural figure has to be considered in the specific context of Freud's argument. He begins his essay by opposing Jentsch's description of the uncanny as "intellectual uncertainty" in which the uncanny is explicitly understood as a spatial condition: "something one does not know one's way about in," an inability to be "orientated" in an "environment." Ibid., 221. He then traces the various meaning of *unheimlich,* which are repeatedly punctuated by the spatial figure of the house ("belonging to the house . . . security as in one within the four walls of his house . . . surrounded by close walls . . . so *heimlig* in the house . . . the cottage . . .") and even the haunted house ("(of a house) haunted,"). But, in opposing Jentsch, he tacitly opposes this spatial sense despite the fact that he goes on to cite his own uncanny experience of spatial disorientation between the small houses in a small town in Italy, losing one's way in a mountain forest, and wandering "about in a dark, strange room, looking for the door or the electric switch, and colliding time after time with the same piece of furniture." Ibid., 237. He extracts from his own examples the principle of repetition rather than that of space itself. In fact, it can be argued that Freud finds the theme of the uncanny itself disorienting in precisely the way he attempts to bracket out. The text stages but also denies his experience of

intellectual uncertainty in the face of the uncanny. Significantly, the essay is only able to gain control over the uncanny by bracketing out space. The example of the haunted house, with which he says he perhaps should have begun, only comes up, to be immediately bracketed away again, at the precise moment he has regained control, a recovery of the principles of psychoanalytic theory announced in the very spatial terms he has attempted to bracket out: "And now we find ourselves on familiar ground." Ibid., 236. Having been disorientated in the strange space of the uncanny he returns to the familiar home. Nevertheless, he is forced to invoke the haunted house in order to gain explicit access to the theme of death, specifically that of "spirits, demons, and ghosts," which has been as tacitly inscribed into the text as the theme of space from the beginning. In the end, the uncanny turns out to be a ghost story, a story of the subject haunted by what it has repressed, a story in which the haunted house is central even, if not especially because it is explicitly and systematically suppressed only to return again late in the essay in its penultimate example as a "naive enough" story about the haunting of a "furnished house" haunted by crocodiles which come to life out of the carvings of its furniture. Ibid., 244.

57. Jacques Derrida, "Living On: *Border Lines,*" 96.

58. Ibid., 108.

59. Ibid., 137.

60. Ibid., 76.

61. Jacques Derrida, "Cartouches," 195.

62. Ibid., 217.

63. Ibid., 244.

64. Jacques Derrida, "To Speculate—on Freud," 300.

65. Ibid., 369.

66. Ibid., 342.

67. Jacques Derrida, "Telepathy," *Oxford Literary Review,* vol. 10, nos. 1–2, 1988, 3–42, 28–33.

68. Derrida's "How to Avoid Speaking: Denials," for example, describes how a particular political topography is established to the extent that the shared language that constitutes it is "haunted" by that which "exceeds" any "position" in the space and yet leaves its secret mark within it. The essay explores the strange relationship "between the place and the place of the secret, between the secret place and the topography of the social." Jacques Derrida, "How to Avoid Speaking: Denials," 21. Likewise, in "Shibboleth," Derrida identifies how a political space is constituted by the "*unheimlich*" "spectral return" into it of that which has been excluded from it but is encrypted within it. Jacques Derrida, "Shibboleth," 394.

69. Jacques Derrida, "Force of Law: The 'Mystical Foundation of Authority'," 965.

70. Derrida's introduction to his first reading of the second half of "Force of Law," (published in a supplementary footnote to the text) argues that Benjamin's text is a "ghost story" that is itself haunted: "haunted by *haunting* itself, by a quasi-logic of the phantom which, because it is the more forceful one, should be substituted for an ontological logic of presence, absence or representation. . . . the law of the phantom, the

spectral experience and the memory of the phantom, of that which is neither dead nor living, more than dead and more than living, only surviving . . ." Ibid., 973.

71. Ibid., 1005.

72. Ibid.

73. Ibid., 1009. "The secret without secret of resistance, for deconstruction, is perhaps a certain connivance with ruin." Jacques Derrida, "Biodegradables: Seven Diary Fragments," trans. Peggy Kamuf, *Critical Inquiry*, vol. 15, no. 4, 1989, 812–873, 851.

74. "I don't feel that I'm in a position to *choose* between an operation that we'll call negative or nihilist, an operation that would set about furiously dismantling systems, and the other operation. I love very much everything that I deconstruct in my own manner; the texts I want to read from the deconstructive point of view are texts I love, with that impulse of identification which is indispensable for reading. . . . my relation to these texts is characterized by loving jealousy and not at all by nihilistic fury (one can't read anything in the latter condition) . . ." Jacques Derrida, "Roundtable on Autobiography," 87.

75. Jacques Derrida, "Violence and Metaphysics: An Essay on the Thought of Emmanuel Levinas," 117.

76. Jacques Derrida, "At This Very Moment in·Whose Work Here I Am," trans. Rubin Berezdivin, in Robert Bernasconi and Simon Critchley, eds., *Re-Reading Levinas* (Bloomington: Indiana University Press, 1991), 11–48, 18.

77. Ibid., 19.

78. Ibid., 11.

79. Ibid., 18.

80. Ibid., 42.

81. Jacques Derrida, "Violence and Metaphysics: An Essay on the Thought of Emmanuel Levinas," 88.

82. Jacques Derrida, "The Deaths of Roland Barthes," trans. Pascale-Anne Brault and Michael Naas, in Hugh J. Silverman, ed., *Philosophy and Non-Philosophy Since Merleau-Ponty* (New York: Routledge, 1988), 259–296, 267.

83. Ibid., 268.

84. Ibid., 267.

85. Jacques Derrida, *Glas*, 144.

86. Ibid., 214.

87. "De quelle exclusion est-elle faite? Et de quelle envie de vomir? . . . Le ni-avalé-ni-rejeté, ce qui reste dans la gorge comme autre . . ." Jacques Derrida, "Ja, ou le faux-bond," 94.

88. "Quand je dis que *Glas* travaille au paradoxe de 'l'effet de lecture,' j'etends en particulier qu'il fait l'un de ses thèmes principaux de la réception (assimilation, digestion, absorption, introjection, *incorporation*), ou de la non-réception (exclusion, forclusion,

rejet et encore, mais cette fois comme expulsion intestine, *incorporation*), donc du vomis-sement interne ou externe, du travail-du-deuil et de tout ce qui vient ou revient à *dé*gueuler. Mais *Glas* ne traite pas seulement de ces thèmes, il se propose d'une certaine manière à toutes ces opérations." Ibid., 93.

89. ". . . il faut adjoindre ou plutôt identifier la question du "rythme," des délais rythmés, etc." Ibid.

90. Jacques Derrida, *Glas*, 15. On Nietzsche opposing literature to those who write when they cannot digest something, see Jacques Derrida, "Living On: *Border Lines*," 106.

91. For Derrida, desire has no place without spacing. Jacques Derrida, "Aphorism Coun-tertime," 418. *Of Grammatology* speaks of the necessary "spacing" between desire and pleasure. Jacques Derrida, *Of Grammatology*, 280.

92. Jacques Derrida, "'Eating Well,' or the Calculation of the Subject: An Interview with Jacques Derrida," interview with Jean-Luc Nancy, trans. Peter Connor and Avital Ronell, in Eduardo Cadava et al., eds., *Who Comes after the Subject?* (New York: Routledge, 1991), 96–119. "Carnivorous sacrifice is essential to the structure of subjectivity, which is also to say to the founding of the intentional subject . . ." Jacques Derrida, "Force of Law: The 'Mystical Foundation of Authority,'" 953.

93. Jacques Derrida, "'Eating Well,'" or the Calculation of the Subject: An Interview with Jacques Derrida," 99.

94. "Où a lieu un 'effet de lecture,' s'il a lieu?" Jacques Derrida, "Ja, ou le faux-bond," 92.

Dislocating Space

1. Jacques Derrida, "Choreographies," 69.

2. Ibid., 68.

3. Jacques Derrida, "Deconstruction in America: An Interview with Jacques Derrida," 4.

4. "What strikes me when the question you raise is centered around the question of place is a certain type of deconstructive thinking, at least the kind that has interested me personally more and more for some time now: that is, precisely, the question and the enigma of event as that which takes place [qui a *lieu*], the question of the enigma of place. And here we have to proceed very, very slowly and very, very cautiously when we ask ourselves what we really mean by place. Thinking about the question of place is a very difficult thing—as is thinking about event as something which takes place." Ibid., 4.

5. For Derrida, "position" is not simply something addressed by discourse but is the effect of discourse. To rethink position is therefore to rethink discourse: "As you know, *decon-struction* means, among other things, the questioning of what synthesis is, what thesis is, what a position is, what composition is, not only in terms of rhetoric, but what *position* is, what *positing* means. Deconstruction questions the *thesis*, the theme, the positionality of everything . . .," Jacques Derrida, "Jacques Derrida on Rhetoric and Composition: A Conversation," 8. "The very idea of a thetic presentation, of *Setzung* or *Stellung* . . . was one of the essential parts of the system that was under deconstructive questioning." Jacques Derrida, "The Time of a Thesis: Punctuations," trans. Kathleen McLauglin, in

Alan Montefiore, ed., *Philosophy in France Today* (Cambridge: Cambridge University Press, 1983), 34–50, 42. Deconstructive discourse repeatedly identifies examples "athetic" or "nonthetic" writing "beyond the logic of position" (of which the most extended and detailed example is Freud in Derrida's "To Speculate—On Freud") and its own athetic condition, which significantly determines its political status: "the deconstructive jetty in itself is no more propositional than *positional;* it deconstructs precisely the *thesis,* both as philosophical thesis . . . and as *theme.* . . . Hence the necessity for deconstruction to deal with texts in a different way than as discursive contents, themes or theses, but always as institutional structures and, as is commonly said, as being political-juridical-sociohistorical—none of these last words being reliable enough to be used easily, hence their relative rare use in the most cautious texts called deconstructive. . . . Using an outdated language, one might thus say that the deconstructive jetty isn't essentially theoretical, thetic, or thematic because it is also ethical-political." Jacques Derrida, "Some Statements and Truisms about Neo-logisms, Newisms, Postisms, Parasitisms, and Other Small Seismisms," 86.

6. Jacques Derrida, "*Fors:* The Anguish Words of Nicolas Abraham and Maria Torok," xliv.

7. Ibid., xxi.

8. Ibid., 119.

9. Ibid., xlviii.

10. Jacques Derrida, "Limited Inc., a b c . . . ," 76.

11. Ibid., 82.

12. Ibid., 90. "The parasite parasites the limits that guarantee the purity of rules and of intentions, and this is not devoid of import for law, politics, economics, ethics . . . etc." Ibid., 98.

13. Ibid., 103.

14. "What is the place, the taking-place, or the metaphoric event, or of the metaphoric?" Jacques Derrida, "The *Retrait* of Metaphor," 17. "Does the preface take place, then? Where would it take place?" Jacques Derrida, "Outwork, Prefacing," 11. "Does the signature take place? Where? How? Why? For Whom?" Jacques Derrida, *Glas,* 3. "Does the title take place?" Jacques Derrida, "Title (To Be Specified)," 17.

15. "That does not mean (to say) that there is no castration, but that this *there is* does not take place." Jacques Derrida, *Glas,* 229.

16. Jacques Derrida, "Le facteur de la vérité," 436.

17. Ibid., 441.

18. Ibid., 426.

19. Ibid., 492.

20. Ibid., 420.

21. "All the '*unheimlich*' relations of duplicity, which unfold without limit in a dual structure, find themselves omitted or marginalized in the Seminar. They are of interest

only at the moment when they appear neutralized, dominated, mastered in the constitution of the triangular symbolic system . . . What thus finds itself controlled is *Unheimlichkeit*, and the anguishing disarray which can be provoked—without any hope of reappropriation, of closure, or of truth." Ibid., 460.

22. "Le concept de crise signerait un dernier symptôme, l'effort convulsif pour sauver un 'monde' que nous n'habitons plus: plus d'*oikos*, d'économie, d'écologie, de site habitable 'chez nous'. . . . La "représentation" de crise et la rhetorique qu'elle organise ont toujours au moins cette finalité: déterminer, pour la limiter, une menace plus grave et plus informe, en vérité sans figure et sans norme." Jacques Derrida, "Economies de la crise," *La Quinzaine Littéraire*, 339, August 1983, 4–5, 4.

23. "N'épargnant aucune région, ce mal-être et cette menace affectent bein la destination de l'humanité, et moins que jamais depuis cinquante ans nous ne saurions les localiser, leur assigner, pour les contenir, un lieu propre." Jacques Derrida, "Ce que j'aurais dit . . .," 85.

24. Jacques Derrida, "The Double Session," 213.

25. Jacques Derrida, "Shibboleth," 335.

26. Jacques Derrida, *Of Grammatology*, 145.

27. Ibid.*, 314.

28. Jacques Derrida, "Ja, ou le faux-bond," 62

29. Jacques Derrida, "Living On: *Border Lines*," 104.

30. Ibid., 138.

31. Ibid., 146.

32. Jacques Derrida, "Shibboleth," 409.

33. Ibid., 407.

34. Jacques Derrida, "Deconstruction and the Other," 107.

35. Ibid., 112.

36. Jacques Derrida, "Tympan," xii.

37. Jacques Derrida, "Some Questions and Responses," 261.

38. See, for example, the discussion of "dis-closure" in the lectures on Parmenides: "According to the obvious meaning, when we think of the 'open,' we think of something opened versus something closed. And what is open and opened is 'a space.' The open refers to the essential domain of space . . . the open refers to what is spatial." Martin Heidegger, *Parmenides*, 156. It is not simply opposed to the enclosure it opens. On the contrary, it produces it: "Disclosure, however, does not simply result in something disclosed as unclosed. Instead, the dis-closure [Ent-*bergen*], is at the same time an en-closure [*Ent*-bergen] . . . Disclosure—that now means to bring into a sheltering enclosure . . ." Ibid., 133.

39. Martin Heidegger, *The Basic Problems of Phenomenology*, 300.

40. "This openess exclusively and primarily provides the space in which space as we usually know it can unfold. The self-extending, the opening up, of future, past and present is itself prespatial; only thus can it make room, that is, provide space." Martin Heidegger, *On Time and Being*, trans. Joan Stambaugh (New York: Harper and Row, 1972), 14.

41. Martin Heidegger, "Art and Space," trans. Charles H. Seibert, *Man and World*, vol. 6, 3–8, 4.

42. Jacques Derrida, "Positions," 84.

43. Jacques Derrida, "The Time of the Thesis: Punctuations," 47.

44. Jacques Derrida, "Deconstruction and the Other," 109.

45. Jacques Derrida, "Ulysses Gramophone: Hear Say Yes in Joyce," 257.

46. Jacques Derrida, "Some Statements and Truisms about Neo-logisms, Newisms, Postisms, Parasitisms, and Other Small Seismisms," 82.

47. "I don't know what today we should call, strictly speaking, a philosopher or an artist. I am sure that there are interesting things today that must connect something philosophi-cal and something artistic without being additional to one or the other. But this doesn't make a diagram, this doesn't draw a sort of chart, or cartography of their positions. If we rely on given traditional positions, we know what to say, we know that for a philosopher as such, art is not essential. A philosopher, in principle, doesn't write works of art, which means that he is interested in the meaning, he is interested in the concept, not in the form, not in the composition. But—in principle, from the point of view that Plato was also an artist, and Spinoza was also an artist—for Schelling and for Nietzsche philosophy was a form of art. But since what I am interested in is the essence of philosophy, the essence of art, and I don't know what philosophy and art should be, I have no answer to what we have to do. I am sure that the writing of something which has to do with thought, I didn't say with philosophy but with thought, this writing can *not* be an objective writing having nothing to do with the signifiers, with the form, with the composition. So thinking has an essential link with writing. So here I will paraphrase Schelling—any new form of thinking implies a new way of writing—an originality in form, but I am not sure that this originality is what you call artistic originality—deconstruction in thought, it there is such a thing, is not strictly speaking philosophical or artistic." Jacques Derrida, "Artists, Phi-losophers and Institutions: A Talk with Jacques Derrida," *Rampike*, vol. 3, no. 3–vol. 4, no. 1, 1984–85, 34–36, 34.

48. Jacques Derrida, "Freud and the Scene of Writing," 214.

49. Ibid., 222.

50. Jacques Derrida, "Voice II . . .," trans. Verena Andermatt Conley, *Boundary II*, vol. 12, no. 2, 1984, 76–93, 77.

51. Jacques Derrida, "'Genesis and Structure' and Phenomenology," 155

52. "It remains that Being, which is nothing, is not a being, cannot be said, cannot say itself, except in the ontic metaphor. And the choice of one or another group of meta-

phors is necessarily significant. It is within a metaphorical insistence, then, that the interpretation of the meaning of Being is produced." Jacques Derrida, "The Ends of Man," 131.

53. Ibid., 133.

54. "My reference to Heidegger is often a reference to those places in Heidegger's thought where the question of place is very alive and very mysterious too. All this means that the question of place is absolutely essential, but all the more difficult to circumscribe and to isolate." Jacques Derrida, "Deconstruction in America: An Interview with Jacques Derrida," 4.

55. Jacques Derrida, "Restitutions: The Truth of Pointing," 257.

56. Ibid., 261.

57. "The ghostly is not far away. The relation which unsticks being from the existent without making something else of it, another existent, but merely a nothingness, a nonexistent which is there without being there as being present, this relation has some connivance with haunting. *Unheimlickeit* is the condition—take this word however you will—of the question of being, of its being-on-the-way, inasmuch as it (does not) pass(es) via nothing. In *Zeit und Sein,* the experience which relates presence to absence (*Anwesen/Abwesen*) is called *unheimliche.*" Ibid., 378.

58. "The *unheimlichkeit* of the thing." Ibid, 373.

59. Ibid., 360.

60. Jacques Derrida, "The Deaths of Roland Barthes," 267.

61. Ibid., 295.

62. Jacques Derrida, "*Ousia* and *Grammé:* Note on a Note from *Being and Time,*" 41.

63. Martin Heidegger, *Being and Time,* 138.

64. Jacques Derrida, "*Ousia* and *Grammé:* Note on a Note from *Being and Time,*" 41.

65. Jacques Derrida, "Geschlecht: Sexual Difference, Ontological Difference," 73.

66. Ibid., 77.

67. Ibid.

68. Jacques Derrida, "Plato's Pharmacy," 132.

69. Ibid., 133.

70. Ibid., 69.

71. Ibid., 128.

72. Ibid., 81.

73. Ibid., 103.

74. Jacques Derrida, "Languages and the Institutions of Philosophy," 130.

75. Ibid., 132.

76. Ibid., 146.

77. Ibid., 134. "In the western tradition, especially in the modern tradition, since the beginning of the nineteenth century—philosophy is located at the top of the pyramid, it is a point from which the philosopher can watch the whole field, every regime of the encyclopedia. It is the philosopher who knows what the physicality of physics is, what the psychology of the psyche is. The philosopher is at the top of the hierarchy, or what I call the ontological encyclopedia. But being at the top, he is reduced in fact to almost nothing, to a point, a point at the top of the pyramid. In principle he has the right—to look over everything. And he is reduced, as we know, to almost nothing. The philosophy department is nothing. The discourse on the death of philosophy in the western countries, a discourse which started a long time ago in the nineteenth century, the discourse on the death of philosophy has to do, to some extent, with this institutional situation, which is not only institutional in the external sense, it is institutional in the deepest sense." Jacques Derrida, "Artists, Philosophers and Institutions," 36.

78. Jacques Derrida, "Languages and the Institutions of Philosophy," 133.

79. "Il faut protester contre l'enfermement de la philosophie. Nous refusions légitimement l'assignation à résidence . . ." Jacques Derrida, "Les antinomies de la discipline philosophique: Lettre préface" in Jacques Derrida, *Du droit à la philosophie* (Paris: Galilée, 1990), 511–524, 517.

80. "De son *chez-soi* propre." Jacques Derrida, "Les événements? Quels événements?," *Nouvel Observateur*, 1045 H.S., 1984, 83–84, 84.

81. Jacques Derrida, "Les antinomies de la discipline philosophique," 518–521.

82. Jacques Derrida, "At This Very Moment in Whose Work I Am," 33.

83. "It leaves place for the other in a taking-place of *this* book where *this here* no longer shuts in upon itself, upon its own subject." Ibid., 31.

84. Ibid., 11.

85. Ibid., 16.

86. "From the moment in which the work of deconstruction makes some progress, the risks of domestication increase." Jacques Derrida, "The Derridean View: An Inter-View with Jacques Derrida," trans. Mary Ann Caws, *BM104*, vol. 2, no. 1, Sept. 1988, 4–5, 5.

87. Jacques Derrida, "Ja, ou le faux-bond," 108.

88. "In any case, deconstruction is not a project, which could just be present in front of no matter whom, after some prior decision. Nor is it a method, or a field, which one can try to appropriate for oneself, or to reduce to a homogenous space. My work would be rather inscribed in a configuration larger than itself, a mobile, plural configuration sometimes far from the places most familiar to me (for example: architecture, film, legal studies)." Jacques Derrida, "The Derridean View: An Interview With Jacques Derrida," 4.

89. Jacques Derrida, "Force of Law: The 'Mystical Foundation of Authority,'" 931.

90. Jacques Derrida, "Mnemosyne," trans. Cecile Lindsay, in Jacques Derrida, *Memoires for Paul De Man* (New York: Columbia University Press, 1986), 1–43, 18.

91. "But is there a proper place, is there a proper story for this thing? I think it consists only of transference, and of a thinking through of transference, in all the senses that this word acquires in more than one language, and first of all that of the transference between languages." Ibid., 14.

92. Jacques Derrida, "Deconstruction in America: An Interview With Jacques Derrida." 21.

93. Ibid., 3. This involves a displacement of the classical concept of "symptom": "deconstructions are not an enterprise. It is already a symptom of the situation you're describing: this change in the twentieth century in technology, in economics, in military strategies, these transformations in languages, etc. I consider deconstruction to be a symptom, but at the same time, the concept of 'symptom' has to be deconstructed, has to be analyzed; it's not a symptom in the sense of a sign at the surface of what is *signified* by the sign. It's a sign which *transforms* this situation, so the concept of symptom is not pertinent enough." Jacques Derrida, "Some Questions and Responses," 262.

94. On the "translation" of deconstruction in America: "You are supposing that the original of deconstruction is not to be found in America. I don't know how true that is. I don't know if there is an original of deconstruction." Jacques Derrida, "Deconstruction in America: An Interview with Jacques Derrida," 22. Derrida goes on to argue that if it was originally named as such in France, it was so already by way of a "deforming translation" of Heidegger.

95. "There is something French in deconstruction, and it will be interesting to analyze this. Nevertheless, my feeling is that deconstruction is not French at all, and that it is not so well received in France. It comes from outside." Jacques Derrida, "Deconstruction: A Trialogue in Jerusalem." *Mishkenot Sha'ananim Newsletter,* no. 7, December 1986, 1–7, 6.

96. Jacques Derrida, "Some Statements and Truisms about Neo-logisms, Newisms, Postisms, Parasitisms, and Other Small Seismisms," 93.

97. Jacques Derrida, "Letter to a Japanese Friend," 4.

98. Jacques Derrida, "The Time of a Thesis: Punctuations," 45.

99. Jacques Derrida, "An Interview with Derrida," interview with Catherine David, trans. David Allison et al., in David Wood and Robert Bernasconi, eds., *Derrida and Différance* (Coventry: Parousia Press, 1985), 107–127, 81.

100. Jacques Derrida, "Some Statements and Truisms about Neo-logisms, Newisms, Postisms, Parasitisms, and Other Small Seismisms," 72.

101. Ibid., 75.

102. Jacques Derrida, "Afterword: Towards an Ethic of Discussion," 141.

103. Jacques Derrida. "Limited Inc. a b c . . .," 46.

104. Ibid., 29.

105. Ibid., 107.

106. Ibid., 38.

107. "This force of rupture is due to the spacing which constitutes the written sign: the spacing which separates it from other elements of the internal contextual chain (the always open possibility of its extraction and grafting), but also from all the forms of present referent (past or to come in the modified form of the present past or to come) that is objective or subjective. This spacing is not the simply negativity of a lack, but the emergence of the mark." Jacques Derrida, "Signature, Event, Context," trans. Alan Bass, in Jacques Derrida, *Margins of Philosophy* (Chicago: University of Chicago Press, 1982), 307–330, 317.

108. Jacques Derrida, "Limited Inc. a b c . . . ," 76.

109. Ibid., 55.

110. Ibid., 82.

111. Ibid., 97.

112. Derrida argues that the sense in which theory "cannot be apolitical or politically neutral. And the analysis of political dimension of all contextual determination is never a purely theoretical gesture. It always involves a political evaluation, even if the code of this evaluation is overdetermined, resists classifications [such as right/left], and is yet to come—promised—rather than given." Jacques Derrida, "Afterword: Towards an Ethic of Discussion," 132. "What I am saying implies a rather profound transformation of the concept of the 'political.'" Ibid., 136.

113. Ibid., 111.

114. Ibid., 112. When Derrida reflects upon this argument elsewhere, he insists on the necessity of rethinking violence: "I'm not sure if there is a pure and general strict rule for avoiding violence in argumentation. . . . there is a problem with violence. Some violence cannot be avoided, so we have to elaborate simply, explicitly the problem of violence, violence in academic discussion and so on . . . You can't avoid—and you should not avoid—any violence in order to avoid violence. . . . I say that perhaps we have only the choice between different kinds or qualities of violence, depending on the context. Sometimes a violent gesture is less violent, more disarming than another and so on. A non-violent gesture is possible. . . . we are thinking of a good violence, which would be non-violent with regards to the bad violence, the evil one. So I am thinking of something non-violent and we are trying to discuss this and to share this thinking so as to try to do what we can to avoid the worst violence, and even if we cannot determine the rules and do anything positive to avoid any violence whatsoever, perhaps in this shared thinking of non-violence, some non-violence happens without our calculation. Non-violence, or pure non-violence cannot be calculated, but perhaps it happens. . . . So from that point of view 'deconstruction' would be a dream of such a non-violence." Jacques Derrida, "A Discussion with Jacques Derrida," *Writing Instructer*, vol. 9, no. 1/2, 1989, 7–18, 10.

115. Jacques Derrida, "Afterword: Towards an Ethic of Discussion," 125.

116. Ibid., 135.

117. Ibid., 133.

118. Jacques Derrida, "The Law of Genre," trans. Avital Ronell, *Glyph* 7, 1980, 202–229, 219

119. Ibid., 204.

120. Ibid., 206.

121. Ibid., 213.

In-Conclusion

1. "I would try to elaborate the problem of violence and to think what violence is. And again if I say what violence is, I would have to transform the question because the concept of 'being' already involves some violence. Even the question 'What is?' is not totally devoid of violence. So I would like to think beyond—here we come back to deconstruction—to think beyond a tradition in which even the most neutral and innocent and ontological question conveys some violence." Jacques Derrida, "A Discussion with Jacques Derrida," 12. "Deconstruction is first of all a way of not letting yourself be imposed on by a program of answers in the form of questions. It's a manner of interrogating the question itself; the question and questions: and even the authority of questioning." Jacques Derrida, "The Derridean View: An Interview with Jacques Derrida," 5. The "style" of deconstruction is "not a propositional one, but I wouldn't say that it's totally interrogative. Of course, it's more interrogative than propositional, OK, but the form of the questions, the questioning syntax, is not taken for granted, not taken for the first and last form of thinking. So we have to question the form of questioning, in a sense which is not positive: I would distinguish between the positive, or positions, and affirmations. I think that deconstruction is rather affirmative than questioning; this affirmation goes through some radical questioning, but is not questioning in the final analysis." "Jacques Derrida on the University," interview with Imre Salusinsky, *Southern Review*, 19, 1986, 3–12, 9. This questioning of the authority of the question begins as a sustained questioning of "the privilege of *questioning* in Heidegger's thought." See Jacques Derrida, "On Reading Heidegger: An Outline of Remarks to the Essex Colloquium," *Research in Phenomenology*, vol. 17, 1987, 171–188, and Jacques Derrida, *Of Spirit: Heidegger and the Question*, trans. Geoffrey Bennington and Rachel Bowlbey (Chicago: University of Chicago Press, 1989). On the way in which the space of philosophy is both established as an "enclosure" or "founded dwelling" inasmuch as philosophy is a "community of the question" but is radically complicated by the ambiguous status of the question, see, particularly, "Violence and Metaphysics: An Essay on the Thought of Emmanuel Levinas," 79–80.

References

Works by Jacques Derrida Cited

"Afterword: Toward an Ethic of Discussion." Trans. Samuel Weber. In Jacques Derrida, *Limited Inc.* Evanston: Northwestern University Press, 1988, 111–160.

"Les antinomies de la discipline philosophique: Lettre préface." In Jacques Derrida, *Du droit à la philosophie.* Paris: Galilée, 1990, 511–524.

"Aphorism Countertime." Trans. Nicholas Royle. In Derek Attridge, ed., *Acts of Literature.* New York: Routledge, 1992, 414–433.

"Architecture Where the Desire May Live." *Domus* 671, 1986, 17–25.

"The Art of *Mémoires*," Trans. Jonathan Culler. In Jacques Derrida, *Memoires for Paul De Man.* New York: Columbia University Press, 1986, 45–88.

"Artists, Philosophers and Institutions: A Talk with Jacques Derrida." *Rampike,* vol. 3, no. 3–vol. 4, no. 1, 1984–85, 34–36.

"At This Very Moment in This Work Here I Am." Trans. Rubin Berezdivin. In Robert Bernasconi and Simon Critchley, eds., *Re-Reading Levinas.* Bloomington: Indiana University Press, 1991, 11–48.

"Before the Law." Trans. Avital Ronell and Christine Roulston. In Derek Attridge, ed., *Acts of Literature.* New York: Routledge, 1992, 181–220.

"Biodegradables: Seven Diary Fragments." Trans. Peggy Kamuf. *Critical Inquiry,* vol. 15, no. 4, 1989, 812–873.

"Cartouches." Trans. Geoff Bennington and Ian McLeod. In Jacques Derrida, *The Truth in Painting.* Chicago: University of Chicago Press, 1987, 183–253.

"Ce que j'aurais dit . . ." In *Le complexe de Léonard ou la Société de création.* Paris: Editions de Nouvel Observateur, 1984, 77–92.

References

"Choreographies." Trans. Christie V. McDonald. *Diacritics,* vol. 12, no. 2, 1982, 66–76.

Cinders. Trans. Ned Lukacher. Lincoln: University of Nebraska Press, 1991.

"Cogito and the History of Madness." Trans. Alan Bass. In Jacques Derrida, *Writing and Difference.* Chicago: University of Chicago Press, 1978, 31–63.

"The Deaths of Roland Barthes." Trans. Pascale-Anne Brault and Michael Naas. In Hugh J. Silverman, ed., *Philosophy and Non-Philosophy Since Merleau-Ponty.* New York: Routledge, 1988, 259–296.

"Declarations of Independence." Trans. Tom Keenan and Tom Pepper. *New Political Science,* no. 15, Summer 1986, 7–15.

"Deconstruction and the Other." In Richard Kearney, ed., *Dialogues with Contemporary Continental Thinkers,* Manchester: Manchester University Press, 1984, 105–126.

"Deconstruction: A Trialogue in Jerusalem." *Mishkenot Sha'ananim Newsletter,* no. 7, December 1986, 1–7.

"Deconstruction in America: An Interview with Jacques Derrida." Interview with James Creech, Peggy Kamuf, and Jane Todd. *Critical Exchange,* no. 17, Winter 1985, 1–33.

"The Derridean View: An Inter-view with Jacques Derrida." Interview with Edward Marx. Trans. Mary Ann Caws. *BM104,* vol. 2, no. 1, Sept. 1988, 4–5, 8.

"Desistance." Trans. Christopher Fynsk. Introduction to Christopher Fynsk, ed., *Typography: Mimesis, Philosophy, Politics.* Cambridge: Harvard University Press, 1989, 1–42.

"Différance." Trans. Alan Bass. In Jacques Derrida, *Margins of Philosophy.* Chicago: University of Chicago, 1982, 1–27.

"A Discussion with Jacques Derrida." *Writing Instructor,* vol. 9, no. 1/2, 1989, 7–18.

"Dissemination." Trans. Barbara Johnson. In Jacques Derrida, *Dissemination.* Chicago: University of Chicago Press, 1981, 287–366.

"The Double Session." Trans. Barbara Johnson. In Jacques Derrida, *Dissemination.* Chicago: University of Chicago Press, 1981, 287–366.

"Du Tout." Trans. Alan Bass. In Jacques Derrida. *The Post Card: From Socrates to Freud and Beyond.* Chicago: University of Chicago Press, 1987, 497–521.

"Economies de la crise." *La Quinzaine Littéraire,* 339, August 1983, 4–5.

"Economimesis." Trans. R. Klein. *Diacritics,* vol. 11, no. 2, 1981, 3–25.

"'Eating Well,' or the Calculation of the Subject: An Interview with Jacques Derrida." Interview with Jean-Luc Nancy. Trans. Peter Connor and Avital Ronell. In Eduardo Cadava et al., eds., *Who Comes after the Subject?* New York: Routledge, 1991, 96–119.

Edmund Husserl's 'Origin of Geometry': An Introduction. Trans. John P. Leavy, Jr. Brighten: Harvester Press, 1978.

"The Ends of Man." Trans. Alan Bass. In Jacques Derrida, *Margins of Philosophy.* Chicago: University of Chicago Press, 1982, 109–136.

265

References

"Entre crochets: entretien avec Jacques Derrida, première partie," *Digraphe* 8, April 1976, 97–114.

"Les événements? Quels événements?," *Nouvel Observateur,* 1045 H.S., 1984, 83–84.

"Le facteur de la verité." Trans. Alan Bass. In Jacques Derrida, *The Post Card: From Socrates to Freud and Beyond.* Chicago: University of Chicago Press, 1987, 411–496.

"Force and Signification." Trans. Alan Bass. In Jacques Derrida, *Writing and Difference.* Chicago: University of Chicago Press, 1978, 3–30.

"Force of Law: The 'Mystical Foundation of Authority'." Trans. Mary Quaintance. *Cardozo Law Review,* vol. 11, no. 5/6, July/August 1990, 919–1046.

"Fors: The Anguish Words of Nicolas Abraham and Maria Torok." Trans. Barbara Johnson. Foreword to Nicolas Abraham and Maria Torok. *The Wolf Man's Magic Word.* Trans. Nicholas Rand. Minneapolis: University of Minnesota Press, 1986, xi–xlviii.

"Freud and the Scene of Writing." Trans. Alan Bass. In Jacques Derrida, *Writing and Difference.* Chicago: University of Chicago Press, 1978, 196–231.

"From Restricted to General Economy: A Hegelianism without Reserve." Trans. Alan Bass. In Jacques Derrida, *Writing and Difference.* Chicago: University of Chicago Press, 1978, 251–277.

"'Genesis and Structure' and Phenomenology." Trans. Alan Bass. In Jacques Derrida, *Writing and Difference.* Chicago: University of Chicago Press, 1978, 154–168.

"Geschlecht: Sexual Difference, Ontological Difference." *Research in Phenomenology,* XIII, 1983, 65–84.

"The Ghost Dance: An Interview with Jacques Derrida." Interview with Mark Lewis and Andrew Payne. Trans. Jean-Luc Svoboda. *Public,* 2, 1989, 60–73.

Glas. Trans. John P. Leavy, Jr., and Richard Rand. Lincoln: University of Nebraska Press, 1986.

"How to Avoid Speaking: Denials." Trans. Ken Frieden. Sandford Budick and Wolfgang Iser, eds., *Languages of the Unsayable: The Play of Negativity in Literature and Literary Theory.* New York: Columbia University Press, 1989, 3–70.

"Implications." An interview with Henri Rose. Trans. Alan Bass. In Jacques Derrida, *Positions.* Chicago: University of Chicago Press, 1981, 1–14.

"Interpretations at War: Kant, the Jew, the German." *New Literary History,* vol. 22, no. 1, 1991, 39–95.

"An Interview with Derrida." Interview with Catherine David. Trans. David Allison et al. In David Wood and Robert Bernasconi, eds., *Derrida and Différance.* Coventry: Parousia Press, 1985, 107–127.

"Ja, ou le faux-bond." *Digraphe,* 11, March 1977, 83–121.

"Jacques Derrida in Conversation." Interview with Raul Mortley. In Raul Mortley, ed., *French Philosophers in Conversation: Derrida, Irigary, Levinas, Le Doeuff, Schneider, Serres.* London: Routledge, 1990, 92–108.

References

"Jacques Derrida on Rhetoric and Composition: A Conversation." Interview with Gary A. Olson. *Journal of Advanced Composition,* 10, 1990, 1–21.

"Jacques Derrida on the University." Interview with Imre Salusinsky, *Southern Review,* 19, 1986, 3–12.

"La Parole Soufflée." Trans. Alan Bass. In Jacques Derrida, *Writing and Difference.* Chicago: University of Chicago Press, 1978, 169–195.

"Languages and Institutions of Philosophy." Trans. Sylvia Soderlind et al., *Semiotic Inquiry/Researches Semiotiques,* vol. 4, no. 2, 1984, 92–154.

"The Law of Genre." Trans. Avital Ronell, *Glyph* 7, 1980, 202–229.

"Letter to a Japanese Friend." Trans. David Wood and Andrew Benjamin. In David Wood and Robert Bernasconi, eds., *Derrida and Differance.* Coventry: Parousia Press, 1985, 1–5.

"Limited Inc. a b c . . ." Trans. Samuel Weber. In Jacques Derrida, *Limited Inc,* Evanston: Northwestern University Press, 1988.

"Living On: *Border Lines.*" Trans. James Hulbert. In Harold Bloom et al., eds., *Deconstruction and Criticism.* London: Routledge and Kegan Paul, 1979, 75–176.

"Mallarmé." Trans. Christine Roulston. In Derek Attridge, ed., *Acts of Literature.* New York: Routledge, 1992, 110–126.

"Me-Psychoanalysis: An Introduction to the Translation of *The Shell and the Kernal* by Nicolas Abraham." Trans. R. Klein. *Diacritics,* vol. 9, no. 1, 4–12.

"Mnemosyne." Trans. Cecile Lindsay. In Jacques Derrida, *Memoires for Paul De Man.* New York: Columbia University Press, 1986, 1–43.

"Mochlos ou le conflit des facultés." *Philosophie,* 2, April 1984, 21–53.

Of Grammatology. Trans. Gayatri Chakravorty Spivak. Baltimore: Johns Hopkins University Press, 1976.

Of Spirit: Heidegger and the Question. Trans. Geoffrey Bennington and Rachel Bowlby. Chicago: University of Chicago Press, 1989.

"On Colleges and Philosophy." Interview with Geoff Bennington. *ICA Documents 4: Postmodernism,* 1986, 66–71.

"On Reading Heidegger: An Outline of Remarks to the Essex Colloquium," *Research in Phenomenology,* vol. 17, 1987, 171–188.

"Otobiographies: The Teaching of Nietzsche and the Politics of the Proper Name." Trans. Avital Ronell. In Christie V. McDonald, ed., *The Ear of the Other: Otobiography, Transference, Translation.* New York: Schocken Books, 1985, 1–38.

"*Ousia* and *Grammé:* Note on a Note from *Being and Time.*" Trans. Alan Bass. In Jacques Derrida, *Margins of Philosophy.* Chicago: University of Chicago Press, 1982, 26–67.

"Outwork, Prefacing." Trans. Barbara Johnson. In Jacques Derrida, *Dissemination.* Chicago: University of Chicago Press, 1981, 1–59.

References

"Parergon." Trans. Geoff Bennington and Ian McLeod. In Jacques Derrida, *The Truth in Painting*. Chicago: University of Chicago Press, 1987, 15–147.

"La Parole Soufflée." Trans. Alan Bass. In Jacques Derrida, *Writing and Difference*. Chicago: University of Chicago Press, 1978, 169–195.

"The Pit and the Pyramid: Introduction to Hegel's Semiology." Trans. Alan Bass. In Jacques Derrida, *Margins of Philosophy*, Chicago: University of Chicago, 1982, 69–108.

"Plato's Pharmacy." Trans. Barbara Johnson. In Jacques Derrida, *Dissemination*. Chicago: University of Chicago Press, 1981, 61–172.

"The Politics of Friendship." *Journal of Philosophy*, vol. 75, no. 11, 1988, 632–645.

"Popularitiés: Du droit à la philosophie du droit." In Jacques Derrida, *Du droit à la philosophie*. Paris: Galilée, 1990, 525–535.

"Positions." Interview with Jean-Louis Houdebine and Guy Scarpetta. Trans. Alan Bass. In Jacques Derrida, *Positions*. Chicago: University of Chicago Press, 1981, 37–96.

"The Principle of Reason: The University in the Eyes of its Pupils." Trans. Catherine Porter and Edward P. Morris. *Diacritics*, vol. 13, no. 3, 1983, 3–20.

"Proverb: 'He that would pun . . . ,'" Trans. John P. Leavy, Jr. In John P. Leavy, Jr., *Glassary*. Lincoln: University of Nebraska Press, 1986, 17–21.

"Psyche: Inventions of the Other." Trans. Catherine Porter. In Lindsay Waters and Wlad Godzich, eds., *Reading De Man Reading*. Minneapolis: University of Minnesota Press, 1989, 25–65.

"Restitutions of the Truth in Pointing [*pointure*]." Trans. Geoff Bennington and Ian McLeod. In Jacques Derrida, *The Truth in Painting*. Chicago: University of Chicago Press, 1987, 255–382.

"The *Retrait* of Metaphor." Trans. by editors. *Enclitic*, vol. 2, no. 2, 1978, 5–34.

"Roundtable on Autobiography." Trans. Peggy Kamuf. Christie V. McDonald, ed., *The Ear of the Other: Otobiography, Transference, Translation*. New York: Schocken Books, 1985, 39–90.

"Roundtable on Translation." Trans. Peggy Kamuf. In Christie V. McDonald, ed., *The Ear of the Other: Otobiography, Transference, Translation*. New York: Schocken Books, 1985, 91–162.

"Scribble (Writing-Power)." Trans. Cary Plotkin. *Yale French Studies*, 59, 1979, 116–147.

"Semiology and Grammatology." Interview with Julia Kristeva. Trans. Alan Bass. In Jacques Derrida, *Positions*. Chicago: University of Chicago Press, 1981, 15–36.

"Shibboleth." Trans. Joshua Wilner. In Derek Attridge, ed., *Acts of Literature*. New York: Routledge, 1992, 370–413.

"Signature, Event, Context." Trans. Alan Bass. In Jacques Derrida, *Margins of Philosophy*. Chicago: University of Chicago Press, 1982, 307–330.

References

"Some Questions and Responses," Nigel Fabb et al., eds., *The Linguistics of Writing: Arguments between Language and Literature.* Manchester: Manchester University Press, 1987, 252–264.

"Some Statements and Truisms about Neo-logisms, Newisms, Postisms, Parasitisms, and other Small Seismisms." Trans. Anne Tomiche. In David Carroll, ed., *The States of "Theory": History, Art and Critical Discourse.* New York: Columbia University Press, 1990, 63–94.

Speech and Phenomena and Other Essays on Husserl's Theory of Signs. Trans. David B. Allison. Evanston: Northwestern University Press, 1973.

"Structure, Sign, and Play in the Discourse of the Human Sciences." Trans. Alan Bass. In Jacques Derrida, *Writing and Difference.* Chicago: University of Chicago Press, 1978, 278–294.

"Telepathy," Trans. Nicholas Royle. *Oxford Literary Review,* vol. 10, nos. 1–2, 1988, 3–42.

"The Theatre of Cruelty and the Closure of Representation." Trans. Alan Bass. In Jacques Derrida, *Writing and Difference.* Chicago: University of Chicago Press, 1978, 232–250.

"The Time of a Thesis: Punctuations." Trans. Kathleen McLauglin. In Alan Montefiore, ed., *Philosophy in France Today.* Cambridge: Cambridge University Press, 1983, 34–50.

"Title (To Be Specified)." Trans. Tom Conley. *Sub-Stance,* 31, 1981, 5–22.

"To Speculate—on "Freud."" Trans. Alan Bass. In Jacques Derrida, *The Post Card: From Socrates to Freud and Beyond.* Chicago: University of Chicago Press, 1987, 257–409.

"Des Tours de Babel." Trans. Joseph F. Graham. In Joseph F. Graham, ed., *Difference in Translation.* Ithaca: Cornell University Press, 1985, 165–207.

"Tymphan," Trans. Alan Bass. In Jacques Derrida, *Margins of Philosophy.* Chicago: University of Chicago, 1982, ix–xxix.

"Ulysses Gramophone: Hear Say Yes in Joyce." Trans. Tina Kendall and Shari Benstock. In Derek Attridge, ed., *Acts of Literature.* New York: Routledge, 1992, 253–309.

"Violence and Metaphysics: An Essay on the Thought of Emmanuel Levinas." Trans. Alan Bass. In Jacques Derrida, *Writing and Difference.* Chicago: University of Chicago Press, 1978, 79–153.

"Voice II . . ." Trans. Verena Andermatt Conley. *Boundary II,* vol. 12, no. 2, 1984, 76–93.

"White Mythology: Metaphor in the Text of Philosophy." Trans. Alan Bass. In Jacques Derrida, *Margins of Philosophy.* Chicago: University of Chicago, 1982, 207–271.

Works by Martin Heidegger Cited

"Art and Space," Trans. Charles H. Seibert. *Man and World,* vol. 6, 3–8.

The Basic Problems of Phenomenology. Trans. Albert Hofstadter. Bloomington: Indiana University Press, 1982.

References

Being and Time. Trans. John Macquarrie and Edward Robinson. New York: Harper and Row, 1962.

"Building, Dwelling, Thinking." Trans. Albert Hofstadter. In Martin Heidegger, *Poetry, Language, Thought*. New York: Harper and Row, 1971, 143–161.

The Essence of Reasons. Trans. Terrence Malick. Evanston: Northwestern University Press, 1969.

History of the Concept of Time: Prolegomena. Trans. Theodore Kisiel. Bloomington: Indiana University Press, 1985.

Identity and Difference. Trans. Joan Stambaugh. New York: Harper and Row, 1969.

An Introduction to Metaphysics. Trans. Ralph Manheim. New Haven: Yale University Press, 1959.

Kant and the Problem of Metaphysics. Trans. Richard Taft. Bloomington: Indiana University Press, 1990.

"Language." Trans. Albert Hofstadter. In Martin Heidegger, *Poetry, Language, Thought*. New York: Harper and Row, 1971, 187–210.

"Letter on Humanism." Trans. David Farrell Krell. In *Martin Heidegger: Basic Writings*. New York: Harper and Row, 1977, 193–242.

The Metaphysical Foundations of Logic. Trans. Michael Heim. Bloomington: Indiana University Press, 1984.

Nietzsche Vol. I: The Will to Power as Art. Trans. David Farrell Krell. San Francisco: Harper and Row, 1979.

Nietzsche, Vol. III: The Will to Power as Knowledge and as Metaphysics. Trans. David Farrell Krell. San Francisco: Harper and Row, 1987.

On Time and Being. Trans. Joan Stambaugh. New York: Harper and Row, 1972.

"The Origin of the Work of Art." Trans. Albert Hofstadter. In Martin Heidegger, *Poetry, Language, Thought*. New York: Harper and Row, 1971, 15–87.

"Overcoming Metaphysics." Trans. Joan Strambaugh. In Martin Heidegger, *The End of Philosophy*. New York: Harper and Row, 1973, 84–110.

Parmenides. Trans. André Schuwer and Richard Rojcewicz. Bloomington: Indiana University Press, 1992.

". . . Poetically Man Dwells . . . ," Trans. Albert Hofstadter. In Martin Heidegger, *Poetry, Language, Thought*. New York: Harper and Row, 1971, 211–229.

The Principle of Reason. Trans. Reginald Lilly. Bloomington: Indiana University Press, 1991.

"Remembrance of the Poet," Trans. Douglas Scott. In Martin Heidegger, *Existence and Being*. Washington: Gateway, 1949, 233–269.

References

"The Question Concerning Technology." Trans. David Farrell Krell. *Martin Heidegger: Basic Writings.* New York: Harper and Row, 1977, 283–317.

Schelling's Treatise on the Essence of Human Freedom. Trans. Joan Stambaugh. Athens: Ohio University Press, 1985.

"The Way to Language." Trans. Peter D. Hertz. In Martin Heidegger, *On the Way to Language.* New York: Harper and Row, 1971, 111–136.

"What Are Poets For?" Trans. Albert Hofstadter. In Martin Heidegger, *Poetry, Language, Thought.* New York: Harper and Row, 1971, 89–142.

What Is a Thing? Trans. W. B. Barton and Vera Deutsch. Chicago: Henry Regnery Company, 1967.

What Is Called Thinking? Trans. J. Glenn Gray. New York: Harper and Row, 1968.

Other Authors Cited

Abraham, Nicolas, and Maria Torok. "Introjection-Incorporation: Mourning or Melancholia." In Serge Lebovici and Daniel Widlander, eds., *Psychoanalysis in France.* New York: International University Press, 1980, 3–16.

Abraham, Nicolas, and Maria Torok. "A Poetics of Psychoanalysis: The Lost Object—Me." *Substance,* vol. 13, no. 2, 1984, 3–18.

Benjamin, Walter. "The Task of the Translator." Trans. Harry Zohn. In Hannah Arendt, ed., *Illuminations.* New York: Schocken Books, 1968, 69–82.

Descartes, René. "Seventh Set of Objections with the Author's Replies." Trans. John Cottingham et al. *The Philosophical Writings of Descartes Vol. II.* Cambridge: Cambridge University Press, 1984.

Freud, Sigmund. "Three Essays on the Theory of Sexuality." Trans. James Strachey. *The Standard Edition of the Complete Psychological Works of Sigmund Freud,* London: Hogarth Press, 1955, vol. 7, 1959, 125–243.

Freud, Sigmund. "Mourning and Melancholia," Trans. James Strachey. *The Standard Edition of the Complete Psychological Works of Sigmund Freud,* London: Hogarth Press, 1955, vol. 14, 243–258.

Freud, Sigmund. "The Uncanny." *The Standard Edition of the Complete Psychological Works of Sigmund Freud,* London: Hogarth Press, 1955, vol. 17: 217–256.

Kant, Immanuel. "An Answer to Question: 'What is Enlightenment?' Trans. H. B. Nisbet. In *Kant's Political Writings.* Cambridge: Cambridge University Press, 1970, 54–60.

Kant, Immanuel. *Anthropology from a Pragmatic Point of View.* Trans. Mary J. Gregor. The Hague: Martinus Nijhoff, 1974.

Kant, Immanuel. *The Critique of Judgement.* Trans. James Creed Meredith. London: Oxford University Press, 1952.

References

Kant, Immanuel. *Critique of Pure Reason*. Trans. Norman Kemp Smith. London: MacMillan and Co., 1929.

Kant, Immanuel. *Education*. Ann Arbor: University of Michigan Press, 1960.

Immanuel Kant. *The Metaphysical Principles of Virtue. II. The Metaphysics of Morals*. Trans. James Ellington. Indianapolis: Bobbs-Merrill, 1964.

Kant, Immanuel. *Observations on the Feeling of the Beautiful and the Sublime*. Trans. John T. Goldthwait. Berkeley: University of California Press, 1965.

Kant, Immanuel. "On Philosopher's Medicine of the Body." In Lewis White Beck, ed., *Kant's Latin Writings*. New York, Peter Lang, 1986, 217–243.

Kant, Immanuel. "On the Common Saying: 'This May be True in Theory, But It Does Not Apply in Practice'." Trans. H. B. Nisbet. In Hans Reiss, ed., *Kant's Political Writings*. Cambridge: Cambridge University Press, 1970, 61–92.

Kant, Immanuel. "Perpetual Peace: A Philosophical Sketch." Trans. H.B. Nisbet. In Hans Reiss, ed., *Kant's Political Writings*. Cambridge: Cambridge University Press, 1970, 93–130.

Kant, Immanuel. *The Philosophy of Law*. Trans. W. Hastie. Edinburgh: T. T. Clark, 1887.

Nietzsche, Friedrich. *The Gay Science*. Trans. Walter Kaufman. New York: Vintage Books, 1974.

Panofsky, Irwin. *Idea: A Concept in Art Theory*. Trans. Joseph J. S. Peake. New York: Harper and Row, 1968.

Rousseau, Jean-Jacques. "A Discourse on the Moral Effects of the Arts and Sciences." Trans. G. D. H. Cole. In Jean-Jacques Rousseau, *The Social Contract and Discourses*. London: Dent, 1973, 1–26.

Rousseau, Jean-Jacques. "A Discourse on the Origin of Inequality." Trans. G. D. H. Cole. In Jean-Jacques Rousseau, *The Social Contract and Discourses*. London: Dent, 1973, 27–113.

Rousseau, Jean-Jacques. "A Discourse on Political Economy." Trans. G. D. H. Cole. In Jean-Jacques Rousseau, *The Social Contract and Discourses*. London: Dent, 1973, 115–153.

Rousseau, Jean-Jacques. *Emile*. Trans. Barbara Foxley. New York: Dent, 1973.

Rousseau, Jean-Jacques. "Essay on the Origin of Languages." Trans. John H. Moran and Alexander Gode. In *On the Origin of Language*. New York: Frederick Ungar, 1966, 1–74.

Rousseau, Jean-Jacques. "The Social Contract." Trans. G. D. H. Cole. In Jean-Jacques Rousseau, *The Social Contract and Discourses*. London: Dent, 1973, 164–278.

Wigley, Mark. "Architecture after Philosophy: Le Corbusier and the Emperor's New Paint," *Journal of Philosophy and the Visual Arts*, no. 2, 1990, 84–95.

Wigley, Mark. "Heidegger's House: The Violence of the Domestic." *D: Columbia Documents in Architecture and Theory*, no. 1. 1992, 91–121.

Index